# Oregon Farmers' Markets
## Cookbook & Guide

### Kris Wetherbee

— *A Maverick Publication* —

Copyright © 1998 by Kris Wetherbee

All Rights Reserved. No part of this book may be reproduced or transmitted in any form or by any means, electronic or mechanical, including photocopying, recording, or by any information storage and retrieval system without permission in writing from the publisher.

ISBN 0-89288-272-7

Library of Congress Catalog Card Number: 98-66243

Photographs on pages 21, 26, 32, 41, 47, 49, 59, 69, 85, 95, 101, 110, 121, 125, 147, 155 and 159 courtesy of Rick Wetherbee

Maverick Publications
P.O. Box 5007
Bend, Oregon 97708

**For Rick,**
**my husband and best friend,**
**who helps make life fun**

# Acknowledgments

A big thank you goes to the farmers' market vendors and market directors who helped make this book possible by taking time out of their busy schedule to contribute these delicious recipes and market information and for making them available to *Oregon Farmers' Markets Cookbook & Guide*. I wish to thank all of them for their participation.

I'm extremely grateful to my husband Rick for his abiding support and help with the book; my mom and dad for the fax machine which turned into a great time saver; and to Gary Asher for recognizing the need and giving me the opportunity. A special thank you to Territorial Seed Company for their contribution of the fruit and vegetable slides.

I also would like to thank:
- Inge Winters
- Judy Lovett
- Nancy Brown
- Ron & Judy Bennett
- Chris Peterson
- Jerry Mires
- Laura Napruszewski
- Carolyn Raab
- Bridget Wise

# Table of Contents

Introduction     9

Shopping The Market     11

Beaverton Farmers' Market     13

Corvallis Saturday Farmers' Market     25

Douglas County Farmers' Market     41

Grants Pass Growers' Market     57

Independence Farmers' Market     69

Indoor Farmers' Market     81

Lane County Farmers' Market     97

People's All-Organic Farmers' Market     115

Portland Farmers' Market     131

More Farmers' Markets     151

Listing of Farmers' Markets In Oregon     177

Resource Listing     181

Bibliography     183

Index     185

*Courtesy of Lane County Historical Museum.*

# Introduction

Farmers' markets have always been an important part of people's lives, both for shoppers and producers. An integral part of history, farmers' markets have also been an important element throughout the community by keeping farmlands in production, supplying jobs, establishing community interaction, helping the local economy and also providing the community with locally grown, just picked produce in a fun and enjoyable atmosphere.

Before the 1950's, farmers' markets were often known as public markets. Quite commonplace, public markets have been a universal element of everyday life since the beginning of time. By 1918 public markets were located in more than 50% of American cities having populations of 30,000 or more. They continued to keep their standing as the main market center up until the 1930's. Unfortunately however, by World War II, public markets were becoming a thing of the past.

New methods of transportation took the country by storm—first the railroads, then the interstate highway system after 1955, bringing with it mass trucking. Refrigeration, corporate controlled supermarkets and processing plants dominated the food industry and changed the way Americans shopped.

Then with the early 70's came the 'back to the land' movement and the growing concern for pesticide-free produce that was fresh and flavorful. A resurgence began and over the next 20 years, farmers' markets spread like wildfire. Every year new markets continue to spring forth and there are now well over 2,000 farmers' markets nationwide with over 30 markets located in Oregon.

The small family farm remains a vital part of the food production in this country today, in fact they produce nearly one-third of the food that's grown. And even though the thought of working the land and growing food may sound picturesque or glamorous to some, what it does involve is a lot of hard work in conditions that the farmer often has no control over. Yet despite bugs and critters, temperature extremes of sunny, hot weather soaring near 100 degrees, or piercing cold winds blowing through driving rains, the farmer perseveres bringing delicious fresh produce from the farm, to the market, to your table.

The farmers' markets in Oregon offer a wealth of experience and family-tested recipes from a diversity of growers and producers. They found ways to cook with the seasons that the whole family enjoys, and I'm sure you will too. That's why this book came about.

This book will not only provide the smart shopper with many unique and wonderful recipes, but also help spread and increase the awareness and benefits of shopping at your local farmers' market. The market is a common ground for the community, attracting people from many different walks of life. Many markets also become involved in one project or another, be it cooking demonstrations, providing educational services through master preservers and gardeners, or even participating in special events or charity projects like WIC Farmers' Market Nutrition Programs or food banks.

Selection is boundless with heirlooms and other quality varieties that you wouldn't find in the supermarket because of their rigorous handling and transportation time involved with packing sheds and wholesalers. Unusual and hard-to-find vegetables and specialty items are available at farmers' markets, along with grower expertise on how to store it and use it. Freshness, flavor and nutrition are much higher with prices often being generally lower (especially during the peak harvest season) than for most comparable items found in the supermarket. And many farmers are growing their food without the use of pesticides and other harmful chemicals, not only providing healthy food for your family, but also growing it in a way that is good for the land.

Bring the family and enjoy a new experience that includes vine and tree ripened foods, a wide selection of plants, local crafts and lots of activities. Farmers' markets are a great place to shop and a fun place to be.

# Shopping the Market

Trips to the farmers' market have become an anticipated event all over the country. For many, it's a weekly get together with good friends and great food. As a market vendor myself for six years, my husband and I look forward to seeing familiar faces and hearing the latest news from our customers. I've also learned, through observation and feedback, some valuable tips to help make the shopping day productive and fun.

First, get to know your vendors. Walk through the market to see what each vendor has to offer. Things can change weekly so make the rounds each time. You'll soon discover what is available and when it's available. If you want to purchase only organically grown food, by talking with the vendors you'll learn which farms are certified organic. And vendors are always willing to share their knowledge with you whether it's how to grow a plant or how to cook a vegetable. They'll often have cooking and preparation tips, including the best variety for your intended use.

By talking with vendors, you'll also find out which ones can sell produce in bulk amounts. Perhaps you want to put up dill pickles for the season. You can often get a discount when buying large amounts. Every year at our booth we get a request for 10 to 20 pounds of green tomatoes. Maybe you're looking for the perfect fruits and vegetables for an upcoming party. Ask your vendor. If they can, they'll be happy to take orders in advance and bring you the best for your guests. And if you don't see what you're looking for, ask. The vendor may have it and just hasn't restocked the display, or can bring it for you next week.

Shop with the seasons and be flexible on your menu choices. You're not likely to find fresh blackberries in June for that pie, but cherries are in season and make a wonderful pie. Sugar snap peas and asparagus may not be on your list but they may be at the market, for a limited time only. You may also see something you've never tried before. Ask the vendor how to prepare it, then cook up a surprise for your family. It may become one of their favorites.

For the best selection of produce at its prime, shop early. Growers may have a limited supply, particularly when it's the first of the season. Late in the day shopping may find several items that are sold out. While shopping the market, if you see what you're looking for don't wait too long to buy it, especially if there are just a few left. By the time you've finished looking and go back for the item you want, it may be sold out. You can often leave purchases with the vendor when space allows until you're done shopping.

Bring your own bags or baskets, and a ready cooler in the car comes in handy on hot days or when buying perishables like cheese or fish. Plan your day so that you can bring your purchases home right after you're done shopping. You bought them fresh, you want to keep them fresh.

To make your farmers' market experience complete, use this book. It was created with you in mind. There's a listing for all the farmers' markets in Oregon so you can be sure to find the one nearest you. Information is given about the participating markets and vendors to bring awareness about special events and specialty items and produce available. A resource listing of participating vendors is a significant tool for you to learn about those offering mail order catalogs, Community Supported Agriculture (CSA), farm stand purchases and other services. And best of all are the "fresh from the farm" recipes that will make not only shopping for produce fun, but also bring new life and excitement to your family meals. See you at the market!

Arugula Mayonnaise  •  Mushroom-Leek Gravy

Judy's Smoked Fish Dip

Helmi's Smoked Salmon Chowder

Potato-Leek Soup  •  Butternut Ginger Soup with Kale

Sweet and Sour Red Cabbage

Steamed Green Cabbage and Potatoes

Shell Bean Succotash  •  Greens and Beans with Pasta

Watermelon Burritos  •  Summer Harvest Casserole

Elin's Creamed Albacore Tuna on Toast

Swedish Open-Face Salmon Sandwiches

Laura's Mom's Strawberry Pie  •  Swiss Apple Tart

# BEAVERTON FARMERS' MARKET

**LOCATION:**
5th & Hall Blvd., behind the Fire Station,
between Hall & Tucker and 3rd Avenue & 5th
May through October
Saturdays, 8:00 - 1:30

**SECOND LOCATION:**
Same location as above
July through September
Wednesdays, 3:00 - 7:00

WITH JUST SEVEN VENDORS, THE BEAVERTON FARMERS' MARKET FIRST OPENED IN June 1988. The market has grown considerably since that first day and now offers a great variety of products with over 100 participating vendors.

If it's in season it can be found at the Beaverton Farmers' Market. The "Five-A-Day" fruit and vegetables rule is easy to follow while shopping at the market—strawberries, raspberries, blueberries, boysenberries, New Zealand berries, and marionberries are followed by cherries, peaches, melons and apples. Some of the vegetable growers are known for their specialties with fresh English peas in June, first local sweet corn picked at the right moment, salad mixes, artichokes, wonderful peppers, homegrown tomatoes, green beans, new potatoes, juicy carrots of all sizes, many different herbs, even chestnuts toward the end of October. Advice on how to store and prepare the vegetables or fruit is freely given.

The chocolate-covered Oregon Hazelnuts from Stickney Orchards never last long on a Saturday. Susan, the lamb lady, brings different cuts of lamb while The Astoria Fish Company displays salmon, halibut, crab and more. Antonia's hand-made pasta, risotto and biscotti are the best this side of Italy, and Meadowcharm Dairy's Chocolate Milk is to die for (definitely not low-calorie). When all the shopping makes you hungry, a freshly grilled bratwurst or bierwurst from Fetzer's German Deli will help make the day complete.

There are booths with honey, jams, goat cheese, mushrooms, home-made salad dressings, baked goods, wine and more. The shopper can also choose from a great assortment of cut flowers or the perfect bouquet, and the home gardener will find the market the perfect place for their planting needs with plenty of vegetable starts, herbs, bulbs, trees, shrubs, annuals and perennials.

Listen to the Bluegrass music of Endangered Species, or let the group *Music of the Andes* delight you with some lively tunes from South America. Whether you're looking for one item or many, the market will turn your trip into an adventure in shopping.

# Arugula Mayonnaise

*Gathering Together Farm is an eleven year old certified organic farm located on the Mary's River. They specialize in greens, potatoes, onions, leeks, shallots, winter squash and kale, and also grow produce for Organically Grown Co-op, a restaurant, and seed crops for Seeds of Change. Last year they sold over 40 distinct types of vegetables at the Beaverton, Philomath, Corvallis, and Lane County farmers' markets.*

*This may make your regular mayonnaise obsolete.*

1 cup arugula leaves, lightly packed (no stems)
1 clove garlic
1 large egg yolk
1/2 cup olive oil
1 to 2 tablespoons fresh lemon juice
salt & pepper to taste

IN A BLENDER OR FOOD PROCESSOR, combine and puree arugula, egg yolk, 1 teaspoon olive oil, 1 tablespoon lemon juice, salt and pepper. With blender still running, add remaining oil in a fine stream till thickened. Add more lemon juice, salt and pepper if necessary. Keep refrigerated. Makes 3/4 cup.

**Sally Brewer**
GATHERING TOGETHER FARM

# Mushroom-Leek Gravy

*Delicious served over mashed yellow potatoes, greens, pasta, or rice.*

3 cups leeks, finely chopped (stem only)
3 cups shitake mushrooms, thinly sliced
2 cups nutritional yeast
1/2 cup plus 2 tablespoons canola oil, divided
1 tablespoon minced garlic
2 tablespoons cornstarch
1/4 cup water
4 cups water, milk, or beer
1/3 cup tamari (may substitute soy sauce)

IN SMALL SKILLET, sauté leeks, mushrooms, and garlic in 2 tablespoons oil until tender. In a heavy bottomed pan, dry-sauté yeast until it turns color and starts to smoke. (This part requires constant stirring! Walking away for even a few seconds may mean disaster). Once yeast is cooked, add 1/2 cup oil and stir for 3 more minutes. Stir in tamari and liquid of choice and bring to slow boil. Thoroughly mix cornstarch with 1/4 cup water, add to gravy and stir until thickened. Amount of cornstarch may be adjusted to alter thickness of gravy. Serve over mashed yellow potatoes, pasta, or rice. Yields about 8 cups.

**John Eveland**
GATHERING TOGETHER FARM

# Judy's Smoked Fish Dip

*Oregon Ocean Seafoods, home of SKIPANON BRAND, has been a family business since 1978. Norman Kujala contributes 50 years of fish processing experience. His oldest son, Mark, is chief smoker. Mark's mentors are "giants" in the art of fish smoking, in this community renown for its fishing traditions. Norman and Judy Kujala sell smoked, canned and fresh seafood at the Beaverton market.*

*A good smoked fish dip that can be made with any of Skipanon Brand's smoked fish.*

1 cup flaked smoked fish and its liquid

4 oz. cream cheese
2 tablespoons milk

MASH CREAM CHEESE with milk. Add flaked fish and combine well. Serve on crackers or with chips.

**Norman & Judy Kujala**
OREGON OCEAN SEAFOODS

# Helmi's Smoked Salmon Chowder

*Enjoy a delicious, old-country meal that's simple to make.*

2 potatoes, grated
1/4 cup minced onions
2 tablespoons butter
3 tablespoons flour

3 cups milk
1 can smoked salmon, flaked with liquid
salt and pepper to taste

BOIL POTATOES AND ONIONS in water just to cover. In a 2 quart saucepan, melt butter and stir in flour. Add milk and heat, stirring until thickened. Add potatoes and onions with water and smoked salmon. Salt and pepper to taste. Serves 4

**Norman & Judy Kujala**
OREGON OCEAN SEAFOODS

---

**how to spot a ripe watermelon**

Unlike other fruits, watermelons do not continue to ripen once they've been picked. Tell-tale signs the grower looks for are a slight hazing of the rind and a dried-up tendril opposite where the fruit stem attaches to the vine. Also the term 'yellow belly' is a good thing when it comes to watermelons. The 'belly' is the side that rests on the ground. This will turn from white to a shade of yellow when the melon is ready. You can also look for this 'yellow belly' when shopping for a vine-ripened watermelon. Thumping is a matter of personal choice, some swear by it and others scoff at it. If you feel lucky, the thump should sound deep and hollow, like you're thumping your chest as opposed to your stomach. A good grower will usually know how to spot a ripe melon.

# Potato-Leek Soup

*For autumn and winter fare, potato-leek soup is a sure crowd pleaser.*

| | |
|---|---|
| 6 cups water or stock | 1 1/2 teaspoons dried dill weed |
| 6 cups diced potatoes (about 5 large) | 1 teaspoon salt |
| 4 tablespoons butter | black pepper to taste |
| 2 cups leeks, thinly sliced (about 3) | 2 tablespoons unbleached wheat flour |
| 1 cup celery, chopped | 1 cup milk or cream |
| 1 teaspoon dried thyme | 1/2 cup fresh parsley, minced |

IN LARGE SOUP POT, bring water to boil, then add potatoes. Cover and cook until potatoes are tender, about 20 minutes. Puree 3/4 of the potatoes in a blender or food processor; add back to soup pot. In a 10-inch skillet, melt 2 tablespoons butter over low heat. Add leeks, celery, thyme, and dill weed, sautéing until leeks are tender, about 10 to 15 minutes. Add to soup pot along with salt and pepper. In same pan, melt remaining 2 tablespoons butter, then add flour, stirring for about 1 minute. Whisk in milk or cream, then turn off heat. Add mixture to soup along with fresh parsley. Simmer uncovered for 10 to 15 minutes. Ladle into individual soup bowls and enjoy. Serves 8.

**John Eveland**
GATHERING TOGETHER FARM

# Butternut Ginger Soup with Kale

*Flavorful and hearty, fresh ginger is a great compliment to beans and butternut squash.*

| | |
|---|---|
| 1 cup uncooked white beans | 2 tablespoons fresh ginger root, minced |
| 11 cups water | 4 cloves garlic, minced |
| 6 cups peeled, seeded, and diced butternut squash | 1 tablespoon salt |
| | black pepper to taste |
| 2 tablespoons canola oil | 1 bunch kale, washed and chopped |
| 1 cup onion, chopped | |

IN LARGE POT, cover beans with water and soak overnight. Drain and rinse thoroughly. Bring beans to boil in 8 cups of water and then simmer, covered for 1 1/2 hours or until tender. In separate covered pot, cook squash in remaining water until tender. Add to blender and puree until smooth, then add to cooked beans. In a skillet, heat the oil and lightly sauté onion, ginger, and garlic till tender, then add to soup pot. Stir in chopped kale at the end and cook until the kale is wilted. Serves 8.

**Sally Brewer**
GATHERING TOGETHER FARM

BEAVERTON FARMERS' MARKET

# Sweet and Sour Red Cabbage

*At the west end of the Columbia Gorge situated on a high hill is Winters Farms, a family farm first begun in the 1940s by Howard and Ruth Winters. The Winters family grows an assortment of popular and unique berries along with many vegetables including green and wax beans, pickling and slicing cucumbers, sweet onions, beets, English peas and sweet corn. Summer and winter squash, tomatoes, red and green cabbage and many herbs top the list. In addition to growing for the Beaverton and Portland Farmers' Markets, their wholesale customers and brokers remain an important part of their business.*

*Our red cabbage is frequently requested at the market and so is this recipe.*

4 cups red cabbage
1 tart apple
4 tablespoons butter
1 heaping tablespoon brown sugar
1 cup onions, minced

6 tablespoons red wine vinegar
1 cup beef or chicken broth or water
1 teaspoon salt
1/2 cup red currant jelly

WASH, DRY AND SHRED the cabbage. Chop the apple. Melt the butter in a large frying pan and stir in the brown sugar. Add the apple and onions, cover and cook over low heat for 4 to 5 minutes or until wilted. Stir in cabbage and vinegar, cover and braise for 10 minutes.

Pour in the broth or water and salt; cook, covered, over low heat for 2 hours (or bake in a preheated 300 degree oven for 2 1/2 hours). Stir in the jelly before serving. Depending on the freshness of the cabbage, cooking time can be reduced. Start checking texture after 1 hour of cooking. Makes 6 cups

**Inge Winters**
WINTERS FARMS

---

**history of the smoking process**

Before there were freezers and canning jars, the earliest method of food preservation was simply drying. There were obstacles but soon answers were discovered to pest problems and better preservation. Smudge fires under drying racks kept pests away from the food while it was drying. The smoke from these fires actually made the food last longer and taste even better.

Then came the breakthrough of salt curing, resulting in yet better tasting, and longer lasting food. In fact, weeks of "cold-smoking" prepared salted meat or fish could last indefinitely. With the lack of refrigeration, this method became essential for families, armies and sailing ship crews.

Unfortunately food preserved this way needed lengthy soaking and cooking to make it palatable. Without this it would be far too tough and salty to eat.

With the 20th century came refrigeration and quick transportation, reducing the need for heavily smoked and salted meats and fish. Today the smoking process is mainly to cook and add flavor. Instead of 15% salt content, today's meats and fish are lightly salted at just 2 to 3%. Now foods are ready to eat after being cold-smoked for less than 20 hours, or "hot-smoked" in just a few hours.

OREGON OCEAN SEAFOODS

## Steamed Green Cabbage and Potatoes

*The yellow-fleshed Yukon Gold potatoes are excellent in this dish.*

2 pounds green cabbage; washed, cored and chopped or sliced into 1/2-inch pieces
2 large potatoes, peeled and thickly sliced
1/4 cup olive oil
1 cup onions, sliced
sliced pepperoni (or bacon)
salt and freshly ground black pepper to taste
broth or water

HEAT OLIVE OIL in a large saucepan; add the onions and pepperoni, cooking until onions are wilted. Add the cabbage and potatoes, then season to taste with salt and pepper. Cover and steam over low heat for 20 to 30 minutes or until the potatoes are tender. Stir frequently. If the vegetables start to brown, add some broth or water. Serves 4.

**Inge Winters**
WINTERS FARMS

## Shell Bean Succotash

*Fresh summer savory is the perfect compliment to beans and really enhances this dish.*

2 cups horticultural beans (shell beans)
1 strip bacon
1 teaspoon salt
2 tablespoons onions, chopped
1 cup water
1 cup tomatoes; peeled, seeded and chopped
2 cups corn kernels (preferably fresh)
2 tablespoons butter
salt and freshly ground black pepper
fresh summer savory or other favorite fresh herb

PUT BEANS, BACON, SALT AND ONIONS in a saucepan; add water. Bring water to boil, cover and simmer for 20 minutes. Stir in tomatoes and corn. Simmer for 10 minutes longer. Remove bacon, stir in butter, and season to taste with salt, pepper and fresh herbs. Serves 4 to 6.

**Inge Winters**
WINTERS FARMS

---

**cooking with garlic**  Roasted, baked, sautéed, or fresh; garlic can be cooked in many ways. The character of a dish can change depending on how garlic is prepared and when it is added. For a stronger garlic flavor, add fresh minced garlic to the dish after it is cooked. A milder flavor will develop if the garlic is cooked along with the dish, and for a really mellow flavor, try roasting or baking garlic first to bring out a nutty sweetness. When cooking garlic on the stove, be careful to not let it over brown or burn. The result can be bitter and the flavor may ruin the whole dish.

BEAVERTON FARMERS' MARKET

# Greens and Beans with Pasta

*The arugula adds a wonderfully distinct flavor to this quick and easy pasta dish.*

16 ounce package whole wheat fettucine (or other pasta)
1/4 cup virgin olive oil
4 cloves garlic, chopped
1/2 teaspoon red pepper flakes

8 cups arugula (rocket) leaves, coarsely chopped
15 ounce can cannelloni or red beans
parmesan cheese

BOIL WATER IN A LARGE POT and then add the pasta. Cook according to package directions. In a separate skillet, lightly sauté the chopped garlic and red pepper flakes in olive oil, about 2 to 3 minutes. Add the beans and greens with enough water to keep them from sticking to the pan. Cook, stirring until the greens are wilted. Toss with cooked pasta, adding in a little extra virgin olive oil. Serve on large platter and top with parmesan cheese. Serves 4.

**NOTE:** The rocket can be older and spicier than what you would put in a salad. Other greens such as mustard, collard, beet, or spinach can also be substituted.

**John Eveland**
GATHERING TOGETHER FARM

**what is arugula?** If you've ever had a spicy mesclun or salad mix, you've probably eaten arugula. This spicy green also goes by the names of salad rocket, roquette or rocket cress. Belonging to the mustard family, its peppery flavor has undertones of a nutty, sesame taste.

Younger and larger leaves alike are rich in vitamin C, phosphorus, calcium, and potassium, with larger leaves being stronger tasting. As the leaves get older they become seemingly bitter, but all is not lost. The flowers are not bitter and can add a distinctively sesame-type flavor to salads.

# Watermelon Burritos

*Tom Denison has been farming in Corvallis since 1978. Denison Farms grows a wide variety of certified organic fruits and vegetables year-round. Some of their more popular items include cold-frame tomatoes during June and July, and a dozen different melon varieties in August and September. Many other vegetables and fruits such as figs and persimmons can be found at any of the 7 different markets they sell at, including Beaverton, Corvallis, and Lane County.*

*It's simple to make and easy to remember. You won't even need to write it down.*

NO, WE'RE NOT KIDDING. Substitute watermelon chunks for tomato pieces in your favorite bean burrito recipe. Unusual, but great!

**Tom Denison & Elizabeth Kerle**
DENISON FARMS

# Summer Harvest Casserole

*The eggplant really fills out this casserole dish.*

2 medium eggplant, cut in 1/4-inch slices
3 orange or yellow sweet bell peppers, cut in 1/4-inch slices
6 fresh tomatoes, cut in 1/4-inch slices
1 large sweet onion, sliced in rings
1 bunch fresh basil, chopped
4 cloves garlic, chopped
1/4 cup olive oil
1/2 pound mozzarella, jack, or cheddar cheese, grated

OIL THE BOTTOM of a 9x13-inch pan with 1 tablespoon olive oil. Spread a layer of eggplant slices on bottom of pan. Add a layer of peppers, tomato, then onion slices. Top with half the chopped basil. Repeat layers. Sauté garlic in remaining olive oil; drizzle over vegetables. Top with grated cheese. Cover and bake in a pre-heated oven at 350 degrees for 45 minutes. Serves 4 to 6.

**Tom Denison & Elizabeth Kerle**
DENISON FARMS

---

**looking for leeks**

There was a time when leeks were hard to find. Then in early 1900's, a French chef in New York created vichyssoise, the exquisite cold potato and leek soup. Now it seems most people prefer their potato and leek soup hot, but hot in taste leeks aren't. Looking somewhat like gigantic scallions, leeks taste sweeter and are more delicate than onions. Look for leeks beginning in late August to early May. The prized part is the white and pale green stem. Leaves should be dark green, crisp and fresh-looking. Although the leaves are tough, they can add flavor to the stockpot. Because leeks are hardy, they winter over quite well here though sometimes they will develop a hard central core from the developing seed stalk. No matter how long a leek is cooked, this core will remain tough. As the leeks grow, dirt usually gets caught between the leaves and will need to be removed before cooking. The simplest way to do this is to split the leek lengthwise and rinse well under cool running water.

BEAVERTON FARMERS' MARKET

# Elin's Creamed Albacore Tuna on Toast

*Tuna never tasted so good.*

2 tablespoons butter
3 tablespoons flour
1 1/2 cups milk

1 can Albacore tuna, flaked, with liquid
salt and pepper to taste

IN A QUART SAUCEPAN, melt butter and stir in flour. Add milk and heat, stirring until thickened. Add tuna, then salt and pepper to taste. Spoon on warm bread or toast. Delightful. Serves 3 to 4.

**Norman & Judy Kujala**
OREGON OCEAN SEAFOODS

# Swedish Open-Face Salmon Sandwiches

*Be sure to make plenty for seconds of this colorful and delicious sandwich*

ONTO BUTTERED RYE BREAD, layer the following:

mayonnaise (generous amount)
thinly slices cucumbers, onions
flaked canned salmon (reserve the liquid for soups)

fresh or dried dill weed to taste
thin slice of red bell pepper

**Norman & Judy Kujala**
OREGON OCEAN SEAFOODS

| leafy kale | One of the most nutritious greens, kale is very rich in Vitamin A, calcium and iron; with amounts of vitamin C, B vitamins, phosphorus and potassium. After removing the midrib and tough stem, chop the leaves and use fresh in salads, or lightly steam, braise or stir fry. The midribs can be diced like celery and saved for soups and stews. When touched by frost, kale becomes very sweet. |
|---|---|

BEAVERTON FARMERS' MARKET

# Laura's Mom's Strawberry Pie

*This recipe works with any berry that's in season.*

1 9-inch baked pie shell                whole berries

### Glaze:

1 cup crushed berries           1/2 cup water
1 cup sugar                     pinch of salt
3 tablespoons cornstarch        2 tablespoons butter

FILL BAKED PIE SHELL with whole berries. Mix glaze ingredients (except butter) in saucepan and bring to a boil; boil for 2 minutes. Remove from heat and add the butter. Pour glaze over berries and refrigerate at least two hours before serving. Serves 6 to 8.

**Inge Winters**
WINTERS FARMS

---

**potato lore**

The potato didn't start off getting the same welcome reception with the rest of the world as it did in its original home, the Andes of Peru. Pizarro brought the potato to Spain in the early sixteenth century, and soon it traveled into France and Italy. The potato was an oddity to the people of this time and they looked upon the lumpy, bumpy tubers as diseased because they reminded them of leprous hands.

Sir Francis Drake discovered the potato in Columbia where he stocked his vessel and sailed home for England, but only after stopping and leaving samples in Virginia. At first, the English didn't seem to know what to do with the potato. When given to the cooks to prepare for the royal table of Queen Elizabeth, they threw the tubers away and served up a dish of boiled potato greens instead. Since potato greens have a high concentration of the poisonous alkaloid solanine, one could only imagine how "green" everyone at that Royal Banquet must have been.

The value of the potato became evident to some, especially Germany's Emperor Frederick Wilhelm. After a sequence of Prussian crop failures, the Emperor issued the "Brandenburg Potato Paper". Simply put, it stated that all peasants were to plant potatoes or suffer the loss of their ears and noses.

In every country there were those few brave souls that tested, and tasted the potato. Eventually it became accepted worldwide and at times was heavily relied upon to sustain people through crop loss and famine. So much so that when potato blight struck in the mid 1800's, the resulting famine affected more than just the Irish, though they suffered the most.

Now potatoes are as accepted, widely used, and commonplace as people, and the "proof is in the pudding" so to speak because it has become one of the world's major food crops. In the United States alone, over 49 billion pounds were produced in 1996. Today potatoes have made their way into a multitude of dishes, and restaurants everywhere are serving mashed potatoes, baked potatoes, French fries and potato skins. With over 5,000 varieties, the potato has probably become the number one vegetable in production. The rest is just history.

BEAVERTON FARMERS' MARKET

# Swiss Apple Tart

*This recipe can be used for many different fruits like peaches, apricots or fresh plums, but not berries.*

9-inch pie shell, unbaked
several apples (Kings are best)
finely chopped nuts (optional)
6 tablespoons sugar
1 egg
1 teaspoon cornstarch
2/3 cup cream or milk
   (use less liquid if using milk)
1/2 teaspoon cinnamon

PREHEAT OVEN TO 425 DEGREES. Sprinkle unbaked pie shell with hazelnuts. Peel and quarter apples, then slice quarters in half, lengthwise. Arrange apple slices in a circular fashion on pie shell. Beat together in a small bowl; sugar, egg, cornstarch, cream and cinnamon. Pour over apples. Bake for 15 minutes at 425 degrees. Reduce to 375 degrees and bake an additional 25 to 30 minutes or until custard is set and begins to brown slightly. Sprinkle with a little sugar if desired. Serves 6 to 8.

**Inge Winters**
WINTERS FARMS

**pick a peck of sweet peppers**

Sweet peppers come in a variety of different shapes and vivid colors. A green pepper is a sweet pepper that just hasn't fully matured and ripened to its final color. Most all sweet peppers begin growing as a green pepper although there are a few varieties where the pepper will start growing its fruit in colors like purple, pale yellow or greenish-yellow. A pepper will be its sweetest after it has fully developed and turned its final color, and that can be shades of red, gold, yellow, orange or even chocolate depending on the variety.

BEAVERTON FARMERS' MARKET

Blueberry Salsa • Apple Butter

Potato, Green Bean and Garlic Soup • Zucchini Quiche

Broccoli Bacon Salad • Collard Greens with Pasta and Feta

Kuta and Onion Stir Fry • Delicata Boats

Tabouli-Stuffed Grape Leaves Casserole

Migas • Ballymaloe Brown Bread

Irish Soda Bread • Grape Pie

Monine's Incredible Apple Pie • Honey of an Apple Cake

One Bowl Apple Cake • Vanilla Caramel Sauce

Lekvar • Lekvar Bars

Prune Snow

# CORVALLIS SATURDAY FARMERS' MARKET

**LOCATION:**
Riverfront Park "Blue Lot"
First Street between Jackson and Monroe Avenue
Mid-April through
late November
Saturdays, 9:00 a.m. to 1:00 p.m.

ESTABLISHED IN 1991, THE CORVALLIS SATURDAY FARMERS' MARKET PROVIDES A highly visible, centralized location for shoppers to experience quality produce. The focus is on local organic and conventionally grown produce, nursery plants, herbs, cut flowers, honey and eggs. Baked goods and other specialty foods were added in 1995, and the market now features two restaurant booths. Samples of melons, tomatoes, apples and other pomes help customers learn about differences in taste, color, texture and shape among the many varieties offered at the market.

Corvallis, home to the state's land-grant university, is set in the Willamette Valley, formed by Oregon's Coast Range and the Cascades. The market operates from Corvallis' lively and historic downtown in a parking lot on the riverfront. In 1999, the market expects to move temporarily near City Hall during construction of a sewer project and redesign of First Street and public spaces adjacent to the river.

At the market, the shopper will find some unique resources relating to seeds. Vendors include Alan Kapuler, research director for Seeds of Change, and Jean Frazier Geist, daughter of renowned vegetable breeder W.A. "Tex" Frazier. Rose Marie Nichols McGee of seed purveyor Nichols Garden Nursery in Albany, and Carol Deppe, author of "Breed Your Own Vegetable Varieties" both attend the market as customers.

Results of a market tomato tasting in 1996 prompted McGee to add an heirloom called "Cherokee Purple" to her catalog's tomato offerings. The Nichols catalog is designed by Janet O'Doherty Hessel, a market vendor and graphic artist who created the market's horse-and-wagon logo from an historic photo.

Live acoustic music recently became a weekly feature of the market. And for a possible first among Oregon farmers markets, the Corvallis market has a homepage on the World Wide Web. Come visit at http://www.peak.org/farmers-market. Better yet, bring the family and join in the fun.

# Blueberry Salsa

*Over three years ago the Steele family bought Blueberry Bottom, a Corvallis farm with a blueberry patch that was planted nearly 40 years ago. This 1/2 acre patch has quite a reputation for its sweet berries which are also featured at the Corvallis Saturday Market and the Indoor Thursday Market along with the Steele family's garden produce.*

*A surprising blend of combinations results in this beautifully colored salsa. I took a batch of blueberry salsa to the Philomath Thursday Market for sampling. People were hesitant to try it at first, but once they did all I could hear was "can I have the recipe!"*

2 cups fresh blueberries
1/2 medium red onion, diced
2 jalapeno peppers, seeded and minced
1 red bell pepper, cored and diced
3 tablespoons chopped fresh cilantro
1/4 cup fresh lime juice
1 teaspoon salt

COARSELY CHOP 1 1/2 cups of the blueberries. In a bowl, combine the chopped and the whole blueberries and the remaining ingredients. Let stand for 1 hour. Great as a condiment for the barbecue, or try it with tortilla chips.

**The Steele Family**
**Tina, Russell, Daniel, Chase, & Jared**
BLUEBERRY BOTTOM

| **selecting summer squash** | Harvested during the warm weather of summer, it's best eaten when the fruit is small, tender and the seeds are still immature. Zucchini, scallop, and crookneck are the types of squash familiar to most. |
|---|---|
| | Shaped like a baseball, long like a bat or even club-shaped, zucchini also comes in a variety of colors. From the palest green to a dark green almost as black as the night, zucchini can also be colored gold, yellow, or even striped. |
| | The old-time varieties of yellow crooknecks are full of flavor, slightly warted and bright yellow. Newer varieties are milder in flavor, wartless, and range in yellow hues from light to dark. |
| | Scallop squash is also referred to as "pattypan", and can be white, pale green or deep yellow. |
| | To enjoy squash at its tender best, choose those that have good color, are firm but not hard, and still quite small. |

# Apple Butter

*For a variety of fresh-picked apples, Monine & Bob Stebbins only have to go as far as their own farm, Brooklane Specialty Apples. The orchard was planted in 1988 using the French Axis system with emphasis on new varieties developed by Bob Stebbins, retired extension tree fruit specialist. Covering 1 1/2 acres of their farm are 1500 apple trees on dwarf rootstock, producing plenty to sell at the Corvallis Wednesday and Saturday Markets where they also sell fresh cider. Each season the Stebbins host 2 or 3 cider making parties filled with guests from their mailing list.*

*This butter can be stored in the refrigerator for up to 3 weeks. To keep longer, freeze or heat to boiling, put in clean canning jars and process in a boiling water bath for 10 minutes. You can make the apple butter in the microwave or the oven. The microwave is faster, but the oven makes a slightly better colored product. They both taste delicious and make about 1 1/2 cups apple butter.*

1 quart applesauce
1/4 cup frozen apple juice concentrate, thawed
1 teaspoon cinnamon
1/2 teaspoon allspice
1/4 teaspoon cloves
1/2 teaspoon nutmeg
1 tablespoon cornstarch

### Microwave preparation

USE A ROUND 2 or 3 quart glass casserole with a lid. Combine all ingredients thoroughly. Cover and cook at full power for about 35 minutes. The cover can be placed slightly off center so steam can escape, but the sauce won't splatter on the oven. Stir every 10 minutes. Cook until it is thick enough to spread easily.

### Oven preparation

Combine all ingredients thoroughly in a 9x13-inch glass cake pan. Cover with foil, cutting 4 or 6 slits about 2-inches long into the foil covering. Bake in a 400 degree oven for about 1 hour and 15 minutes, stirring every half hour. Cook until desired consistency is reached.

**Monine & Bob Stebbins**
BROOKLANE SPECIALTY APPLES

**tahini terminology** — A natural creamy puree of sesame seeds, tahini's nutty flavor is used in many dishes like Baba Ganoush, a traditional Middle Eastern spread served with pita bread squares. Tahini can also be used in dressings, with fish entrees, noodles or vegetable dishes.

# Potato, Green Bean and Garlic Soup

*Jeff Falen and Elanor O'Brien grow a wide selection of certified organic vegetables on 10 acres at Persephone Farm, located on the banks of the South Santiam River between Lebanon and Sweet Home. Farming since 1985, their decision to diversify their markets and crops from the wholesale markets led them to the Portland market in 1992.*

*Quick! Simple! So Good!*

| | |
|---|---|
| 1 1/2 pounds russet potatoes, cut into 2-inch cubes | 1 pound fresh green beans, cut into 2-inch lengths |
| Kosher salt | 6 tablespoons olive oil |
| 6 cups water | 6 large cloves garlic, thinly sliced |
| | Freshly ground black pepper |

BRING THE POTATOES, 1 tablespoon salt and the water to a boil in a large, covered pot. Reduce heat and cook until the potatoes are nearly soft, about 15 minutes. Add the green beans and cook, uncovered, until they turn bright green and start to get tender. While potatoes and beans are cooking, heat the olive oil in a small saucepan until hot but not smoking. Add sliced garlic and cook, stirring constantly until golden brown. Remove from heat and set aside. When beans and potatoes are cooked, add browned garlic to soup. Season to taste with salt and pepper and enjoy. Serves 4.

**Elanor O'Brien**
PERSEPHONE FARM

# Zucchini Quiche

*You can never have too many zucchini recipes and this one is quick, easy, and very tasty.*

| | |
|---|---|
| 4 eggs, slightly beaten | 1/2 teaspoon mayonnaise |
| 1/2 cup oil | 3 cups zucchini, thinly sliced or shredded |
| 1/2 cup parmesan cheese | 1 cup Bisquick mix |
| 1/2 teaspoon each pepper, dried basil, oregano, and seasoned salt | 1/2 cup chopped onion |
| | 1/4 cup fresh parsley, snipped |

In a large bowl, mix all ingredients together and pour in a 9x13-inch baking dish. Bake in a preheated 325 degree oven for 25 minutes. Yum! Serves 6 to 8.

**Carol Shenk & Shirley Wainwright**
YUMMY HONEY

# Broccoli Bacon Salad

*Carol Shenk's sons started raising bees as a 4-H project and the result was more than just honey. She soon began selling honey at the Corvallis Wednesday and Saturday Markets, then added her garden produce of flowers, herbs, fruits, and vegetables.*

*Broccoli is one of the richest vegetables sources of calcium and this salad is packed with many vitamins and minerals*

3 stalks broccoli
1/4 pound sliced bacon
(reserve 2 teaspoons drippings
for dressing)

1 medium onion, diced
1 cup cheddar cheese, grated

### Dressing

1/2 cup mayonnaise
1/4 cup sugar

3 tablespoons white wine vinegar
2 teaspoons bacon drippings

CUT BROCCOLI FLOWERETTES into bite size pieces. Peel broccoli stalks and cut into bite size pieces as well. Cut bacon strips into 1/4-inch pieces and fry until crisp; set aside. Mix together broccoli, onion, cheese and bacon.

For dressing, combine mayonnaise, sugar, white wine vinegar and bacon drippings. Top the salad with dressing and chill for 1 to 3 hours. Serves 4.

**Carol Shenk & Shirley Wainwright**
YUMMY HONEY

| **too hot to handle** | Oils from the hot pepper can cause great discomfort and irritation to the eyes and skin. Even with careful washing, the oils can sometimes remain on the skin for hours and cause pain later when you touch your eyes, nose or skin. To prevent undue pain, wear rubber gloves when working with hot peppers. For those that prefer to be adventurous and go gloveless, wash hands when finished and rinse with vinegar to remove any last traces of the oil. You also may be one of those lucky few who are seldom bothered by the irritating oils from the pungent peppers. |
|---|---|

# Collard Greens with Pasta and Feta

*Denison Farms sells their certified organic fruits and vegetables at 7 different farmers' markets including Beaverton, Corvallis, and Lane County.*
*A tasty and nutritious 'fast-food' for any occasion.*

6 tablespoons olive oil
1 large leek, thinly sliced
1 bunch collard greens,
    coarsely chopped
2 red or yellow sweet peppers,
    chopped
2 large tomatoes, chopped
1 16 ounce package of pasta penne,
    fusili, or shells
1 cup feta cheese, crumbled
freshly ground black pepper

BRING PASTA WATER to a boil in a large pot and cook pasta until al dente. Drain and reserve. Heat oil in deep skillet. Add leek and cook over medium heat for 10 minutes. Add collards, stirring for 2 minutes; then add peppers and tomatoes. Cover and cook 10 minutes over medium-low heat. Crumble feta into vegetables and mix gently. Add cooked pasta to vegetables and feta. Simmer over low heat for 3 minutes. Serve with freshly ground pepper. Serves 4 to 6.

**Tom Denison & Elizabeth Kerle**
DENISON FARMS

### connoisseur's guide to seedless grapes

| variety | color | comments |
|---|---|---|
| Canadice | Red | Delicious grapey spicy flavor with medium sized berries. Fantastic table grape, also used for juice, jelly and wine. |
| Concord seedless | Bluish-black | Same distinctive concord taste with a sweet flavor. Great juice and also used for pie making. |
| Einset | Bright red | Wonderful, mild strawberry flavor. Stores well. |
| Glenora | Blue-black | Some describe it as a spicy blueberry-like flavor, others say highly flavored and spicy. I think concord-like with a hint of spice. |
| Himrod | Amber-white | Excellent quality, crisp flavor with a hint of spiciness. Excellent for raisins as well as fresh eating. |
| Interlaken | Greenish/white | Small fruit size. Sweet and crisp, tight skinned with excellent flavor and great for raisins. |
| Reliance | Pink | Very sweet grape with an almost champagne-like flavor. Wonderful fresh, for wine, juicing or jellies. |
| Vanessa | Red | Medium sized berries with a tangy-sweet fruity flavor. Great for juice and jams. |
| Venus | Blue | Large clusters of big grapes with a slight muscat flavor. |

# Kuta and Onion Stir Fry

*Harry McKormick of SunBow Farm originally helped launch the Corvallis market along with Rebecca Landis and Ron Spisso. Now SunBow Farm owners McKormick and Bine Schulte grow over 90 different certified organic vegetables and herbs.*

*Kuta is a unique summer-type squash with a mild, sweet buttery nutty flavor. Young fruit is light green and somewhat pear shaped, while mature fruits turn dark green and can be used for baking or stuffing, like winter squash.*

1 pound cubed Kuta
1/3 pound sweet Walla Walla onions, sliced or diced
sunflower seeds
olive oil
1 to 2 tablespoons fresh cilantro, chopped

IN A LARGE SKILLET, stir fry the onions in olive oil until tender. Add sunflower seeds and stir in the cubed Kuta. Stir until seeds are golden and squash is tender. Add chopped cilantro. Serve over rice with traditional German cream sauce (recipe follows). Serves 4.

## Traditional German Cream Sauce

1/2 stick butter
1 to 2 tablespoons unbleached flour
1 cup vegetable cooking stock
1/2 to 1 cup heavy cream
dash of nutmeg
sprinkle of salt
fresh or dried summer savory

In a saucepan, melt butter over medium heat. Add enough flour to make a paste. Slowly whisk in the vegetable cooking stock, adding more if needed. Stir until somewhat thickened. Whisk in remaining ingredients, stirring well to make a creamy sauce. Serve over Kuta and Onion Stir Fry, or over favorite rice and vegetables.

**Bine Schulte**
SUNBOW FARM

---

**prune plums are so wonderful!!** Whether you dry them, freeze them, can them, or just plain eat them—prune plums are just wonderful. For a great low-fat substitute, use pureed prune plums in place of butter. Try substituting the same amount of pureed prune plums for butter in brownie, cake, and cookie recipes. The fat in these baked goods can be reduced by 75-90% when you use pureed prune plums instead of butter, and you'll get more vitamins, minerals, and fiber too. For a good source of iron, vitamin A, potassium, and phosphorus, you just can't beat prune plums.

# Delicata Boats

*A wonderful squash with an acorn-butternut like taste,
delicata's are the ideal shape for these tasty boats.*

2 medium delicata squash
1 medium onion, chopped
1 apple, thinly sliced
2 teaspoons curry powder

1/2 pound sausage (vegetarians may substitute marinated and seasoned tofu)
1/2 cup sharp cheddar cheese, grated
1/2 cup wheat germ or bread crumbs

IN MEDIUM SKILLET, sauté onions until translucent. Add sausage and brown. Cut squash lengthwise and scoop out seeds. Set squash boats in large baking dish with 1/2-inch water added. Sprinkle squash with curry powder. Fill each boat with sausage mixture and arrange apple slices on top. Sprinkle with cheese and wheat germ or crumbs. To prevent drying, make sure apples are completely covered with cheese and crumbs. Cover with foil and bake in pre-heated oven at 375 degrees for 1 hour. Serves 4.

**Elanor O'Brien**
PERSEPHONE FARM

# Tabouli-Stuffed Grape Leaves Casserole

*Cloud Run Farm grows 200 varieties of grapes in red, green, and blue, all available at the Corvallis Wednesday Farmers' Market where they also sell apples, pears, quinces, plums, and tanned sheepskins. This farm originally had Oregon's largest collection of grape varieties. The previous owner was a grape hobbyist with a 'green' thumb, a 'red' thumb, and a 'blue' thumb.*
*Here's a quick and easy meal that's a sure hit with friends as well as family.*

2 boneless chicken breasts
Tabouli salad
    (from mix or from scratch)

grape leaves

GRILL CHICKEN on barbecue until cooked. Cool and cut into thin slices. Place fresh grape leaves in a pot of boiling water for 30 seconds. Remove and lie leaves flat until cooled. Stuff grape leaves with tabouli (parsley-wheat salad). Alternate in layers, chicken and stuffed grape leaves in casserole. Place in a low heat oven at 325 degrees for about 15 minutes, or until heated.

**Amy Schoener**
CLOUD RUN FARM

# Migas

*In an urban backyard jungle just south of Oregon State University lies The Calico Garden, the farm of Larry and Rebecca Landis. Here at the farm they grow organic vegetables, herbs, and flower bouquets. They sell through the Corvallis market's community table, and also offer specialties like heirloom tomatoes and peppers, antique roses, and hardy geraniums. Talk about keeping heirloom vegetables alive. They also grow a pepper indigenous to the Huichol people of Mexico, their going-away present when they moved here to Oregon.*

*A brunch and dinner favorite in Austin, Texas where we lived for 8 years. This dish solves an important environmental problem: what to do with the rubble left at the bottom of bags of tortilla chips.*

8 large or 10 medium free-range eggs
A splash or dollop of milk or yogurt to blend with the eggs (optional)
1 medium onion, chopped
4 cloves garlic, chopped
4 small potatoes, cubed after softening by parboiling, steaming, or microwaving
2 tablespoons canola oil
ground cumin to taste
black pepper to taste

1 or 2 chile peppers, depending on pepper availability and hotness, chopped
1 large tomato, chopped
1/2 cup zucchini or sweet pepper, chopped
1/2 cup tortilla chip 'rubble' (leftover chip pieces)
1 tablespoon fresh cilantro, chopped
1/2 cup grated or chopped white cheddar or jack cheese
fresh salsa, red or green, to serve at the table
flour tortillas

BEAT THE EGGS, adding a little milk or yogurt if desired. In a large nonstick pan, sauté the potatoes, garlic, and onion in canola oil until the potatoes begin to brown. Add the chile peppers, cumin and black pepper and sauté until the peppers intensify in color. Add tomatoes and any optional vegetables.

Crumble chip 'rubble' directly into the pan. Sauté a few minutes, then add cilantro just before pouring in the eggs. Add eggs and scramble. When the eggs are fully cooked but not bone dry, top with cheese and turn off the burner; residual heat should be sufficient to melt the cheese.

Serve with heated flour tortillas and fresh salsa. Place a band of migas down the middle of a tortilla, add salsa and roll into an impromptu burrito. Serves 4 to 6.

**Rebecca Landis**
THE CALICO GARDEN

---

**irish soda bread story**

The great potato famine destroyed more than the luck of the Irish and was far reaching into many other countries. Soon many were driven from their land and along with the Irish immigrants to America also came Irish Soda Bread. Traditionally this bread was baked over a smoldering open peat fire because of the scarcity of wood in Ireland for cooking and fuel. Once in America the recipe was slightly modified to adapt to oven baking.

# Ballymaloe Brown Bread

*Francie O'Shea baked up Cooking At The Cafe and began selling her delicious home-baked goods in 1983 at the Corvallis and Albany Farmers' Markets. Sales took off and her creations found their way into her restaurant and cookbook. Now she's back at the Corvallis Saturday Market selling her baked goods and loving it.*

*Easy to make and simply delicious.*

3 1/2 cups whole wheat flour
1/4 cup unbleached flour
2 teaspoons salt
1 1/2 packages (3 1/2 teaspoons) active dry yeast
2 tablespoons molasses
2 cups warm water, 100 degrees

MIX TOGETHER in large bowl all dry ingredients, except yeast. Mix molasses into warm water. Sprinkle yeast on top and stir. When it starts to foam, add to dry ingredients and mix well. Pour batter in a greased 9-inch loaf pan. Let rise in a warm place until the bread reaches the top of the pan, about 1/2 hour. Bake in a 450 degree oven for 10 minutes. Reduce heat and bake 35 to 40 minutes more until richly browned and hollow sounding when tapped on the bottom of bread. Makes one 9-inch loaf.

**Francie O'Shea**
COOKING AT THE CAFE

# Irish Soda Bread

*A rustic loaf with traditional Irish flavor.*

3 1/4 cups whole wheat flour
1 1/2 cups unbleached flour
2 teaspoons salt
1 1/2 teaspoons baking soda
1/2 cup oats (not instant)
2 1/2 cups buttermilk

IN LARGE BOWL, mix together dry ingredients. Stir in the buttermilk until the mixture comes together to form a soft, moist dough. Turn out onto a lightly floured surface and form into a 10-inch diameter, round disk. With a sharp knife, cut a deep cross through the dough, almost cutting the dough into quarters. Bake at 425 degrees on a greased sheet pan for 15 minutes, then reduce heat to 350 degrees and bake 20 to 25 minutes more or until crusty and richly browned. Makes 1 large round loaf.

**Francie O'Shea**
COOKING AT THE CAFE

CORVALLIS SATURDAY FARMERS' MARKET

# Grape Pie

*For a great pie try this one with grapes for a surprisingly dramatic taste.*

### Filling

4 cups concord-type grapes, seedless or seeds removed
1/4 cup sugar
1/3 cup flour
1 tablespoon lemon juice

### Topping

1/2 cup flour
1/4 cup sugar
1/4 cup margarine, softened

COMBINE ALL INGREDIENTS for filling in a mixing bowl. Spoon filling into homemade or prepared pie crust. For topping, cut margarine into sifted flour and sugar until crumbly. Spread topping over filling. Bake pie in a pre-heated 400 degree oven for 40 minutes.

**Amy Schoener**
CLOUD RUN FARM

# Monine's Incredible Apple Pie

*Feature your own favorite pie apple with this recipe. Good pie apples include a mix of Jonagold, Cox's Orange Pippin, Melrose, Newtown Pippin, Gravenstein, and Idared.*

7 or 8 good pie apples
1/2 cup sugar
1 rounded tablespoon cornstarch
1 rounded tablespoon flour
3/4 teaspoon cinnamon
1/4 teaspoon nutmeg
pastry for pie

MIX SUGAR, cornstarch, flour and spices together in a large bowl. Peel, core and quarter apples, cutting into 1/4-inch thick slices. Add apple slices to sugar mixture, stirring well to coat slices.

Line a 10-inch pie pan with pie crust. Pour apple filling into pie pan. Cover with additional pastry and sprinkle with sugar. Put foil around the edges to prevent crust from over browning. Bake at 425 degrees for 1 hour or until pie bubbles and a toothpick goes into apples easily. Let cool for several hours before serving. Serves 4 to 8.

**Monine & Bob Stebbins**
BROOKLANE SPECIALTY APPLES

# Honey of an Apple Cake

*This cake is delicious and very moist.*

3 cups grated apples
1 1/2 cups sugar
2 tablespoons honey
2 teaspoons cinnamon
1 teaspoon nutmeg
1 teaspoon salt
2 teaspoons baking soda

2 eggs
1 cup oil
2 teaspoons vanilla
1 cup raisins
1 cup chopped walnuts
whipped cream (optional)

MIX TOGETHER in a large bowl the apples, sugar, cinnamon, nutmeg and salt. Add flour and baking soda, mix well then set aside. In another bowl, thoroughly beat eggs until creamy, then add oil and vanilla. Blend egg mixture into apple-flour mixture. Fold in raisins and nuts, then pour into a greased and floured 9x13-inch baking pan. Bake in a preheated oven at 350 degrees for 45 to 50 minutes. Serve warm or let cool, and top with a dollop of whipped cream if desired. Serves 12.

**Carol Shenk & Shirley Wainwright**
YUMMY HONEY

# One Bowl Apple Cake

*Here's where less is best—less dishes that is!*

4 cups apples, chopped and unpeeled
1/2 cup oil
1/2 cup applesauce
1 1/2 cups sugar
2 eggs

2 cups flour
1 teaspoon salt
2 teaspoons cinnamon
2 teaspoons baking soda

### Topping

1/4 cup sugar

1/2 cup nuts, chopped (your favorite)

MIX OIL, applesauce, sugar, and eggs in a large bowl. Add dry ingredients to oil mixture and stir to combine. Fold in apples then pour into a greased 13x15-inch baking dish. Sprinkle with sugar and nuts. Bake at 350 degrees for 55 minutes or until toothpick inserted comes out clean. Serve warm or cooled, plain or with sauce.

**Monine & Bob Stebbins**
BROOKLANE SPECIALTY APPLES

# Vanilla Caramel Sauce

*This sauce can be stored in a covered container in the refrigerator for several weeks. Serve with fresh apple slices for an easy to eat caramel apple flavor.*

2 cups sugar
1 cup brown sugar
1 cup light corn syrup
1 can sweetened condensed milk

1 cup milk
1/3 cup butter or margarine
1/4 teaspoon salt
2 teaspoons vanilla

COMBINE SUGARS, corn syrup, condensed (not evaporated) milk, and milk in a 3 quart heavy saucepan. Cook over medium heat, stirring until sugars are dissolved and syrup starts to boil. Reduce heat to low and simmer, stirring occasionally to prevent scorching, until mixture reaches 230 degrees on a candy thermometer.

Remove from heat and add butter or margarine and salt. Stir well. After about 2 minutes, add vanilla and stir. When it is slightly cooled, add 1/2 cup milk and stir until well mixed.

**Monine & Bob Stebbins**
BROOKLANE SPECIALTY APPLES

**growing organically**

The term "growing organically" is often used to describe plants or produce grown without chemical pesticides, herbicides and fertilizers. For those who are serious about being organic, it goes far beyond that. It's not only what isn't done, but also what is done to the soil. What is taken from the soil in the way of nutrients is returned back from natural sources like compost, cover crops and animal manures. Living microorganisms are an important part of soil health and by applying compost, mulch, and other organic matter, the soil has better tilth, is healthy and full of life.

Anytime plants are growing, disease and insects can be a problem, but the organic grower is careful to use only safe organic controls that are harmless to important beneficial insects and crop pollinators. Many diseases and insect pests can be controlled by fostering a healthy soil and an abundance of beneficial insects. Also important is crop rotation to prevent soil from becoming depleted of certain nutrients and keep specific insects and diseases from gaining a foothold. The end result is a balanced eco-system, an environmentally friendly method of growing, a responsible caretaking of the land, and healthy, great-tasting produce.

# Lekvar
## (Prune Butter)

*Lekvar is so versatile and can be used in many different recipes.*

3 pounds pitted prunes
 (or pitted prune plums)
1/4 cup lemon juice

2 cups water (if using dried prunes only)
1/2 cup light corn syrup (optional)

PUT ALL INGREDIENTS into a sauce pan and bring to a boil. Reduce heat and simmer until prunes are soft. Cool slightly and put through a sieve, food mill or "squeezo". Pack into jars and freeze, or process in a hot water bath for 20 minutes. Use in any of your favorite recipes, or even with biscuits or toast.

**Mike Jordan & Joan Noyce**
JORDAN'S VALLEY FRUIT

# Lekvar Bars

*Jordan's Valley Fruit evolved over 35 years ago when Mr. Smith first planted Oscar prune plums. Since then, Mike Jordan bought the farm and inherited these unique plum trees with fruit that is similar to Brook's prune plums but much larger and tastier. "The fella that developed this species took his secrets to his grave", says Jordon. "I know of no more Oscar prune plum trees anywhere". In addition to prune plums, Mike and Joan sell Bartlett pears and Gravenstein apples at the Corvallis Saturday Market.*

*The recipes here were from an elderly u-pick client and originated from Europe. The lekvar bars are absolutely delicious!*

1 cup brown sugar
1/2 cup butter or margarine
1/2 teaspoon salt

1 cup flour
1 1/2 cups rolled oats
1 cup lekvar (recipe above)

CREAM SUGAR and butter together in a large bowl until light and fluffy. Beat in salt, flour, and oats. Mix well. Line the bottom of a 9-inch square pan with half the mixture. Spread lekvar over all, then cover with the remaining oat mixture. Bake at 350 degrees for 30 to 40 minutes, or until crisp and browned. Cut into squares and enjoy. Serves 4 to 8.

**Mike Jordan & Joan Noyce**
JORDAN'S VALLEY FRUIT

# Prune Snow

*This makes a wonderful, exotic special treat.*

1 cup lekvar (prune puree)          sugar
2 egg whites

SWEETEN PRUNE PUREE to taste. Beat egg whites until stiff, then beat in puree. Continue beating until mixture is very fluffy. Turn into a serving dish and chill thoroughly. Also makes an excellent topping. Serves 4.

**Mike Jordan & Joan Noyce**
JORDAN'S VALLEY FRUIT

### apples and their uses

| variety | best uses | taste |
| --- | --- | --- |
| Braeburn | Snacking, salads | Sweet-tart |
| Cortland | Snacking, baking | Slightly tart |
| Crispin/Mutsu | All-purpose | Sweet |
| Empire | All-purpose | Sweet-tart |
| Fuji | Snacking, salads | Sweet |
| Gala | Snacking, salads | Sweet |
| Ginger Gold | Snacking, salads, baking | Sweet-tart |
| Golden Delicious | All-purpose | Sweet, slightly tart |
| Granny Smith | All-purpose | Tart |
| Gravenstein | Baking, cooking, sauces | Tart |
| Idared | Salads, baking, cooking | Moderately tart |
| Jonagold | Snacking, salads | Sweet, slightly tart |
| Jonathan | All-purpose | Moderately tart |
| Macintosh | Snacking, baking | Sweet-tart |
| Newtown Pippin | Salads, baking, cooking | Slightly tart |
| Northern Spy | Snacking, salads, baking | Slightly tart |
| Paulared | Snacking, baking | Slightly tart |
| Red Delicious | Snacking, salads | Sweet |
| Rome | Baking, cooking | Slightly sweet |
| York | Snacking, baking | Moderately tart |
| Winesap | Snacking, baking, cooking | Tart |

Pesto • Salsa

Nancy's Salsa • Salsa De Tomatillo

Chicken Noodle Soup • Beef Stew

Cabbage Vegetable Soup • Gazpacho A La Seville

Squash Bisque • Green Bean Tossed Salad

Thai Pasta Salad • Steamed Daikon

Oriental Style Pac Choi • Italian Style Pac Choi

Tiella • Roasted Vegetable Pasta

Lasagna with Fresh Veggies and Tomato Sauce

Baked Chiles Rellenos • Fresh Enchilada Sauce

Lemon Basil Grilled Chicken • No Cholesterol Squash Pie

Fresh Apple Cake

# DOUGLAS COUNTY FARMERS' MARKET

**LOCATION:**
Roseburg Valley Mall by "The Bon Marche"
Stewart Parkway & Garden Valley Blvd.
April through last Saturday of October
Saturdays, 9:00 a.m. to 1:00 p.m.

TUCKED WITHIN THE LOW ROLLING HILLS OF ROSEBURG, THE DOUGLAS COUNTY Farmers' Market gives the community the opportunity to purchase fresh, in-season, locally grown and produced goods in an outdoor setting. The market originally began when the desire of a few growers met with the experience of Judy Lovett.

Their first season began in 1994 with only 9 vendors, and soon grew to over 40 members and an expanded new mid-week market on Tuesday's from 4:00 p.m. to 8:00 p.m. Each year brings more vendors and diversity to interested shoppers. To keep their association members current, educational opportunities are provided in the way of ongoing updates in pertinent information.

You'll find quality and freshness with lots of certified organic, and herbicide and pesticide free produce. There's also an assortment of plants for any garden including vegetables, herbs, and flowers, plus plenty of delicious baked goods, jams, candies and pastries that conveniently await the savvy shopper.

# Pesto

*Buck & Judy Lovett first began their agricultural adventure while living in the Sierra mountains of California. When they relocated to Mountain Spring Farms in Myrtle Creek, they drove to Eugene and Grants Pass to sell their produce because there wasn't a farmers' market in their community. But that didn't stop Buck & Judy. Remember the saying "if you build it they will come"? That's what happened because in 1994 the Lovett's helped start the Douglas County Farmers' Market. In addition to selling their organic produce, they also have a community supported agriculture (CSA) project on the farm.*

*At the market fresh basil is always in demand because everyone just loves pesto.*

1/2 cup pine nuts
1 teaspoon salt
3 to 4 cups fresh basil leaves
1/4 pound freshly ground romano cheese

1 1/2 to 2 cups fine olive oil
4 cloves garlic, peeled
1/2 teaspoon freshly ground black pepper
1/4 pound freshly ground parmesan cheese

USING 1/2 CUP OF THE OLIVE OIL, process all remaining ingredients in a blender or food processor until smooth. Add remaining oil and process until smooth and creamy. Serve with hot pasta, using about 1/2 to 3/4 cup pesto for each pound (before cooked) of pasta.

**Buck & Judy Lovett**
MOUNTAIN SPRING FARMS

**picking and storing winter squash**

The term 'winter squash' can sometimes be misleading since it's usually harvested in late summer or early autumn. Winter squash is so named because with proper storage, it can often be kept through winter. The ideal storage conditions are between 50 to 60 degrees with low humidity. A cool storage room, enclosed patio, garage, or unplugged freezer work well as long as it's not damp or the squash will soon rot. Keep the squash from touching each other and do not wash before storing.

The gardener can tell when winter squash is ready to be picked due to a subtle color change (depending on the variety). Also the stem will be slightly shriveled and brown, and the skin or rind should not pierce easily with a thumbnail.

When selecting squash, look for ones with good color (there should be no hint of green on non-green colored squash), and a nice firm skin or rind. Be sure the stem is 1-inch or longer if you plan to store your squash for any length of time.

# Salsa

*Dawn Warren and Tamera Croucher, partner and daughter, started Warrens Gardens just 2 years ago and now offer an array of fresh garden produce, herbs, flowers, perennials, shrubs and trees. In addition to other vegetables, they specialize in tomatoes, peppers, thyme, oregano, and mint. The Warrens are always experimenting by growing unusual plants for this area, and also offer custom orders for plant starts.*

*Salsa goes beyond just chips and burritos. Use salsa in your favorite stew or even toss it with pasta.*

3 large tomatoes
1/2 onion, chopped
1/2 green pepper, cut into chunks
4 sprigs fresh cilantro
3 cloves garlic
1/4 teaspoon salt
2 tablespoons lemon juice

PUT ALL INGREDIENTS into a blender or salsa maker and mix to your personal preference; course, medium or fine. Serve and enjoy.

**Dawn Warren**
WARRENS GARDENS

# Nancy's Salsa

*Variety is the spice of life and that's exactly what Dennis and Robin O'Neill of Tipton Farm grow on their two acres. Along with their two children, they produce plenty of vegetables, fruits, herbs, and flowers for the Douglas County Farmers' Market. They also bring along dried flower arrangements and wreaths. Of course growing all this food has its rewards as the O'Neills noted, "our knowledge about healthy, natural food has grown tremendously. We are committed to healthy eating!"*

*Our sister-in-law, Nancy Leisner, gave us her recipe for salsa. This salsa is delicious and very easy to make. Most of the time we triple this recipe and we always add extra cilantro.*

2 medium tomatoes, diced
1/4 medium onion, diced
4 sprigs cilantro, diced
2 cloves garlic, minced
1 teaspoon garlic salt
2 tablespoons lemon juice
1 tablespoon lime juice
1 jalapeno pepper, diced

MIX ALL INGREDIENTS in a bowl and serve. You can also skip the step of dicing the vegetables and put them into a food processor instead.

**Dennis and Robin O'Neill**
TIPTON FARM

# Salsa De Tomatillo
## (Mexican Green Tomato Sauce)

*For a refreshing change of pace, try this green salsa instead.*

3/4 cup cooked tomatillos (prepared as below)
1 tablespoon white onion, finely chopped
1/2 clove garlic, chopped
2 or more serrano chiles, chopped
1 tablespoon fresh cilantro, minced
salt to taste

THOROUGHLY MIX all the ingredients, mashing the cooked tomatillos. Heat in sauce pan on stove top. Serve warm or at room temperature.

**To prepare tomatillos for sauce:**

Strip off the papery husks and rinse tomatillos in cold water. Put in saucepan and cover with hot water. Simmer on low until the fruits are soft and the skins are tender. (Depending on size, this can take from 10 to 20 minutes.) Do not let them boil or they will split open and lose their seeds and pulp in the cooking water.

**Dennis and Robin O'Neill**
TIPTON FARM

# Chicken Noodle Soup

*Use only fresh herbs for this recipe to really bring out the flavor.*

4 pieces of chicken (any pieces you want)
2 quarts water or broth
1/2 cup celery, chopped
1 cup onion, chopped
2 tablespoons snipped parsley
1 bay leaf
1/2 cup carrots, grated
2 teaspoons fresh thyme
1 teaspoon salt
pepper to taste
3 cups egg noodles

IN LARGE SOUP POT, add water or broth and boil chicken gently with celery, onion, herbs, spices, and carrots until chicken comes away easily from the bone. If desired, pull meat off bone and return the chicken back to the pot. Add 3 cups egg noodles and continue to cook for 20 minutes more. Serve while hot.

**Dawn Warren**
WARRENS GARDENS

# Beef Stew

*Serve this robust stew along with cornbread for a satisfying meal*

1 1/2 pounds beef stew meat
2 tablespoons oil
1 cup onion, chopped
1 clove garlic, minced
4 medium potatoes, peeled and cubed
4 large carrots, sliced
1 cup celery, chopped
1 teaspoon dried thyme
3 cups V-8 juice or other vegetable-type juice
salt and pepper to taste

BROWN THE MEAT WITH OIL in a large pot. Add remaining ingredients and simmer until meat and vegetables are tender, about 1 1/2 hours. Ladle into soup bowls and serve while hot. Serves 4 to 6.

**Dawn Warren**
WARRENS GARDENS

**tamari vs. soy sauce**   Fermented soybeans are what they have in common. The difference lies in the "other" ingredients that are used. Tamari is a natural soy sauce that is free from additives, while most soy sauce products sold at the market may contain additives like caramel coloring, corn syrup, salt, and sodium benzoate as a preservative.

DOUGLAS COUNTY FARMERS' MARKET

# Cabbage Vegetable Soup

*This soup makes a very filling and tasty meal.*

1/2 head cabbage, chopped
3 large Yukon Gold potatoes, cubed
4 carrots, sliced
1 onion, chopped
1 15 ounce can kidney beans, rinsed and drained
1 15 ounce can tomato sauce
1/4 cup tomato paste
1 1/4 cups broth
3 cups water
2 teaspoons chili powder
1 1/2 teaspoons cumin
juice from half a lemon

COMBINE ALL INGREDIENTS in a large pot. Bring to boil, then simmer, covered, for about 2 hours. Serves 4.

**Buck & Judy Lovett**
MOUNTAIN SPRING FARMS

# Gazpacho A La Seville

*This is a refreshing soup you can make in a hurry for those hot and hectic summer days.*

24 ounces tomato juice
1 cup cucumbers, diced
1/4 cup green peppers, diced
2 tablespoons chives
2 to 3 tablespoons fresh basil, chopped (or more to taste)
1 clove garlic, minced
1/4 teaspoon salt
1 cup tomatoes, diced
1/4 cup onions, diced
1 jalapeno pepper, diced
1 teaspoon Worcestershire sauce
1 tablespoon olive oil
1/4 teaspoon pepper
Tabasco sauce, a few drops (optional)

PLACE ALL INGREDIENTS in a blender and blend for a few seconds. Serve in chilled bowl with a dollop of sour cream, or in a mug with a cucumber spear. Serves 6.

**Buck & Judy Lovett**
MOUNTAIN SPRING FARMS

---

**shitake mushrooms** — Delicious and richly flavored, Shitake mushrooms lend a uniqueness to any recipe. Indoor growing kits or "mushroom logs" are available at many nursery centers and occasionally at farmers' markets. Fresh mushrooms can be harvested at 2 week intervals right in your own home.

DOUGLAS COUNTY FARMERS' MARKET

# Squash Bisque

*Smooth, rich and creamy. This will cheer up even the rainiest of days.*

1/2 cup onion, chopped
2 tablespoons celery leaves, chopped
1/4 cup celery, chopped
2 tablespoons butter
1 1/2 cups winter squash or pumpkin, cooked and pureed
1 15 ounce can vegetable stock or chicken stock
2 1/2 cups water
2 slices bread, trimmed of crust and cubed (1 cup)
1 teaspoon salt
1/8 teaspoon pepper
1 small bay leaf
1/4 teaspoon marjoram leaf, crumbled
1/4 teaspoon thyme
1/4 cup milk

COOK ONION, CELERY AND LEAVES in butter in a Dutch oven, uncovered, over low heat. Stir often until vegetables are tender, about 7 minutes. Stir in remaining ingredients except milk. Bring to a boil, then lower heat and simmer uncovered, stirring occasionally, about 45 minutes. Discard bay leaf. Put soup in blender for smoother consistency and return back to Dutch oven. Stir in milk and cook until heated through. Serves 6 to 8.

**Buck & Judy Lovett**
MOUNTAIN SPRING FARMS

**what is a csa?** Called Community Supported Agriculture, CSA might more accurately be described as a connection. It's a consumer connection to a variety of healthy and often organic, fresh-from-the-farm quality produce, to an experience and education of seeing, knowing, and in some cases, being a part of where foods really comes from. It connects the consumer with the farmer in a way that benefits both.

A CSA works on the basis of "shares" and "dividends." Subscribers buy a share in a farm, then receive their dividends in the form of fresh picked fruits and vegetables offered weekly throughout the growing season. Consumers commit to share the expenses and risks encountered by the farmer, but they also share the rewards and any surplus bounty. It connects consumer needs with farmer needs. There are now 300 to 400 CSAs nationwide.

# Green Bean Tossed Salad

*Use the young, tender green beans for this salad*

### Toss together:

1 1/2 pounds fresh green beans, blanched

8 sun dried tomatoes, sliced with some of the oil

1/2 cup pine nuts, toasted (toast on cookie sheet at 300 degrees for 5 minutes)

### Dressing:

2 cloves garlic, minced

1/2 cup fresh basil, chopped and packed

2 tablespoons white wine vinegar

1 tablespoon grated parmesan cheese

salt & pepper to taste

TOSS DRESSING with salad and serve on chilled plates.

**Buck & Judy Lovett**
MOUNTAIN SPRING FARMS

# Thai Pasta Salad

*For a different taste, try substituting Thai basil for the cilantro.*

8 ounce package linguine

8 ounces green cabbage, chopped (about 4 cups)

1 cup carrots, shredded

1 cup sweet onion, sliced

1/3 cup fresh cilantro

### Dressing:

1/4 cup teriyaki sauce

3 tablespoons lemon juice

2 tablespoons olive oil

1/2 teaspoon fresh ginger root, grated

1/4 teaspoon crushed red pepper

COOK PASTA ACCORDING to package directions. Drain in colander and rinse well under cold water.

Whisk dressing ingredients in a large serving bowl until blended. Add rinsed and drained pasta and the remaining ingredients. Toss gently to mix and coat. Serves 4.

**Buck & Judy Lovett**
MOUNTAIN SPRING FARMS

DOUGLAS COUNTY FARMERS' MARKET

# Steamed Daikon

*An obsessed gardener for 7 years, Jon & Akiyo Riggs joined the Douglas County Farmers' Market over 3 years ago where they sell spinach, lettuce, peas, beets, Swiss chard, corn, cucumbers, artichokes, tomatoes, and of course, daikon. At Riggs Family Gardens, everything is grown in raised beds and fertilized with steer, sheep or pig manure. Registered organic growers, as a time-saving measure the Riggs may decide to grow weeds and pull vegetables instead. A word of advice they offer to fellow gardeners is "you can't pick your kids, but your kids can sure pick".*

*Daikon is a long, white winter radish. Steamed daikon is simple to cook, very popular in stir fry and creates quite a surprise for first time diners.*

SLICE A BIG FAT DAIKON (Japanese radish) into 1/2-inch rings and steam them any way you can until you can poke a fork through.

Serve with butter, soy sauce, mayonnaise, or all the above.

**Jon & Akiyo Riggs**
RIGGS FAMILY GARDENS

**the giant radish**

This far out winter-type radish is said to have been growing in the Far East since 500 BC. Reports came back talking of gigantic radishes up to a yard long and a foot in diameter. Most likely this was the Japanese daikon, which translates into "long root." Even though daikons can get quite big, most are harvested at 12 to 18-inches in length. Still a popular staple of the Far East, daikon's are very versatile when it comes to cooking and for eating raw or pickled. Besides, why grow 50 red radishes to serve with that vegetable dip when one daikon will do the job even better.

# Oriental Style Pac Choi

*Pac choi, bok choy, pak choi are all different spellings for the same vegetable.*

pac choi, prepared
olive oil

3 carrots, cut julienne style
1 small onion, sliced

### Sauce—mix together

1 tablespoon tahini or peanut butter
2 tablespoons soy sauce or tamari

3 tablespoons water or apple juice
dash hot sauce or Tabasco to taste

TO PREPARE PAC CHOI, separate the ribs by cutting away the leaf. Reserve the leaf. Slice the rib as you would celery, then roll the leaves together sausage style, then slice. In a large skillet or wok, stir fry the ribs of pac choi, carrot and onion in a little oil until almost tender. Add the leaves of the pac choi and stir until wilted. Add sauce and heat. Serve over rice.

**Buck & Judy Lovett**
MOUNTAIN SPRING FARMS

# Italian Style Pac Choi

*Pac choi is the ultimate green vegetable for stir fry and an excellent source of calcium.*

Pac choi, prepared (see above recipe
    for instructions)
olive oil
4 roma-type tomatoes,
    cut into quarters

3 to 6 cloves garlic, minced
1 small can olives, sliced
parmesan cheese
1 16 ounce package pasta,
    cooked (your choice)

IN A LARGE SKILLET OR WOK, add oil and stir fry the pac choi ribs until almost tender. Add the tomatoes and the pac choi leaves and stir until the leaves are wilted. Next add the garlic and olives. Cook until heated. Toss together with parmesan cheese and cooked pasta. Serves 6.

**Buck & Judy Lovett**
MOUNTAIN SPRING FARMS

---

**basil storage tips**

Unlike other produce, basil should not be stored in the refrigerator. Basil stored this way will usually last only 2 or 3 days and often turns black within the first 24 hours. The only exception would be to wash the leaves, then run them through a salad spinner. Place leaves in a storage bag that zips, pressing out as much air as possible. If prepared this way, basil stored in the refrigerator can keep up to a week.

The easiest way to keep basil fresh once it has been cut is right on the kitchen counter in a glass of water. By changing the water daily, basil can be kept fresh and ready to use for up to two weeks. It's convenient, and the wonderful aroma will continue to freshen and scent your kitchen.

# Tiella

*Last summer we had visitors from Tennessee. One day our male guest (just an old farm boy) announced that he was going to make dinner for us all. Off to the garden he went with bucket in hand. After only a few seconds in the kitchen preparing, and then 45 minutes of cooking, this is what we ended up with. Fantastic!*

USING A FAIRLY HEAVY POT or casserole, layer as follows (a little olive oil on the bottom prevents sticking):

potatoes, sliced
onions, sliced
garlic, minced
parmesan cheese
summer squash, sliced

green tomatoes, sliced
fresh basil, chopped
tomatoes, sliced
parmesan cheese

Cover casserole (don't peek while cooking). Cook on stove on high heat until you hear a sizzle, then turn the burner down to low or medium. That's it, 45 minutes later it's done. Serves 6 to 8.

**Buck & Judy Lovett**
MOUNTAIN SPRING FARMS

# Roasted Vegetable Pasta

*The roasting really brings out the flavor and sweetness of these vegetables.*

2 carrots, trimmed, halved lengthwise
   and cut into 1-inch pieces
2 bell peppers, cut into
   1/4-inch slivers
1 eggplant, cut into 1-inch cubes
1 to 2 red onions, slivered
2 tablespoons garlic, minced

cooking spray or olive oil
thyme, fresh or dried
6 to 8 roma-type tomatoes, quartered lengthwise
2 to 4 zucchini, halved lengthwise and cut
   into 1-inch pieces
salt and pepper to taste
8 ounce penne or rigatoni pasta

PLACE CARROTS, PEPPERS, eggplant, red onion, and garlic in bowl. Sprinkle with olive oil or use cooking spray and toss with thyme. Place vegetables in a single layer on a baking sheet, then bake in a 375 degree oven for 1 hour or until tender. Remove to a bowl and set aside.

In a separate bowl, toss tomatoes and zucchini with olive oil and thyme. Place in a single layer on same baking sheet and bake for 30 minutes. Add to the bowl of reserved vegetables and season with salt and pepper.

Cook pasta until tender. Drain and remove to a large, shallow serving bowl. Add reserved veggies and toss. Serves 4.

**Buck & Judy Lovett**
MOUNTAIN SPRING FARMS

DOUGLAS COUNTY FARMERS' MARKET

# Lasagna with Fresh Veggies and Tomato Sauce

*Not a 'heavy' lasagna, this is just right.*

1/2 cup onion, chopped
1 tablespoon olive oil
2 cloves garlic, minced
4 cups tomatoes, coarsely chopped
1/2 cup meatless spaghetti sauce
1/4 cup tomato sauce
2 cups (or more) summer squash, cut into bite size pieces
1 teaspoon dried basil or 2 teaspoons fresh basil
1 3/4 cups part skim ricotta cheese
1 egg
1/4 teaspoon black pepper
1 package lasagna noodles, cooked
3 ounces shredded mozzarella cheese

TO PREPARE SAUCE, sauté until soft the onion, oil and garlic in a pan. Add tomatoes, spaghetti sauce, tomato sauce, squash, and basil. Continue cooking until tomatoes are soft, but still hold their shape. Set aside.

In medium bowl, combine ricotta cheese, egg and pepper. To assemble lasagna, spread 1/2 cup of the tomato/veggie mixture in a 7x11-inch pan. Top with a single layer of the lasagna noodles, 1/3 of the tomato mixture, 1/3 of the ricotta mixture and 1/3 of the mozzarella cheese. Repeat layers.

Cover pan and bake at 350 degrees for 45 minutes. Serves 6.

**Buck & Judy Lovett**
MOUNTAIN SPRING FARMS

---

**parsley particulars**

Leaf texture and flavor intensity will vary with this bright green herb depending on the kind of parsley you choose. Parsley's warm, gentle flavor works well in combining other flavors around it.

Familiar to most is the curly-leaf parsley (also known as French parsley). Most popular served as a garnish in restaurants, this variety keeps longer once picked. The flat-leaf type (Italian parsley) is similar in appearance to celery leaf. This variety is usually the "chef's choice." Just like Florence fennel, Hamburg parsley is a variety that is grown for its thick, fleshy roots and is used much like parsnips.

Any type of parsley lends fabulous flavor to many culinary dishes. Try parsley pesto, or blend with green onions as a "green sauce" topping for potatoes. An important ingredient in gremolata (Italian dressing for fish made with fresh parsley, garlic and lemon zest), tabbouleh, and salsa verde, it can also be used as a substitute for cilantro.

Fresh parsley is always best, but if you must preserve parsley, frozen is favored over dried. Flat-leafed parsley is best for drying since its taste is stronger than the curled-leaf type. Freeze chopped or whole sprigs of parsley in freezer-type storage bags.

DOUGLAS COUNTY FARMERS' MARKET

# Baked Chiles Rellenos

*Corno Di Toro. Horn of the bull, this Italian sweet pepper is adaptable to any situation. It's as good raw as it is sautéed or grilled, and can be used in any recipe that calls for a bell pepper.*

8 to 10 whole green Corno di Toro
   (or any sweet frying-type pepper)
8 ounces jack cheese, cut into strips
8 eggs
2/3 cup milk

1 cup flour
1 teaspoon baking powder
1 cup shredded cheddar cheese
salsa, olives, sour cream

CUT A SLIT DOWN the side of each pepper, then remove seeds and membranes. Fold or stuff equal amounts of cheese inside each pepper. Arrange peppers side by side in a lightly greased 8x10-inch baking dish. Beat eggs until thick and foamy. Add milk, flour and baking powder; beat until mixture is smooth. Pour egg batter evenly over peppers and sprinkle with shredded cheese. Bake uncovered at 375 degrees for 30 minutes. Garnish with salsa, olives and sour cream. Serves 6 to 8.

**Buck & Judy Lovett**
MOUNTAIN SPRING FARMS

# Fresh Enchilada Sauce

*Double this sauce and freeze half for later use.
It is also a good sauce to make Spanish rice with.*

2 medium onions, chopped
1 green pepper, chopped
2 cloves garlic, minced
1 cup tomato sauce
   (puree of fresh tomatoes is best)

2 jalapeno peppers, seeded and minced
2 teaspoons sugar
1 teaspoon salt
1/4 teaspoon ground cumin
1/8 teaspoon dried oregano

IN A SKILLET, sauté onions, peppers, and garlic until soft. Add remaining ingredients and simmer 10 minutes.

**Buck & Judy Lovett**
MOUNTAIN SPRING FARMS

**DOUGLAS COUNTY FARMERS' MARKET**

# Lemon Basil Grilled Chicken

*They'll be asking for seconds so better make plenty.*

1/2 cup olive oil
2 tablespoons white wine vinegar
2 cloves garlic, minced
1/4 teaspoon ground black pepper
1/4 cup lemon juice
1 teaspoon grated lemon peel
1/2 teaspoon salt (optional)
1/2 cup fresh basil, chopped
1 chicken, cut up or selected pieces
    (about 1 1/2 to 2 pounds)

IN A SMALL BOWL, combine oil, lemon juice, vinegar, grated lemon peel, garlic, salt, pepper, and basil. This will make about 1 cup of marinade. Put chicken pieces in a shallow dish and marinade in refrigerator overnight. Grill or broil chicken until done. Serves 4

**Buck & Judy Lovett**
MOUNTAIN SPRING FARMS

# No Cholesterol Squash Pie

*Squash may be a family favorite, but Merlin & Sally May of Rare Trees Nursery are cooking up more than just pie. They have developed an arboretum of rare trees from many parts of the world. These trees and more are situated on 5 acres by the South Umpqua River. First started in 1990, they now sell nursery stock, spruce, fir, pine and cypress at the Douglas County Market. By the way, walk through tours of the Rare Trees Nursery Arboretum are available. Come see them at the market!*

*Big on taste, not on cholesterol.*

3/4 pound firm tofu
2 cups squash, cooked or baked
3/4 cup fructose or 2/3 cup honey
1/3 cup oil (1/4 cup oil if honey
    is used as sweetener)
2 tablespoons sorghum or
    cane molasses
1 teaspoon vanilla extract
1 1/2 teaspoons cinnamon
3/4 teaspoon nutmeg
3/4 teaspoon ginger
1/2 teaspoon salt
3 teaspoons egg replacer
1 unbaked pie crust

BLEND INGREDIENTS FOR FILLING until smooth and creamy. Pour into a prepared pie crust and bake in a preheated 350 degree oven for 1 hour. Chill and serve.

**Merlin & Sally May**
RARE TREES NURSERY

# Fresh Apple Cake

*It is really not necessary to peel the apples unless you have ones with very tough skins. We use tart green apples and you do not even know the peeling is there. This makes a very moist cake.*

4 cups apples, diced　　　　　　　　2 cups sugar
　(do not dice too fine)

**Mix the above thoroughly
and add:**

1/2 cup oil　　　　　　　　　　　　2 eggs, well beaten
1 cup nuts (optional)　　　　　　　　1 teaspoon vanilla

**Mix these ingredients
and add to the above:**

2 cups flour　　　　　　　　　　　　2 teaspoons cinnamon
2 teaspoons baking soda　　　　　　　1 teaspoon salt

PUT BATTER IN A GREASED 9x13-inch baking pan. Bake in a 350 degree oven for about one hour, time may vary. Cake is done when it shrinks from the edge of pan. Reduce heat to 325 degrees if you use a glass pan.

Frost cake with a butter-frosting or cream cheese frosting. Serves 8.

**Dennis and Robin O'Neill**
TIPTON FARM

---

**the celery craze**

The craze for celery existed long ago, only back in times of old it was more commonly used as medicine. By the sixteenth century is was revived for use in the kitchen, and by the nineteenth century the craze went wild and included celery soft drinks, celery gum and Elixir of Celery offered in the 1897 Sears, Roebuck catalog.

Perhaps now the full merits of celery are understood as it can be found more and more in gardens and at farmers markets. Still gardening books describe celery as a "difficult" crop to grow. Though the demands are high, they can be met. Thought of more as a bog plant, celery demands plenty of water and cool summer growing temperatures. Give it a sunny spot in a rich soil high in nitrogen. It thrives in rabbit manure.

The end results are large hefty stalks that are crisp, juicy and full of wonderful flavor. The leaves can be dried or used fresh and are essential for flavoring those warm, hearty winter soups and stews. The stalks add a delightful crunch to salads, are great in stir fry or even as a snack. A favorite snack many grew up with is peanut butter and celery.

Culinary risk-takers may like to try an unusual French dish from 1659. The recipe includes celery hearts, lemon, pomegranates and beets. As for me, I'll eat mine right out of the garden.

DOUGLAS COUNTY FARMERS' MARKET

Garlic Honey Cough Syrup

Apple-Rose Hip Tea

Zucchini Relish • Refrigerator Pickles

Dilled Onion Slices • Fresh From the Farm

Stuffed Mushrooms

Roasted Garlic Mashed Potatoes • Stuffing for Poultry

Quick 40 Clove Chicken

Chewy Egg Dumplings

Serena's Zucchini Bread • Laurie's Lemon Verbena Cookies

Citrus Candied Walnuts

# GRANTS PASS GROWERS' MARKET

**LOCATION:**
Corner of F and 4th
Mid-March to Mid-November
Saturdays, 9:00 - 1:00

**SECOND LOCATION:**
Same as above
June through September
Tuesdays, 9:00 -1:00

A FAVORITE WITH RESIDENTS AND TOURISTS ALIKE, THE GRANTS PASS Growers' Market is second only to the Rogue River as an area attraction. It showcases the finest fresh fruits and vegetables growing in the Southern Oregon region, as well as secondary wood products, gourmet specialty foods, artists and crafters.

This year begins the 19th season for the Growers' Market. The market first opened in 1980 at the Josephine County fairgrounds with fewer than a dozen vendors. Since that time the market has been transplanted in 10 different locations, and in 1993 it settled permanently behind the Post Office.

Now the market stands at over 100 members strong, with locally grown agricultural goods like season fresh produce, eggs, breads and baked goods, honey, herb and vegetable plants, perennials, trees and shrubs, flowers and more. Secondary wood products, artists and crafters also feature hand-crafted items like stained glass, oil, ceramics, bird houses and other garden-related goods.

Much more than an outdoor produce department or nursery, the Growers' Market is a place where community members congregate and can actually learn a thing or two about their food and where it comes from. And thanks to the mild growing conditions in Grants Pass, patrons can enjoy an exceptionally long season.

# Garlic Honey Cough Syrup

*Eden's Gate is what the early settlers called Oregon, so when Cathy & Bill Dunlap settled into their homestead, they named it Eden's Gate Farm. Now they specialize in garlic, nearly 20 different varieties, many of which have taken first place at the Josephine County Fair and the Oregon State Fair. They learned their garlic growing skills from an expert resident who has been growing garlic for the last 40 years. Garlic and shallots are sold at the Ashland, Medford, and Grants Pass markets, and they recently opened their own farm produce stand/craft store and started selling their garlic in their mail-order catalog.*

*Garlic produces allicin, which is a powerful antibiotic. Try this for cold and flu season.*

12 cloves garlic, peeled and lightly crushed
3/4 cup honey
3 tablespoons brandy
1 tablespoon lemon juice

IN A SMALL SAUCEPAN, combine garlic and honey. Cook over low heat for 15 minutes. Stir in brandy and lemon juice. Let stand until cool and strain into a jar. Refrigerate.

**Cathy Dunlap**
EDEN'S GATE FARM

# Apple-Rose Hip Tea

*Located in the foothills of the Siskiyou Mountains of southwestern Oregon is Goodwin Creek Gardens, owned and operated by Jim and Dotti Becker. Established in 1977, the Beckers sell herb plants and seeds including medicinal and rare lavenders, hummingbird and butterfly plants, scented geraniums and everlastings at the Grants Pass Growers' Market.*

*This tea is certainly not unusual, but what makes it outstanding is the kind of rosehips used. "Rosa villosa" is absolutely the biggest and sweetest rosehips we've ever seen, and it makes all the difference in teas and soups.*

2 cups water
handful of dried hips

BRINGS WATER TO A BOIL; add a handful of dried hips and simmer for 10 minutes. Remove from heat, steep 5 minutes more and sweeten to taste. These hips are very sweet so you may not need any honey. They also make a great rose hip soup.

**Jim & Dottie Becker**
GOODWIN CREEK GARDENS

# Zucchini Relish

*Besides farm fresh produce, the Grants Pass Growers' Market also has a artistic display of wonderful crafts, including Dorothy Maffett's birdhouses, garden signs and her specialty, stencils. You'll never be overwhelmed with zucchini because this recipe uses a lot.*

10 cups zucchini, finely chopped
4 cups onion, finely chopped
1 cup green onion, finely chopped
4 tablespoons salt

MIX ALL INGREDIENTS together in a large pot and let stand overnight. Rinse in cold water and allow to drain. Put drained vegetables back into the pot and add the following:

3 cups cider vinegar
5 cups white vinegar

**Mix these spices together and add to the pot:**

1 tablespoon dry mustard
1 tablespoon turmeric
1 1/2 tablespoons cornstarch
2 teaspoons celery seed
1/2 teaspoon black pepper
1 teaspoon red pepper

Bring all ingredients to a boil and cook uncovered, about 1 1/2 hours or until thick. Pour into hot jars and seal, processing according to canning instructions or store in refrigerator. Makes about 6 pints.

**Dorothy Maffett**

**the sweetest rose**

Apple Rose (Rosa villosa) is a 5 to 7 foot shrub with upright branches and simple, light pink flowers. The bush is distinguished by its large and sweet hips which are used both culinary and medicinally. Pick your apple-rose hips when they are fully red. Our bushes look like Christmas in August when they are ready to harvest. You can dry the hips whole on well-ventilated screens. This takes about 3 weeks. These hips are so large you can also cut them in half and scoop out the seeds and hairs with a spoon, then dry them like small fruits. The cleaned and dried hips are great in baked goods as well as tea.

GOODWIN CREEK GARDENS

# Refrigerator Pickles

*A member of the Growers' Market for 9 years, Serena Oltz grows as much as possible out of her home garden for her processed foods booth known as Serena's. Her booth will be easy to find when shopping the market—just follow your nose towards the aroma of delicious baked breads, cookies, coffee cakes and cinnamon rolls. Save room too for the "fresh-picked" fruity taste of her delicious home made jams and jellies.*

*Great pickles with no fuss or mess. The pickles will keep in the refrigerator for up to 6 weeks.*

8 cups cucumbers, sliced and unpeeled
2 cups onions, sliced
1 cup red bell pepper strips, julienne style
1 tablespoon salt
1 1/2 cups white vinegar
2 teaspoons celery seed
2 teaspoons mustard seed
2 cups sugar

IN A LARGE BOWL, combine cucumbers, onion and red pepper. Sprinkle with salt and mix well. Let stand for 1 hour; drain. In a medium bowl, combine sugar, vinegar, celery seed and mustard seed; stir until sugar is dissolved. Place cucumbers mixture in a nonmetallic container. Pour vinegar mixture over cucumbers. Cover and chill for at least 24 hours to blend flavors. Makes about 8 cups.

**Serena Oltz**
SERENA'S


# Dilled Onion Slices

*A wonderful addition to sandwiches and salads, or use as a garnish for any meal.*

1/2 cup sugar
2 teaspoons salt
1/2 teaspoon dill weed
1/2 cup white vinegar
1/4 cup water
2 large white onions, thinly sliced

BOIL ALL INGREDIENTS except onions for 1 minute. Cool this solution by placing saucepan in a sink or pan of cold water. Pack onions in a canning jar. Pour room temperature pickling solution over onions, leaving a 1/2-inch headspace. Process in a boiling water canner for 10 minutes.

**Serena Oltz**
SERENA'S

# Fresh From the Farm

*Joanne & Bruce Gordon bring lots of quality organically grown bedding plants, vegetable and flower starts, herbs, and cactus to the Grants Pass Growers' Market. With Gordons' Commonwealth Garden, you'll find unusual and easy-to-grow varieties for your old-fashioned flower & gourmet vegetable garden.*

*A favorite recipe for many gardeners, Joanne's favorite involves no cooking, no dishes, and no prep time. Sounds great? It is, and here's what she does.*

"WHEN I HAVEN'T HAD TIME to stop for lunch...I cruise the garden (after washing my hands of course) and pick a few peas, a handful of lettuce and parsley, then snap off some broccoli for an early spring treat. Later in the summer it is on to fresh (yes, raw) corn, beans, tomatoes, and still a handful of lettuce and parsley."

**Joanne Gordon**
GORDONS' COMMONWEALTH GARDEN

# Stuffed Mushrooms

*Garlic lovers will love these stuffed mushrooms.*

12 large mushrooms
1/8 cup onion, chopped
1 teaspoon olive oil
6 cloves garlic, minced

1/8 teaspoon pepper
2 tablespoons parmesan cheese
1/2 tablespoon bread crumbs
dash of lemon juice

WASH MUSHROOMS and separate from stems. Finely chop the stems and sauté in olive oil over low heat for 5 minutes along with garlic and onion. Add remaining ingredients except mushrooms; stir to combine. Lightly spray a baking dish or sheet with nonstick vegetable cooking spray. Place mushroom caps on dish and fill with equal amounts of the mixture. Bake in a preheated 350 degree oven for 12 to 15 minutes. Serve warm.

**Cathy Dunlap**
EDEN'S GATE FARM

| | |
|---|---|
| **egg freshness testing** | You don't need to crack an egg to determine if it's fresh. All you need to do is put the egg in a glass or pan filled with water. A fresh egg will stay on the bottom, laying on its side. If one end of the egg tips slightly upward, it's probably past its prime. When it stands up the egg is old, and the rotten egg always floats to the top. |

GRANTS PASS GROWERS' MARKET

# Roasted Garlic Mashed Potatoes

*Many restaurants are now serving up mashed potatoes with roasted garlic.
Now you can enjoy it anytime.*

2 1/2 pounds baking potatoes, peeled and quartered
coarse salt and freshly ground pepper
8 heads (bulbs not cloves) of roasted garlic, peeled and mashed
4 tablespoons butter
1 cup milk

IN A MEDIUM SAUCEPAN, cover potatoes with water. Bring to a boil and add salt. Reduce to a simmer and cook until tender, about 15 minutes. Drain and mash potatoes.

In a small saucepan, combine garlic, butter, and milk. Cook over low heat, stirring until a smooth paste is formed. Turn heat to low under potatoes and mash in garlic mixture. Season to taste with salt and pepper. Serves 4.

**Cathy Dunlap**
EDEN'S GATE FARM

| **roasted garlic** | When garlic is roasted, an incredible change takes place that compounds into a nutty sweetness slightly tempered by a mellow flavor. Yet this wonderful flavor can be had with very little effort. You don't even have to peel the garlic! On a head (entire bulb) of garlic, cut off the top only enough so that all the cloves are exposed. Put as many cut heads as you'd like in a baking dish and drizzle olive oil (about 1/4 teaspoon a head) over each head. Season to taste with salt, pepper and other fresh herbs if desired. Cover the dish and bake for 30 minutes at 300 degrees. Remove the cover and bake until garlic is tender, about an hour. Check the heads during cooking and baste with extra olive oil if needed. When the husks are golden brown and the cloves are soft, remove and simply squeeze out the garlic for use on freshly baked bread, in mashed potatoes, baked potatoes or on top of pasta. Let your imagination be your guide. |

GRANTS PASS GROWERS' MARKET

# Stuffing for Poultry

*This also makes a great side dish for any time of the year.*

4 cups sourdough bread,
   torn into bite size chunks
1 cup celery, chopped
1 cup onion, chopped
1/8 teaspoon nutmeg
1 tablespoon sage
1 teaspoon salt
1/2 teaspoon pepper
1/2 cup butter, melted
4 tablespoons chopped dried parsley
1 egg, slightly beaten
1 cup boiling water

MIX ALL INGREDIENTS together in a large bowl. Stuff into bird and bake, or for a side dish, put dressing in a buttered casserole dish and bake at 375 degrees for 45 minutes, or until edges are brown.

**Dorothy Maffett**

# Quick 40 Clove Chicken

*Lots of cloves, lots of taste.*

6 boneless chicken breast halves
coarse salt and freshly ground
   pepper
1/4 cup olive oil
40 cloves garlic, peeled
1/2 cup chopped parsley

SEASON CHICKEN ALL OVER with salt and pepper. Drizzle with oil and arrange in a single layer in a 13x9-inch baking dish. Scatter garlic cloves over chicken.

Cover and bake in a preheated 400 degree oven for 20 minutes. Sprinkle with parsley and bake, uncovered, 10 minutes longer. Serves 6.

**Cathy Dunlap**
EDEN'S GATE FARM

---

**the garlic difference**  What's your preference? Do you want garlic that's easy-to-peel or long on storage? How garlic performs depends in part on which type of garlic you have—hardneck or softneck. Believed to be the original descendants from wild garlic, the cloves of the hardneck are usually larger. Because its skin isn't as tight, it's also easier to peel. For this same reason hardneck garlic won't store as well and depending on the quality, that can be anywhere from 1 month to 5 months from when it was harvested. Softnecks are harder to peel because their skin is tighter, but this is what makes them great for storing. Given the right conditions, they can keep up to a year.

GRANTS PASS GROWERS' MARKET

# Chewy Egg Dumplings

*In 1993, Arlene and Steve Sarver Sr. moved into their Grants Pass home. Little did they know that when their friend gave them seven chickens, it would hatch out into a new business. Just three years later, over 200 chickens reside at their home, now so suitably named The Cackle Factory. Their chickens have even won many best of breeds as well as best American chicken at the Josephine County Fair. Going into their fourth year at the Grants Pass Growers' Market, they have eggs in every size plus colors like blue and green, and last year they began to sell baby chicks.*

*These dumplings will not puff up, they will be compact and chewy. They are ideal for chicken and dumplings, stews, hot potato salad, and any other use you might have. German dishes such as Tupfenuckel and Poprekash use these type of dumplings.*

3 large eggs
3 cups flour (not self-rising)
water (just enough to moisten)
dash of salt

IN A LARGE BOWL, measure out the flour and make a well in the top. Break the eggs into the well and mix, adding cold water a little at a time until you can just stir it. Put in a dash of salt if desired.

Take a flat plate and soup spoon and mound some of the mixture on the plate. Holding the plate above boiling liquid (water, soup, stew, etc.), pinch off about a half spoonful against the edge of the plate and dip the spoon into the liquid to remove the dough. Repeat until all the mixture is used.

Allow the dumplings to boil until done. They will float to the top and usually take about 10 minutes. (The center should be a little dry looking.) If you are using water to boil them, drain it off and then put them into your favorite recipe.

You can alter the amount of cups of flour and eggs to suit your family size.

**Arlene Sarver**
THE CACKLE FACTORY

---

**sourdough starter**

Starters have been used as a way of leavening bread for thousands of years. Today we call this method sourdough. Starters that are continually used and replenished can keep going a long, long time. There have been reports of original starters passed down through families that are still in existence today. There's nothing complicated about getting a starter going, there are plenty of wild yeasts in the air that will do the job.

The texture and flavor of a starter may vary depending on how and where it is made. Beginning a starter can be as simple as mixing a cup of flour with a cup of water and adding about 1 tablespoon of yogurt, or other ingredients can be used like bread, milk, leftover cereal, commercial yeast and sugar. Put the ingredients for your starter in a clean glass or ceramic jar placed in a warm spot and cover with a light cloth for up to 5 days. Stir the starter daily. When the starter is ready for use, the recipe you're using will indicate where to begin, usually by making a "sponge" the night before. Replace any starter you use by adding 1 cup of lukewarm water, 1/2 cup flour and 1 teaspoon sugar to the jar.

# Serena's Zucchini Bread

*This is a good keeper and freezes very well.*

1 cup oil
2 cups sugar
3 eggs, beaten
2 cups shredded zucchini
1 8-ounce can crushed pineapple, well drained
1 cup walnuts, chopped
1 teaspoon vanilla

3 cups flour
1 teaspoon cinnamon
1 teaspoon cloves
1 teaspoon ginger
1 teaspoon baking soda
1/2 teaspoon baking powder
1/2 teaspoon salt

COMBINE TOGETHER in a large bowl the oil, sugar and eggs. Mix in the zucchini, pineapple, walnuts and vanilla. In a separate bowl, sift the remaining ingredients; fold into zucchini mixture. Pour batter in 3 greased medium loaf pans. Bake in a preheated oven at 325 degrees for 1 hour or until done. Makes 3 loafs.

**Serena Oltz**
SERENA'S

# Laurie's Lemon Verbena Cookies

*This cookie recipe is always used whenever we have an open house or classes. For a wonderfully different taste, add a small amount of crushed lavender flowers.*

1 cup butter
1 1/2 cups sugar
2 eggs
1 teaspoon vanilla

2 tablespoons dry lemon verbena leaves, crumbled
2 3/4 cups flour
1 teaspoon baking soda
1/2 teaspoon salt

CREAM TOGETHER butter and sugar in a large bowl. Beat in the eggs, vanilla and lemon verbena. In a separate bowl, stir together the flour, salt and baking soda, then combine with the egg mixture. Drop from a teaspoon onto an ungreased cookie sheet. Bake in a preheated 350 degree oven for 7 minutes. Don't eat too many!

**Jim & Dottie Becker**
GOODWIN CREEK GARDENS

# Citrus Candied Walnuts

*Walnuts grow well here and can be found at most farmers' markets.*

1 egg white
3 cups shelled walnut halves
1 cup powdered sugar
2 tablespoons lemon juice

2 teaspoons grated orange peel
1 teaspoon grated lemon peel
1/8 teaspoon ground nutmeg

PREHEAT OVEN to 300 degrees. Generously grease a 15 1/2 x 10 1/2 x 1-inch jelly roll pan. Beat egg white in a medium bowl with electric mixer on high speed until soft peaks form. Add walnuts; stir until coated. Stir in powdered sugar, lemon juice, orange peel, lemon peel and nutmeg. Turn out onto prepared pan, spreading nuts in a single layer. Bake for 30 minutes, stirring after 20 minutes. TURN OVEN OFF. Let nuts stand in oven for 15 minutes more. Immediately remove nuts from pan to a sheet of foil. Cool completely. Store up to 2 weeks in an airtight container. Makes 3 cups.

**Serena Oltz**
SERENA'S

## garlic lover's guide

| variety | description | type |
|---|---|---|
| California Early | Large with 12-18 cloves per bulb. Clove is tan or off-white. Commonly available in many food stores. | Softneck |
| German Red | Large with 10-15 cloves per bulb. Hot and spicy cloves favored by chefs. | Hardneck |
| Inchelium Red | Top rated softneck at Rodale's garlic taste test. Mild lingering flavor. Taste sharpens with storage. | Softneck |
| Italian Late | Long-storing, strong and pungent with excellent flavor. | Softneck |
| Korean Red | Easy peel, large bulbs with 5-10 cloves. Purple-striped bulb wrappers. Very hot! Poor storing. | Hardneck |
| Northern White | Potent cloves average 5-7 per bulb. Excellent for baking. | Hardneck |
| Purple Italian Easy Peel | Rich, spicy flavor with sweet aftertaste. Large cloves peel easily and store well. | Hardneck |
| Sicilian Silver | One of the best keepers. Strong flavor is great for cooking. | Softneck |
| Silver Rose | Rose-colored cloves with a sharp flavor. Stores well. | Softneck |
| Spanish Roja | Easy-peel, very popular. Rich, spicy true garlic flavor. Northwest heirloom. | Hardneck |

Apricot Balsamic Dressing

Cran-Raspberry Sauce

Piper's Zucchini Relish • Pickled Garlic

Pickled Asparagus • Healthy Green Sauté

Sweet Onion Pie

Pesto Forever • Pesto Stuffed Chicken Breasts

Honey Sandwich Loaf • Pastrami

Honey Walnut Biscotti

Berry Wonderful Clafouti

Fruit Bobbler

# INDEPENDENCE FARMERS' MARKET

**LOCATION:**
Riverview Park on the waterfront,
just north of the boat ramp
May through October
Saturdays, 9:00 - 1:00

THE INDEPENDENCE FARMERS' MARKET BEGAN IN 1995 AS A PROJECT OF THE Independence Downtown Association. A small town on the Willamette River just south of Salem, some say Independence, Oregon is the other end of the westbound trail that started at Independence, Missouri. The town flourishes with historic buildings and houses, wonderful antique shops, and a beautiful park right in downtown on the river. That park, Riverview Park, is the setting for the market and makes the Independence Farmers' Market a great place for a family outing with picnic areas, shady lawns, a playground, and wonderful views of the river.

Fresh from the farm locally grown produce is featured at the market, along with nursery plants including herb and vegetable starts, glorious hanging baskets and a wide variety of perennials, shrubs and trees. As the season progresses, the market offers an abundance of strawberries, raspberries, blueberries, assorted salad greens, peas, beans, corn, tomatoes, peppers, honey, several kinds of garlic, onions, potatoes, fresh herbs, flowers, and so much more. Several outstanding local crafters and artists also sell at the market, and there are home baked goods, handmade candies and other treats.

Finding the market is easy—from Main Street in Independence turn east on 'C' Street at the south end of Riverview Park and go down the hill to the parking lot. There's lots of parking and easy wheelchair access, and just north of the parking lot and under the trees is the market.

# Apricot Balsamic Dressing

*Four acres may not be enough to successfully raise large livestock, especially when over half of it is forested hillside. What is perfect for this property is honeybees, at least that's what Ron and Judy Bennett decided over 7 years ago when they began Luckiamute Bee. They now have nearly 20 hives, most of which are rented out for pollination in the spring and early summer. The resulting honey (and beeswax candles) are sold at the Independence Farmers' Market and includes blueberry, wild blackberry, raspberry, marionberry, clover, alfalfa, rabbit brush, meadowfoam, mint, and wildflower.*

*Perfect over fresh garden greens or on fruits like a mix of melon balls and fresh berries. Also use as a marinade for chicken or rabbit.*

1/2 cup pitted ripe apricots or canned apricots, drained
1/3 cup balsamic vinegar
1/4 cup honey
2 teaspoons Dijon mustard
1 clove garlic, minced
1/2 teaspoon dried tarragon
1/2 teaspoon dried parsley
1/4 teaspoon salt
1/4 teaspoon pepper
1 tablespoon virgin olive oil

PUREE APRICOTS in a blender, add everything except the oil and process until smooth. Slowly dribble in the oil until combined. Makes about 1 cup.

**Judy Bennett**
LUCKIAMUTE BEE

# Cran-Raspberry Sauce

*This is perfect as a dessert topping after an elegant meal. It can be as simple as a topping served over vanilla ice cream, or as involved as a rich custard layered into a puff pastry shell and topped with this brilliant red sauce.*

12 ounce package frozen raspberries
1 1/4 cups fresh cranberries
2/3 cups sugar

HEAT TO BOILING in a saucepan over medium heat raspberries, cranberries and sugar. Reduce heat and simmer 20 minutes, stirring frequently. Fruit will be very soft and will thicken naturally. Press mixture through a fine strainer, discard pulp and seeds. Cover and chill. Can be made a day ahead.

**Judy Bennett**
LUCKIAMUTE BEE

INDEPENDENCE FARMERS' MARKET

# Piper's Zucchini Relish

*There may be nothing unusual about Keith Nelson and Sloan Aagaard, but there is something very unique about Teal Creek Farms. Part of the original A. Brown deeded land claim from the mid 1800's, in 1994 Keith and Sloan accepted stewardship over much more than the farm. They also set up Teal Creek as a reparian recovery zone and have been helping the wildlife reestablish habitat ever since. Besides their uncommon bird feeding ornaments, they also sell organic produce, garlic and garlic braids at the Independence Farmers' Market.*

*When you take a taste of this relish you won't believe it's zucchini.*

10 cups zucchini, finely chopped*
4 cups onions, finely chopped*
1 green pepper, finely chopped*
1 sweet red pepper, finely chopped*
1 yellow pepper, finely chopped*
Salt
4 1/2 cups sugar
2 1/2 cups white vinegar
5 tablespoons pickling salt
1 tablespoon dry mustard
1 tablespoon cornstarch
2 teaspoons celery salt
1 tablespoon nutmeg
1 tablespoon turmeric
1/2 teaspoon pepper

PLACE ALL THE CHOPPED VEGETABLES in a very large bowl. Sprinkle salt over and mix well. Let stand overnight.

The next day, drain veggies. (I use a clean, old pillowcase. Place salted veggies in case, squeeze out liquid, run cold water in case, squeeze again. Repeat 2 or 3 times.)

Put rinsed veggies in large kettle and add remaining ingredients. Bring to a boil, stir and then simmer for 30 to 45 minutes or until thick. Pack hot mixture in jars, leaving a 1/2-inch space on top. Put filled jars in a canner and process in a boiling water bath for 5 minutes. Makes approximately 7 pints.

*A food processor works well for this task.

**Keith Nelson and Sloan Aagaard**
TEAL CREEK FARMS

---

**cranberry chronicles**

Cranberry's tangy, sharp flavor is said to have graced the tables of the first Thanksgiving in 1621. The Northeast American Indians were actually the first to introduce cranberry sauce (made with cooked wild berries and honey or maple sugar) to the early settlers. Cranes lived near the bogs where the berries grew. They also ate the berries and that's why cranberries were first know as "crane berries."

Fresh cranberries are usually available beginning in September, with the season ending in December. Berries should be plump and firm, with a bright and shiny color. As with most berries, avoid those that are shriveled or soft, and do not wash until ready to use. Store in the refrigerator, unwashed, for up to a week.

# Pickled Garlic

*A unique blend of mingling flavors can really spice up your life.*

2 pounds garlic heads, separated into cloves but unpeeled
1/3 pound fresh ginger, peeled and thinly sliced
1 cup coarse salt (sea salt works fine)
7 dried red chilies
2 cups white or red wine vinegar
2 1/2 tablespoons mustard seed
1 cup dry white wine

COMBINE GARLIC in a large non-aluminum saucepan with enough water to cover. Place over medium heat and bring to a boil; boil for 2 minutes, then drain thoroughly. When cool enough to handle, peel each clove without crushing.

Transfer the cloves to a non-aluminum bowl. Add ginger and salt with enough water to cover. Refrigerate mixture for two days, then drain and rinse thoroughly in cold water. Drain again. Meanwhile, wash 7 half-pint jars and keep hot until needed. Combine the vinegar, wine and mustard seed in a medium non-aluminum saucepan and bring to a boil. Keep hot.

Pack the ginger and garlic evenly into one jar at a time, adding 1 chile (if unavailable, use about 1 teaspoon of dried chile flakes per jar). Pour the hot brine into one jar at a time, leaving a 1/2-inch head space. Refrigerate or process in a canner in a boiling water bath for 15 minutes. Yields about 7 half-pint jars.

**Sloan Aagaard**
TEAL CREEK FARMS

---

**bee by-products**

Honey results from the involvement of 3 important players—the honeybee, nectar and enzymes. Once the bees collect nectar, they begin to evaporate excess water from the nectar, then gland enzymes go to work to change the nectar into honey. Once in the hive, the bees soon ripen the honey with ventilation provided by the fanning of their wings and warmth from the bees in the hive. The resulting product is a sweet, easily digestible food enjoyed by many.

Pollen is a highly nutritious food and is sold in many natural food stores. The pollen (male germ cells produced by plants) is collected by a pollen trap located at the entrance of the hive. The trap gathers the pollen before it is changed into honey. The removal of pollen from the hive can place stress on a colony since it is important to the hive's nutrition (especially young bees) by providing a source of protein and fat.

Royal Jelly is a high-protein food produced from glands in the heads of young worker bees. Sometimes called bee milk, this jelly is fed to queen larvae and active laying queens. Yellowish and milky in appearance, royal jelly is mostly water (about two-thirds), with the remainder being about 90% protein.

Propolis has a natural antibacterial effect and is often used in medicines. It is a collection of plant gums and resins, mixed with the bee's enzymes, wax and pollen. Bees use propolis as a hive disinfectant and sealer for any cracks or crevices. Propolis also gives a varnish-like waterproof protection to the hive.

Beeswax contains about 300 components and is secreted by wax-producing bees that are usually two to three weeks of age. Used by bees to build honeycomb, it's been estimated that 8 to 16 pounds of honey are needed to produce just 1 pound of wax.

INDEPENDENCE FARMERS' MARKET

# Pickled Asparagus

*One of the great things about farmers' markets is getting produce that is so very fresh. Asparagus is not something we grow, but it is for sale in the spring at our market. I won't pay the price for imported asparagus, so we eat lots when it is in season locally. One of the beauties of canning and making pickles is that you can enjoy things when they are not in season. I like to pickle asparagus because it retains some of its crispness. Serve it as an accompaniment to a meat or add it to salads in the darkest days of fall and winter.*

*The original recipe came from Washington State Extension in the early 80's. I got it from the Oregon State Extension and have adapted it by using honey rather than sugar. A few hot dried peppers are also tossed in for a bit of zip.*

2 cups fresh asparagus spears or pieces
1/2 cup boiling water
2 to 3 tablespoons honey or sugar
1/2 teaspoon salt
1/8 teaspoon pepper
1/2 cup vinegar
1 clove garlic
1/8 teaspoon dill weed (optional)
1/4 teaspoon dried red pepper flakes or 1 small dried red chile (optional)

COMBINE BOILING WATER, honey, salt and pepper; stir to dissolve. Add vinegar and chill, or leave hot for water bath processing. Wash asparagus, remove bottom scales. Break at tender part of stalk, size into spears to fit your jar, or cut into pieces 1 1/2-inch long. Blanch in boiling water for 2 minutes (3 minutes for stalks), immerse in ice water and cool thoroughly. Pack into pint jar, add garlic clove, dill, and red pepper if desired. Cover with cold pickling solution and refrigerate until ready to use, or pour hot pickling solution to within 1-inch of the top of jar and process in boiling water bath for 10 minutes (pints or quarts).

This recipe makes one pint. Ten pounds of asparagus equals 12 pints of spears plus 1 pint of pieces.

**Judy Bennett**
LUCKIAMUTE BEE

---

**asparagus advice**

Look for fresh, tender asparagus during the peak months of April and May. Stalks should be firm, well-rounded and plump, not flat; and show no signs of shriveling, wilting or moisture loss. Tips should be bright, pointed and tightly closed. The slimmer stalks are thought to be more succulent.

Although some say blanched asparagus (which will appear light green or white) is sweeter, it is less nutritious than the green asparagus and less flavorful. The rich, bright green asparagus (the most common variety) provides lots of vitamins A and C, plus calcium, phosphorus and potassium.

The asparagus base helps to prevent moisture loss by keeping the rest of the stem moist. When storing asparagus, always wrap the base in a damp towel, and store in a plastic bag in the refrigerator, or refrigerate stalks in a glass of water. Use within a few days for best quality.

To prepare asparagus, grasp the stalk mid-way with one hand and hold the base with the other hand, then bend the stalk. Asparagus will snap at the point where it becomes tender. The tough bottom-end pieces can be cooked until tender, pureed, then added to soups or sauces.

# Healthy Green Sauté

*Sometimes when the gardening bug bites, it bites big like it did with Jamie Aster of Sweet Earth. What started off as a family garden soon grew into more raised beds and a greenhouse that produced plenty of surplus to take to the Independence Farmers' Market. Here Aster sells an assortment of vegetable and flower starts, salad greens and stir fry mix plus country majolica pottery.*

*Growing for a family plus the farmers' market can leave you with little extra time. Besides being delicious, this recipe is also fast, easy, and will make a convert out of any "green phobic" person.*

1 bunch greens, chopped (chard, mustards, bok choy, spinach, etc.)
4 cloves garlic, chopped
1 small onion, chopped
1 tablespoon olive oil
1 to 3 teaspoons balsamic vinegar
pepper and salt to taste

SAUTÉ GARLIC AND ONION in olive oil in a large skillet until lightly browned. Add your greens (still wet from being freshly washed), and when they begin to steam, add fresh ground pepper and salt to taste. Toss greens, then add balsamic vinegar. Toss again and serve immediately. Serves 2 to 4.

**Jamie Aster**
SWEET EARTH

# Sweet Onion Pie

*Wonderful as a main dish or served as a side dish,
this sweet pie will bring out the onion lover in us all.*

4 large sweet onions (Walla Walla or equal yellow granex onions)
1 tablespoon extra virgin olive oil
3 tablespoons butter
2 eggs
1 cup cream or half and half
2 tablespoons flour
1 teaspoon salt
1/8 teaspoon hot red pepper (or more to taste)
1/4 teaspoon freshly ground black pepper
1 pinch nutmeg
2 ounces Swiss cheese, grated
chopped fresh parsley
1 9-inch pie crust

PREPARE AND PARTIALLY BAKE a crust to fit a 9-inch pan using a basic pie dough recipe or a purchased pie crust. Sauté the onions in the oil and butter over a low heat until golden brown. Beat together the eggs, cream (or half and half), flour, salt, peppers, and nutmeg, and then add the onions and half of the grated cheese. Pour into the crust and sprinkle remaining cheese on top. Bake at 375 degrees for 25 to 30 minutes or until golden brown. Garnish with parsley. Serves 4.

**Ron Bennett**
LUCKIAMUTE BEE

# Pesto Forever

*If you love Pesto but don't always have time to do the prep or want to create the mess associated with several servings, we have a simple solution—Pesto Cubes. Use your ice cube tray to create cubes of frozen pesto. After freezing, remove and transfer cubes in freezer bags or containers for later use. Each cube is a single serving.*

2 cloves garlic, more if desired
1 cup firmly packed fresh basil, chopped
1 1/2 tablespoons parsley (optional)
1/4 teaspoon salt
3 tablespoons parmesan cheese
3 tablespoons soft butter
3 tablespoons olive oil
2 teaspoons pine nuts or walnuts, chopped

IN A BLENDER, make a paste by adding all the ingredients except nuts; blend until smooth. After well blended, add nuts of your choice and blend if desired, or serve as is.

**Keith Nelson and Sloan Aagaard**
TEAL CREEK FARMS

# Pesto Stuffed Chicken Breasts

*Always make more than you need because leftover breast thinly sliced, makes an excellent sandwich meat.*

4 boneless chicken breasts
2 Pesto Forever ice cubes

lemon pepper seasoning

CREATE A POCKET in the meaty side of the breast. We accomplish this by placing the breast close to the edge of the cutting board, then holding the knife parallel to the board, make shallow slices into the breast until a 1 1/2 to 2-inch pocket is completed. (Helpful hint: It's easier to make the pocket by using slightly frozen breasts.)

Next, take a frozen pesto cube and slice it into 1/4-inch slices. Fill the chicken pocket with several slices of frozen pesto. Close the opening with toothpicks and sprinkle with lemon pepper seasoning. At this point you can barbecue or pan fry. Serve on a bed of rice or pasta, topped with your favorite light sauce.

Serves 2 to 4.

**Keith Nelson and Sloan Aagaard**
TEAL CREEK FARMS

---

**great greens** — Often referred to as "greens," this group includes European greens like sorrel, mache, cress and arugula; Oriental greens like pac choi, kyona mizuna, tah tsai (tatsoi); root vegetable greens like beet and turnip; and others like mustard, kale and chard. Greens should be promptly refrigerated to keep them fresh and crisp. For longer storage, put freshly washed greens in a zip-lock type bag in the crisper section of the refrigerator.

# Honey Sandwich Loaf

*This makes an excellent sandwich meat. Additional spices such as rosemary, garlic, or others can be added to the ground meat prior to cooking if desired.*

- 5 pounds pork butt (about 30% fat)
- 1 cup ice water
- 2 ounces Morton's Tender Quick
- 1 3/4 ounces corn syrup
- 4 ounces honey
- 1/2 cup Walla Walla onions, chopped fine
- 1 1/2 teaspoons ground white pepper
- 1 teaspoon ground celery seed

GRIND THE MEAT TWICE through a fine plate. Mix in all the ingredients by hand, thoroughly mixing spices, honey and onions throughout the ground meat. Form a loaf from the mixture and place in a deep pan (like a Dutch Oven for instance), pour in water and cover.

Bake at 160 degrees until the internal temperature of the loaf reaches 152 degrees. Add more water as it evaporates. Remove loaf and chill in an ice water bath until the internal temperature falls to 70 degrees. Place the loaf in a refrigerator for 24 hours before slicing. Serve chilled.

**Ron Bennett**
LUCKIAMUTE BEE

# Pastrami

*One of the basic necessities of life (my life anyway) is, once in a while, a real pastrami sandwich. Missing in rural Northwest life is a real Jewish deli with real brisket of beef, real corned beef and real pastrami, not some chemically altered turkey loaf or a hard super-lean clod of beef with a texture like a chipboard.*

*After searching out, I found some corning and pastrami recipes and started to work. You can adjust the spices to suite your taste, adding others. As for me, I'll be trying this out with ostrich meat.*

- 3 to 4 pound beef brisket
- 3/4 cup Morton's Tender Quick
- 1/2 cup honey
- 1/4 cup black peppercorns, crushed
- 2 tablespoons coriander seed, crushed
- 1 teaspoon whole clove
- 4 cloves garlic, diced small
- 1 gallon snap and seal type bag
- 2 cups wood chips (hickory, alder, cherry as suited to your taste)

MIX TOGETHER IN A BOWL the coarsely crushed peppercorn and coriander, Tender Quick, honey, garlic and clove. Rub mixture over both sides of the beef brisket and put it in a 1 gallon snap and seal type bag; refrigerate for 7 days, turning the bag once a day to even curing. After 7 days, hang the brisket in a cool dry place for 24 hours, then following the directions for your smoker; smoke for 1 hour on each side. To serve, slice on the bias and steam.

**Ron Bennett**
LUCKIAMUTE BEE

# Honey Walnut Biscotti

*We have two big old English walnut trees on our farm, and although we share generously with the squirrels we still get lots of walnuts for baking. This recipe came originally from the National Honey Board, but it's a favorite.*

- 1/2 cup butter or margarine
- 3/4 cup honey
- 2 eggs
- 1 teaspoon vanilla
- 2 cups all purpose flour
- 3 teaspoons ground cinnamon
- 1 teaspoon baking powder
- 1/2 teaspoon baking soda
- 1/2 teaspoon salt
- 2 cups quick cooking rolled oats (or run regular rolled oats through a blender for a finer texture)
- 1/2 cup chopped walnuts (filberts are good too)

IN A LARGE BOWL, cream butter; beat in honey, eggs and vanilla. Combine flour, cinnamon, baking powder, baking soda and salt in a small bowl; mix well. Stir into butter mixture. Mix in oats and nuts. Shape dough into two 10x3x1-inch logs on a greased baking sheet. (This is easier if the dough is chilled first).

Bake in preheated 375 degree oven 12 to 15 minutes or until lightly browned. Remove to cutting board. Reduce oven temperature to 300 degrees. Cut each log into 1/2-inch strips; place on cookie sheet. Bake 25 to 30 minutes or until crisp throughout. Cool completely on wire racks. Makes 3 dozen.

**Judy Bennett**
LUCKIAMUTE BEE

---

**honey flavors**

Honey can greatly differ in both color and flavor, depending on the source of nectar gathered by the honey bees. Colors can range from the nearly clear to midnight ebony, with most preferred honeys being a light to golden amber. Flavors can also vary from the delicately mild to fragrantly fruity to the distinctively bold.

Light colored honey is usually milder, while the dark colored honey is stronger and more intense in flavor. Alfalfa, clover and wildflower are common honeys suitable for any use. Orange blossom or fruit honeys like blackberry are excellent with fruit or when used in baking. The intense flavor of the darker honey can be used as a marinade for meats or in barbecue sauce.

ALFALFA is ranked as the most important honey plant in Utah, Nevada, Idaho, Oregon and most of the western states. Alfalfa honey is white or extra light amber in color with a fine flavor. The honey also has a good body, which makes it the perfect table honey.

BLACKBERRY is the primary honey in the Pacific Northwest and can make a light, golden-amber, or even ebony colored honey. The fruity, rich and full-flavored honey is slightly reminiscent of blackberries. An excellent all around honey and especially great for baking.

INDEPENDENCE FARMERS' MARKET

# Berry Wonderful Clafouti

*Pat Rogerson creates a unique line of quality painted woodwork and garden accessories. Her plant indicators with cleaver sayings can perk up any garden and are a favorite at the Independence Farmers' Market.*

*This fresh and fruity tasting "pie" is less than 200 calories per serving.*

| | |
|---|---|
| 4 egg whites, slightly beaten | dash of salt |
| 2 whole eggs, slightly beaten | 1 1/2 cups plain nonfat yogurt |
| 1/3 cup granulated sugar | 1 cup all-purpose flour |
| 3 tablespoons honey | 3 cups raspberries, blueberries, and/or strawberries |
| 2 tablespoons fruit liqueur or orange juice | 2 teaspoons powdered sugar |
| 1 teaspoon vanilla | additional whole berries |

BEAT TOGETHER the eggs and whites, sugar, honey, juice, vanilla and salt in a large bowl until light and frothy. Stir in the yogurt until the mixture is smooth. Add and fold in the flour. Arrange the fruit in a 9x13-inch baking dish that has been lightly coated with a nonstick spray. Pour batter over fruit. Bake at 375 degrees for 30 to 35 minutes or until set. Cool on rack for 30 minutes. Garnish with the powdered sugar and whole berries. Serve warm in wedges like a pie. Serves 8.

**Pat Rogerson**
PAT'S PATTERNS

---

**honey flavors**

CLOVERS are the most popular honey plant in the United States. Depending on location and source, clover honey varies in color from water white to extra light amber and has a mild, delicate flavor. Clover honey is generally considered the standard for comparison.

FIREWEED is a tall summer-blooming herb, native to much of the Pacific Northwest. Light in color and mild in flavor, it is an excellent table honey.

MEADOWFOAM is unique to the Willamette Valley area and because of its intense and overpowering flavor, is usually mixed with other honeys while in the hive. The resulting flavor is unrivaled starting off light, followed by a cotton candy flavor and then finishing with a hint of vanilla.

MINT creates a honey that is dark, rich and full-flavored. Referred to as "the stout beer of honeys", its flavor is not suggestive of mint at all. Its sweet honey flavor holds up well in baking and sauces, and it also makes a wonderful topping for waffles.

ORANGE BLOSSOM honey is often a combination of citrus floral sources. It produces a white to extra light amber honey with a distinctive flavor and the aroma of orange blossoms. Although not a source in the Pacific Northwest, it is commonly available in stores throughout the country.

POISON OAK honey is surprisingly delicious. An excellent all around honey, some say it also improves resistance to Poison Oak. Production is found primarily from Yoncalla, Oregon and south, the flavor is light with nice floral tones though not as light as clover.

INDEPENDENCE FARMERS' MARKET

# Fruit Bobbler

*When it comes to competition, gardening can get quite serious and Doris Cook is serious about growing her fresh vegetables and flowers. A well-known gardener, Cook has won many awards both at the local County and State Fairs. As a Master Gardener, her decades of experience is shared with the shoppers of the Independence Farmers' Market.*

*Use a single fruit or create your own special combination*

1 cup sugar
1 cup flour
2 teaspoons baking powder
1/2 teaspoon salt
3/4 cup milk

3 cups cut fruit (rhubarb, berries, or peaches are great)
3/4 cup brown sugar
3/4 cube margarine, cut into pieces

IN A LARGE BOWL, mix together the sugar, flour, baking powder, salt, and milk, then pour into a 8x8-inch pan. Arrange the fruit and brown sugar over the top of the batter, then dot with the margarine. Bake at 350 degrees for 40 to 50 minutes. Serves 8 to 10.

**Doris Cook**

| **bird feeding ornaments** | The bird feeding ornaments and wreaths are made for our wild feathered friends. The wreaths are constructed from Black and Mammouth sunflower heads dried in a solar dehydrator. They are then decorated around the perimeter with black wheat, oats, millets, and small multi-colored Indian corn. The ornaments consist of 12 assorted millets, small multi-colored Indian corn and suet filled pine cones. Each ornament is decorated with a raffia bow and tie, is Earth friendly and designed to be hung on the outdoor living or wildlife Christmas tree.<br>TEAL CREEK FARMS |
|---|---|

Goat Milk Oatmeal Soap

Fresh Anytime Salsa • Fresh Garden Salsa

Cilantro Pesto • Warm Spinach Salad with Arugula

Tabouli with Cilantro

Zucchini Casserole • Baked Stuffed Squash

Chile Rellenos Bake • Aztec Pudding

Salsa Verde • Tarragon Chicken

Lemon Thyme Rub • Key Largo Rub

Dilly Rolls • Blue Corn Bread

Zucchini Bread • Blue Corn-Blueberry Pancakes

Brown Honey Scones • Rose Petal-Lemon Verbena Tea

Super Easy Strawberry Pie

# INDOOR FARMERS' MARKET

**LOCATION:**
Community Center, Old Independent Schoolhouse
Philomath
June through September
Thursdays, 2:30 - 5:30

BEGINNING ITS FOURTH SEASON, THE INDOOR FARMERS' MARKET FIRST BEGAN TO serve local shoppers on their way home from work who couldn't make it to the other markets. Everyone was a little surprised at the response, as people were also coming from Corvallis and other areas. Many shoppers are seniors who welcome the safety of shopping indoors in a small market with a level floor. The children in the community also become involved and set up refreshment stands, selling cookies or brownies to go along with juices and iced tea.

Special events are also featured and last year included a petting zoo with live farm animals, a Holiday Market, master preservers to answer all canning, drying, and freezing needs, fund-raising bake sales and book signings from local authors.

Even though the indoor market is small and a bit out of the way, it has become an important and anticipated weekly event in the community. Chris Peterson, the market manager, feels the reason why is simple. "Farmers' markets are growing in popularity for a very good reason—people want real food grown by people, not corporations."

# Goat Milk Oatmeal Soap

*Originally settled in 1860 by pioneers who had been flooded out of the mid-west, they chose a site up from the valley floor so they would never see their land flooded again. Now over a century later, Jude Sandberg settled into this same place and named it Spirit Springs. Nearly 7 years later, Sandberg and her daughter, Eva, raise sheep and dairy goats to provide the milk for their goat milk soap, shampoo bars and oatmeal soap. Of course they also use the milk for drinking and for feeding orphaned animals. In addition they sell free-range chicken eggs and produce like Asian pears, Bartlett pears, apples, corn meal and raspberries at the Indoor Farmers' Market.*

*This is an excellent soap for the beginner because it does not require any fancy equipment and it makes a very mild soap. This recipe may be enough soap for a small family for a year. You can double the recipe for a large family, but realize that the stirring time will be longer as it takes longer to harden.*

1 can lye*
3 pints goat milk
5 1/2 pounds clear lukewarm fat
5 teaspoons borax
2 cups oatmeal, finely ground
2 ounces glycerin
1 to 3 tablespoons essential oil
   (your preference)

POUR MILK INTO an enamel, crockery, glass or wood container. Using a wooden spoon, add lye and stir to mix. When this is warm (feel the outside of the container), pour in the lukewarm fat. Keep stirring while adding. Mix in borax and finely ground oatmeal, then add the glycerin and stir for 15 to 30 minutes or until the soap starts to harden. At this time, add the essential oil of your choice (optional). Wearing rubber gloves, shape soap into balls and set aside. Let soap ripen 3 or more weeks. The older the soap, the better. If it has a peculiar odor, this will disappear with age.

*****CAUTION:** Lye is a caustic soda and it burns. It is necessary to be careful when using lye. Keep children away while making the soap and wear protective clothing like strong rubber gloves and glasses. It must be made in glass, enamel or crockery containers and stirred only with a wooden spoon. Rinse all utensils after they have been in a lye solution.

**Jude Sandberg**
SPIRIT SPRINGS

---

**old-fashioned soap making**

Here's a real "old-fashioned" recipe for making soap from the Virginia Housewife, 1860, Randolph. "Put on the fire any quantity of lye you choose that is strong enough to bear an egg—to each gallon, add three quarters of a pound of clean grease; boil it very fast, and stir it frequently—a few hours will suffice to make it good soap. When you find by cooling a little on a plate that it is a thick jelly, and no grease appears, put in salt in the proportion of one pint to three gallons—let it boil a few minutes, and pour it in tubs to cool...Next day, cut out the soap, melt it, and cool it again; this takes out all the lye, and keeps the soap from shrinking when dried."

INDOOR FARMERS' MARKET

# Fresh Anytime Salsa

*Walk into a picture of exotic scents, delicate textures and fragrant flowers. The air is filled with the aroma of herbs and you can feel the ambiance of country living. This picture comes to life while walking in The Thyme Garden, a display garden and business run by Rolfe and Janet Hagan. The garden embraces 92 raised beds of medicinal, culinary and dye herbs and flowers. The garden is open to the public from mid-April to mid-August, 10:00 a.m. to 5:00 p.m., and over 500 varieties of herb seeds, plants, teas, seasoning blends, roots and dried herbs are offered in their catalog as well. The Hagans also sell a variety of herb plants, from the common to the exotic, at the Indoor Farmers' Market in Philomath.*

*When we had our restaurant, this was always a very popular item on "Mexican Day." Many extra "sides of salsa" went out.*

7 to 8 fresh ripe tomatoes or one 28 ounce can tomatoes in puree
1 medium onion
2 to 3 cloves garlic
1 jalapeno pepper
1 small serrano pepper
1/2 teaspoon hot chili powder
1 1/2 teaspoons lime juice
1 tablespoon sugar
1/2 teaspoon salt
1/4 to 1/2 cup cilantro, chopped
2 to 3 green onions, both white and green parts

IN FOOD PROCESSOR, whirl the onion, garlic and peppers until fine. Add tomatoes, chili powder, lime juice, sugar and salt. Process again until thoroughly mixed and then add cilantro and green onions. Whirl just long enough to blend.

**Janet Hagan**
THE THYME GARDEN
HERB SEED COMPANY

---

**where to find coriander and cilantro**

Actually the same plant (Coriandrum sativum), coriander and cilantro are used quite differently. The lacy green leaves of coriander are known as cilantro, while the spherically-shaped seed from the mature plant results in the spice, coriander. Some books reference the flavor of cilantro as that of a combination of sage and citrus, while coriander has more of a citrus taste. There's a long history of use for coriander beginning with the Bible, when in the Sinai wilderness the starving Hebrews were fed manna from Heaven and said, "it was like white coriander seed", Exodus 16:31. And when the colonists arrived to America, is was one of the first herbs they grew.

Coriander spice has a warm, sweet and aromatic flavor that is commonly used in curries, spice mixtures, baked goods, pastries and candies. Store the seed in airtight jars where the flavor will improve with age.

Also known as Chinese parsley, cilantro's pungent leaves take a prominent place in many Mediterranean, Chinese, Thai, Cambodian and Mexican dishes. The young leaves are said to have a grassy and citrusy sage-like flavor. The herb is best used fresh. Of cilantro it is said that you either love the herb or you hate it. Now I love the flavor of citrus and sage, but I can't taste either in cilantro.

# Fresh Garden Salsa

*Known as the Pepper Lady, Leslyn Rasmussen joined the Indoor market in 1996 after her husband's passion for chile peppers produced far more than they could use. Besides an impressive variety of peppers, she prepares Salsa Kits for people to make their own at home. The samples she brings along disappear quickly and her kits have become quite popular.*

*Served with chips or pita bread, fresh garden salsa is a hit anytime.*

1 pound ripe tomatoes
1 small onion
1 garden salsa pepper or
   Hungarian wax
2 jalapeno peppers
2 tablespoons cilantro
1 clove garlic, minced
1/2 teaspoon salt

FINELY CHOP TOMATOES and onions. Slice peppers lengthwise and seed and devein peppers. Finely chop peppers and cilantro, then add all ingredients to a serving bowl, mixing well.

**Leslyn Rasmussen**
PEPPER LADY

# Cilantro Pesto

*As we kept upping the amount of cilantro in our "Fresh Anytime Salsa," we knew there could never be too much cilantro and this recipe is a result.*

1 cup cilantro leaves
1 8 ounce can tomato sauce or
   1 to 2 tomatoes, chopped
2 to 3 cloves garlic, minced
1 tablespoon pine nuts, toasted
1/2 teaspoon salt

WHIRL ALL INGREDIENTS in blender and get out the chips!

**Janet Hagan**
THE THYME GARDEN
HERB SEED COMPANY

---

**shopping for blueberries**  Fresh blueberry season begins in July and continues on into September, depending on the area and variety. A nice feature about blueberries is that they can keep longer in the refrigerator than most other berries. Leave fresh berries unwashed until ready to use, or store frozen in sealed freezer bags for winter-time use in syrups, pancakes and muffins. Unlike other berries, blueberries will not stick together when frozen.

# Warm Spinach Salad with Arugula

*An 11 year old certified organic farm, Gathering Together Farm grows over 40 distinct types of vegetables for Organically Grown Co-op, a restaurant, and the Beaverton, Corvallis, Lane County and Indoor Farmers' Markets.*

*A delightful mix of flavors and textures.*

| | |
|---|---|
| 1 large bunch spinach (about 1 pound) | 4 tablespoons vinegar |
| 2 cups arugula leaves | 2 teaspoons sugar |
| 4 tablespoons olive oil | salt and pepper to taste |
| 3/4 pound mushrooms, sliced | 1/3 cup pine nuts, almonds, or walnuts, lightly toasted |
| 4 scallions, sliced | 1/3 cup feta cheese, crumbled |

PREPARE AND WASH arugula and spinach. Heat oil in a skillet and sauté mushrooms and scallions until scallions have softened. Add vinegar, sugar, salt and pepper, stirring until heated through. Pour mixture immediately over arugula and spinach. Sprinkle with nuts and feta. Serves 4.

**Sally Brewer**
GATHERING TOGETHER FARM

**hookers sweet indian corn**

Like all corn, this is a heavy feeder so it needs to be rotated every year. Smaller in size than sweet corn, it still produces 3 nice big ears on each plant. Grow it like you would any other corn, but be sure to keep it far away from other varieties to prevent cross-pollination. It's at its best when young and tender. Husked, it can be boiled on the stove, roasted over low coals on the barbecue, or leave the husks on and put it in the microwave. When growing for cornmeal, let the stalks dry well and then pick the ears and shuck. I let mine dry on a clean sheet in a spare bedroom. Sometimes an electric blanket set on low goes underneath the sheet to speed up the process.

When the corn is thoroughly dry, pick out the most perfect ears for next year's seed. Choose long ears with nice, straight rows. Once dried, always store the corn is a cool, dry and well ventilated location.

The dry corn can be ground in a grinder or in small batches in a very sturdy blender. This cornmeal is the best you will ever taste!

SPIRIT SPRINGS

# Tabouli with Cilantro

*For over 20 years, Don & Chris Peterson have been growing their food organically, and for over 10 years Chris has been interviewing and profiling local farmers. It was their stories that inspired Chris to become even more committed to buying locally. Because of that commitment, the Peterson's organized the Indoor Community Market to encourage and enable people to support local farmers. And, as Chris points out, "both customers and farmers are richly rewarded". The Petersons also sell organic produce like garlic, potatoes, onions, and green, purple and yellow stringless beans.*

*This is sort of a Latin American version of the ever-popular tabouli, substituting cilantro for the mint and parsley, and adding lots of whatever is "in season." This is a great do ahead recipe.*

1 cup bulgur wheat
1 1/2 cups boiling water
1 teaspoon salt
1/4 cup fresh lemon juice
1/4 cup olive oil
6 to 10 cloves garlic, crushed or minced

freshly ground black pepper to taste
5 green onions, minced
1 large carrot, grated
1 cup cilantro, chopped
1/2 cup chopped black olives
1 tomato, chopped

### Garnish:

feta cheese, garbanzo beans, chopped red or green peppers

COMBINE BULGUR, boiling water and salt in a large bowl or pan. Cover and let stand for 30 minutes. In a small bowl, mix together lemon juice, olive oil, and garlic. Add to bulgur along with cilantro and black pepper, mixing thoroughly. Cover tightly and refrigerate until about a half-hour before serving. Shortly before serving, add remaining ingredients and mix well. Serve garnish on the side. Serves 2 to 4.

**Chris Peterson**

---

**what is a scallion?**

The term "scallion" and "green onion" are often used interchangeable. Some say that scallions can be a green onion, but a green onion isn't necessarily a scallion. To a serious cook however, there is a difference. The delicate flavor of a non-bulbing type such as "Lisbon" or "Evergreen White Bunching" is mostly thought of as a scallion, whereas any onion can be a green onion as long as it's harvested while the bulb is still small and immature.

Whether a green onion or scallion, look for tender green tops that show no signs of yellowing. The bulbs should be 1/2 inch or less in diameter with thin and tender skins. Use green tops and bulb in salads and dressings, soups, stir fry and sauces.

# Zucchini Casserole

*When Sally Moore started giving frozen cookie dough to friends as gifts, someone suggested she go into business. She decided to give it a try and Mrs. Moore's Ultimates took off like gangbusters. Currently she makes four kinds of chocolate chip cookies, varying the type of chips and nuts, or even without nuts. Only top of the line ingredients are used like real butter. The dough is shaped in frozen balls so all the customer has to do is plunk them down on a cookie sheet and bake them for 10 minutes. Currently her frozen dough can be found at the Corvallis Farmers' Market and Philomath's Indoor Market on Thursdays. During the off market season, she does take phone orders.*

*Zucchini is no longer to be feared. Plenty can be used for this recipe.*

3 pounds fresh zucchini
1 1/2 cups onion, chopped
1/2 cup butter or margarine
2 cups sharp cheddar cheese, grated
2 teaspoons seasoned salt

1/4 teaspoon Tabasco sauce
4 eggs, beaten
3 cups soft bread crumbs
1/4 cup butter or margarine, melted

WASH ZUCCHINI, cut into 1/2-inch cubes and set aside. Sauté onion in 1/2 cup butter until limp. Combine zucchini, onion, cheese, seasonings and eggs, mixing well. Turn into a 2 1/2 quart buttered casserole. Combine bread crumbs and melted butter; sprinkle over zucchini mixture. Bake uncovered in a preheated 325 degree oven for 1 hour. Serves 6.

**Sally Moore**
MRS. MOORE'S ULTIMATES

| spinach specifics | Spinach is at its best when harvested in the cool weather of spring or autumn. Summer heat causes stress on the plant and tends to make spinach "bolt" faster, so spinach selection in the summertime may be slim pickings. There are those with smooth and flat leaves, and other Savoy types with crinkled, somewhat thicker leaves. |
|---|---|
| | The green leaves should be succulent and crisp, not showing any signs of wilting, yellowing or decay. For bunched spinach, remove the band, wash well to get rid of dirt and sand, remove excess moisture in a salad spinner and refrigerate in plastic bags in the vegetable crisper. For best quality, use promptly or within a few days. |

# Baked Stuffed Squash

*Butternut squash makes this recipe a winner.*

1 medium butternut squash
2 tablespoons sunflower oil
1 cup onions, chopped (about 2 medium)
1 piece fresh ginger root, chopped fine (about 1-inch)
5 cloves garlic, minced
1 teaspoon dill weed
1 teaspoon basil
1 medium sweet pepper, chopped
1 square tofu, mashed (1/2 pound)
3/4 cup tahini
1 1/2 cups water
1 tablespoon flour
1 tablespoon tamari, or to taste
ground black pepper to taste
1/2 cup fresh parsley, minced

CUT SQUASH IN HALF, scoop out seeds, and bake, face down, in a pan at 400 degrees until tender, about 45 minutes. In a 10-inch fry pan, heat oil and sauté onions, ginger root, garlic, dill weed, and basil over medium heat until they begin to brown. Add chopped pepper, cooking about 2 minutes more. Meanwhile, put tofu in a medium-sized saucepan. Add tahini and mix well. Slowly add water and cook over low heat, stirring with a whisk until the sauce is thoroughly combined. Add flour to sautéed vegetables, then combine vegetables with tofu/tahini sauce. Continue to simmer on very low heat. Add tamari and ground pepper to taste and more water if sauce becomes too thick. Mix in parsley and serve over squash. Serves 2 large main dishes or 4 side dishes.

GATHERING TOGETHER FARM

# Chile Rellenos Bake

*You can also stuff the peppers with chicken or turkey which is really good.*

8 green chiles (Anaheim or ancho for example)
6 ounces monterey jack cheese
4 eggs, beaten
1/3 cup milk
1/2 cup flour
1/2 teaspoon baking powder
1/2 teaspoon salt
1/2 cup cheddar cheese, shredded

SLICE PEPPERS DOWN THE MIDDLE, lengthwise, and remove seeds. Cut monterey jack cheese into strips and stuff inside peppers. Place peppers in a greased 8x8-inch baking dish. Combine eggs and milk, beat in flour, baking powder and salt until smooth. Pour over peppers. Sprinkle cheddar cheese on top. Bake at 350 degrees or until golden, about 30 minutes. Serves 4.

**Leslyn Rasmussen**
PEPPER LADY

INDOOR FARMERS' MARKET

# Aztec Pudding

*I learned how to make this in Mexico and it has been a family favorite ever since for over 30 years! It's especially great if you have access to fresh, local, free-range chickens and fresh tomatillos, onions, chiles and cilantro. The measurements are approximations, adjust according to your taste and what you have on hand.*

1 chicken
onion, chopped
garlic, chopped
1 package corn tortillas
1 pound of mild cheese
   (Monterey jack, muenster,
    provolone, or a combination)

salsa verde (homemade is best, recipe follows)
sour cream
sliced onions
cilantro for more flavor and garnish

COOK THE CHICKEN with some chopped onions and garlic for a richer flavor. Let cool, then pull the meat into shreds; set aside.

Lightly fry the tortillas, one at a time, on both sides; drain on paper towels (I sprinkle them with garlic powder for more flavor). Set aside.

Shred the cheese and slice the onions. Set aside.

When all the ingredients are ready, spread a little salsa verde on the bottom of a lightly oiled casserole dish, then begin layering ingredients in the following order: tortillas, chicken, onion slices, cheese, salsa, and sour cream. If you've got lots of cilantro on hand, sprinkle some between the layers of chicken and onion. Continue layering until you've reached the top of the dish or run out of ingredients. Bake at 350 degrees until bubbly, about 30 to 45 minutes. Serves 6 to 8.

**Chris Peterson**

| | |
|---|---|
| **the stand-alone tomatillo** | Not just a "green tomato" the tomatillo (Physalis ixocarpa) is more of a tomato relative. Going by the names of jamberry, husk tomato or tomate verde, fresh tomatillos will store up to a month when kept in their paper husks and a cool, dry location. In its family are some 80 cousins including the ground cherry, but the tomatillo stands alone for the sweet-tart flavor it brings to salsa verde, chili rellenos, guacamole, green taco sauce or other dips and sauces. Left to turn yellow on the vine, it ripens to a mellow flavor that is wonderful when used fresh in salads, tacos, or sandwiches. Or try some freshly diced tomatillos in your next stir fry for an exciting change of pace. |
| **tomatillo types** | Grown like tomatoes but tasting more like the sweet/tartness of a green apple, tomatillos are indispensable in Mexican cooking, especially salsa verde. Although many different strains exist, there are two basic types of tomatillos: green and purple. |
| | The green tomatillo is known in gardening catalogs as "toma verde", or it may be referred to by the particular strain like "Indian". With the purple tomatillo, the skin and flesh turn a deep purple that is intensified with light. Both types can be used for any purpose although the green is preferred for cooking while the purple is said to be the best for eating raw. Once green tomatillos turn yellow they become even sweeter. |

INDOOR FARMERS' MARKET

# Salsa Verde
## (Green Sauce)

*You probably won't need all of this for the Aztec Pudding.
Reserve what's left for quesadillas, scrambled tofu or eggs.*

3 pounds tomatillos
1 cup fresh cilantro, chopped
4 cloves garlic
1 small onion, chopped

4 to 6 fresh jalapeno peppers
   (or 1 cup canned chiles), seeds removed
2 tablespoons fresh lime juice
a pinch of sugar

REMOVE AND DISCARD husks and stems from tomatillos and wash. Gently drop them into a large pan of boiling water and simmer, covered, until tender, about 10 minutes. Drain thoroughly. Put one-third to one-half of the tomatillos in a blender jar. Add cilantro, garlic, onion, chiles, lime juice and sugar. Blend until smooth. Repeat with remaining ingredients. Taste and adjust seasonings to your liking. Makes about 1 1/2 quarts.

**Chris Peterson**

# Tarragon Chicken

*This is a great dish for company, serves up beautifully and the taste is superb!*

8 chicken breasts
2 tablespoons oil and
   2 tablespoons margarine
1 small onion, finely diced
4 carrots, peeled and sliced as coins
1 cup dry white wine
1/3 cup fresh tarragon, chopped
   (or 2 teaspoons dried)
2 tablespoons fresh chervil, chopped
   (or 1/2 teaspoon dried)

1 teaspoon salt
1/2 teaspoon pepper (black or white)
1 cup 1-2% milk
1 egg yolk (optional)
3 tablespoons flour
1/4 pound mushrooms, sliced
2 tablespoons margarine
2 to 3 green onions, chopped

MELT OIL AND 2 tablespoons margarine in Dutch oven. Brown breasts on both sides and remove. Add onion and carrots; briefly sauté until golden. Return chicken, add wine, tarragon, chervil, salt and pepper. Bring to boil, reduce heat and simmer for 1/2 hour, covered. When almost done, melt the other 2 tablespoons butter and lightly sauté sliced mushrooms. Remove chicken and most of the vegetables from pot; bring back to near boiling. Mix milk, egg yolk, and flour in a small bowl; whisk into pot, stirring until thick. Return vegetables to pot and add sautéed mushrooms and chopped green onions. Serve as a sauce for the chicken. Great over noodles. Serves 6 to 8.

**Janet Hagan**
THE THYME GARDEN HERB SEED COMPANY

# Lemon Thyme Rub

*About two years ago, Judy Dark turned her love of plants and their bounty into a business called Dark Horse Botanicals. Living in a small community of Wren, Dark specializes in herbs, heirlooms and scented geraniums. In the spring and early summer she brings vegetable and herb starts to Philomath's Indoor Market, then herbs and herb products at other times of the year.*

*I have discovered a wide variety of flavored thymes that are excellent to crush and combine with other herbs for meat rubs. Try this with poultry or fish.*

2 teaspoons lemon thyme
1 teaspoon dill weed
1 teaspoon fresh cracked pepper
hot red pepper to taste

COMBINE ALL INGREDIENTS together and rub into meat of your choice. This will make a seasoning rub for about 1/2 pound of meat.

**Judy Dark**
DARK HORSE BOTANICALS

# Key Largo Rub

*Try this on grilled beef, pork or lamb.*

1 tablespoon lime thyme
1 tablespoon crushed mint
1 teaspoon hot red pepper
1 teaspoon ground ginger
1 teaspoon black pepper

MIX ALL INGREDIENTS together and rub into meat of your choice. This recipe can also be mixed with 3/4 cup orange juice, 2 tablespoons oil and 1/4 cup honey for use as a marinade.

**Judy Dark**
DARK HORSE BOTANICALS

---

**bulgur beginnings**
Originating from the whole wheat kernel, bulgur is partially cooked and dried cracked wheat. When a recipe calls for cracked wheat, bulgur can be substituted and visa versa. The main culinary difference is that bulgur cooks faster and has a slightly nuttier taste.

Going by the names of parboiled wheat and wheat pilaf, bulgur is essential in many Mediterranean and Eastern European dishes. Use in soups, salads, casserole, as a cereal or side dish in place of rice. Bulgur is also the foundation for any tabouli salad.

# Dilly Rolls

*The dill adds a wonderful flavor to these rolls.*

1 tablespoon yeast
1/4 cup warm water
1 cup cottage cheese, warmed
2 tablespoons sugar
1 tablespoon onion, minced
2 teaspoons dill seed
1 teaspoon salt
1/4 teaspoon baking soda
1 tablespoon margarine
1 egg, beaten
1 1/2 cups flour plus 1 cup flour

DISSOLVE YEAST in warm water in a bowl. Add cottage cheese, sugar, onion, dill seed, salt, baking soda, margarine and egg, stirring to combine. With a mixer set at medium speed or by hand, beat in 1 1/2 cups of flour for 2 minutes. Add another 1 cup of flour and stir together. Cover and let rise in a warm location.

Dough will be sticky. Put a generous amount of flour on counter and knead dough. Form to even-sized balls for rolls, rise again on pan that has been sprayed or coated with margarine. Bake at 350 degrees for about 20 minutes or until done. At end, brush with melted butter, add fresh chopped dill if available and enjoy.

**Janet Hagan**
THE THYME GARDEN HERB SEED COMPANY

# Blue Corn Bread

*Corn grows so well here and this native corn is a part of our heritage. This bread is also good the next day, either warm or cold.*

1 cup blue corn meal, finely ground
1 cup flour
1/4 cup sugar
1 tablespoon baking powder
1 teaspoon salt
1/3 cup oil
1 egg
1 cup milk

COMBINE DRY INGREDIENTS in a large bowl and mix together well. In another bowl, mix together oil, egg and milk. Stir into dry ingredients until just blended. Pour batter into a well buttered 8-inch square baking pan, and bake at 400 degrees for 25 minutes. Serve warm.

**Jude Sandberg**
SPIRIT SPRINGS

# Zucchini Bread

*When you have excess zucchini, make a lot of bread and freeze for later use.*

| | |
|---|---|
| 3 cups flour | 2 cups sugar |
| 1 teaspoon baking soda | 1 cup salad oil |
| 1/4 teaspoon salt | 2 teaspoons vanilla |
| 3 teaspoons cinnamon | 2 cups zucchini, grated with skins |
| 3 eggs | 1 cup nuts, chopped |

SIFT TOGETHER IN A BOWL the flour, baking soda, salt and cinnamon; set aside. In a separate bowl, mix together eggs and sugar. Blend in oil, vanilla and zucchini. Stir in flour mixture and nuts to combine. Grease and flour two 9-inch loaf pans and pour in batter. Bake in a preheated 325 degree oven for 1 hour.

**Sally Moore**
MRS. MOORE'S ULTIMATES

# Blue Corn-Blueberry Pancakes

*These pancakes are very satisfying but ooh so good, make plenty for seconds.*

| | |
|---|---|
| 3/4 cup buttermilk | 1 tablespoon sugar |
| 1 egg | 2 teaspoons baking powder |
| 2 tablespoons oil | 1/4 teaspoon salt |
| 2/3 cup flour | 1/2 cup blueberries |
| 2/3 cup blue cornmeal, finely ground | |

IN A BOWL, mix together the buttermilk, egg and oil. Stir dry ingredients together in a separate bowl. Add to buttermilk mixture and stir until evenly moistened.

Heat griddle to medium-high and lightly oil. Ladle batter onto griddle, then dot pancake with blueberries. Cook until pancake top looks dry and most bubbles have popped. Turn and cook until second side is brown. Serve with maple syrup.

**Jude Sandberg**
SPIRIT SPRINGS

---

**nut storage**  This is storage information for tree fruit nutmeats like walnuts or seeds like cashews, not some crazy relative. All nuts contain oils which can eventually turn rancid. A cool, dry location will usually keep nuts for several months. Refrigeration lengthens the storage life and when frozen, nuts will easily remain in good condition for a year. Shelled vacuum-packed nuts will also stay fresh longer than those packaged in bags.

INDOOR FARMERS' MARKET

# Brown Honey Scones

*You may be familiar with beeswax candles, but the artistic talents of Bertie Stringer really shine in her beeswax animals such as turtles, frogs, cats and owls. For the Christmas holidays she also makes beeswax tree ornaments with intricate details and the wonderful aroma of beeswax. Bertie and her husband Marshall Dunham run Honeystone Candles from their home in Blodgett, Oregon and do several farmers' markets, plus all the fairs and festivals throughout the year. Besides unique candles, they also sell wonderful honey and honey sticks. Bertie and Marshall often take a glass beehive to the markets, which always draws a crowd!*

*This is a favorite recipe of mine from New Zealand. We pronounce them "skonz," not "skoans." For a nice variation, try adding 1/2 cup chopped dried fruit or grated apple. Sprinkle with a mixture of 1 tablespoon sugar and 1/2 teaspoon cinnamon.*

3 cups whole wheat flour
3 teaspoons baking powder
1/2 teaspoon salt
1 tablespoon butter
2 tablespoons honey
1 1/4 cups milk

MIX FLOUR, baking powder and salt together in a bowl. Cut in butter until mixture resembles crumbs. Dissolve honey in milk and mix into dry ingredients with a knife. Add more milk if needed to obtain a soft dough; knead lightly. Roll or pat out to 3/4-inch thickness. Cut into 2-inch squares and place on a cold, floured tray. Bake in a preheated 425 degree oven for 10 to 12 minutes or until golden brown.

**Bertie Stringer**
HONEYSTONE CANDLES

# Rose Petal-Lemon Verbena Tea

*In the spring when we are practically too busy to eat, we never are too busy to get a real thirst going. We have an abundant tree rose of a pale pink old-strain variety that has hundreds of blossoms. In addition to our daughter making rosebeads, we like to make this refreshing tea.*

IN A CLEAN JAR, gather roses (only those that have not been sprayed or treated) and check for critters. Add whole blossoms to a gallon glass jar until it is loosely 2/3 full. To this add a large handful of lightly crushed lemon verbena leaves; fill the jar with hot water and place in the sun to steep. It's a delicious and refreshing cool-down.

**Janet Hagan**
THE THYME GARDEN HERB SEED COMPANY

# Super Easy Strawberry Pie

*One bowl, no time, great pie!*

2 cups fresh strawberries, sliced
1 can sweetened condensed milk
1/4 cup lemon juice
1 8 ounce container cool whip
1 8-inch graham cracker crust

COMBINE FIRST 4 ingredients in a large bowl, stir gently until blended. Pour into graham cracker crust and chill for 6 hours. Serves 6 to 8.

**Sally Moore**
MRS. MOORE'S ULTIMATES

**corn-a-plenty**

Maize, as corn was called long ago, comes in fascinating colors and varieties. Sweet corn is the type you eat on the cob or off and today comes in shades of white, yellow, orange or bi-colored. Named after Ira Hooker of Olympia, Washington, Hooker's Sweet Corn came to this area nearly 70 years ago. It can be eaten fresh when the kernels are a milky white, or it can be allowed to mature and dry to a blue-black color and used to make the sweetest cornmeal.

Field and/or flour corn goes by many names including starch, dent, ornamental corn and Indian corn. Their colored kernels develop brilliant mixtures or solitary shades of pink, red, brown, blue, gray, black, yellow, gold, and purple. It can be used for cornmeal or flour, decorating or animal feed. The young immature ears of some varieties can be eaten like sweet corn.

Another type of corn is popcorn. Not just any corn will pop, it needs to be an extra-hard form of flint corn. There are pink, white, yellow, and a multi-colored calico mix but don't get too excited, the "popped" corn will not be the color of the kernel. Today it is a popular snack food but in colonial America it was eaten for breakfast with milk and maple sugar. Could this be the next breakfast of champions?

Horton's Fluffy Pesto • Green Garlic Pesto

New Potato Waffles Divine • Chanterelle Frittata

Garlic Green Soup • Cottage Cheese Potato Salad

Green Bean Salad • Zucchini Rounds

Looks Don't Count Zucchini • Zucchini Bake

Tomato Pie • Sweet Italian Peppers

Quiche Lorainne • Honey-Spiced Rabbit

Italian Rabbit Sausage • Pigeon Pie

Whole-Grain Asian Pear Muffins • Broccoli Cornbread

Spoon Bread • Blackberry Pie

Gram's Rhubarb Pie • French Vanilla Ice Cream

Rose Geranium Ice Cream • Lavender Ice Cream

Lemon Ice Cream • Chocolate Mint Ice Cream

# LANE COUNTY FARMERS' MARKET

**LOCATION:**
E. 8th and Oak Streets in Downtown Eugene
April through November
Saturdays, 9:00 - 5:00

**SECOND LOCATION:**
Same as above
July through October
Tuesdays 10:00 - 4:00

THERE'S A BUSTLE OF ACTIVITY GOING ON AT THE CORNER OF EIGHTH AND OAK in Downtown Eugene. The streets are lined with produce of all different shapes, textures and colors, and hungry shoppers explore the brilliant display of fruits and vegetables, deciding what to buy. This is the beginning of the first public market in Eugene, the Eugene Producers' Market which started in 1915.

Decades later the growth of large supermarkets and other conditions led to the closure of the original market in 1959, but a great idea never dies. In 1979, the Lane County Farmers' Market reorganized at the same location, and now has grown at a robust pace. Today the Market is comprised of nearly 150 growers and producers, bringing everything from favorite and unique fresh vegetables and fruits, fresh fish, goat cheese, mushrooms, fresh herbs, free range chicken eggs, baked goods and breads; to jam, jellies, honey, herb and vegetable starts, perennials, plants, fresh and dried flowers, bouquets and crafted wreaths and braids. The Market also has live cooking demonstrations, and shoppers can enjoy the convenience of live entertainment and crafters displaying their wares from the neighboring Saturday Market.

The support of the community keeps the Market flourishing. The Lane County Farmers' Market is the place where paths cross and people meet, and the Market's mission statement is a testament to that common ground. "The Mission of the Lane County Farmers' Market is to further the health of the entire community by enhancing the viability of producing and marketing Oregon grown fruits, vegetables, herbs, flowers, plants and animal products through a democratic association which advances the shared values of the market community."

# Horton's Fluffy Pesto

*If you want to taste the unique blends of different salad mixes, then come visit Debra Martin and Bill Booth of Horton Road Organics. They grow a wide array of certified organic vegetables, cut flowers and some fruits for the Lane County Farmer's Market, local natural food stores, and a 65 member CSA group. Besides salad mixes, you'll also find assorted greens, broccoli, new potatoes, cauliflower, carrots, beets, and basil. Partners Bill & Debra bring over 30 years of farming experience with them to their 5 acre coast range farm.*

*We have a certain way of making this dish that creates a balanced spread both in flavor and nutrition as well as texture. Our sweet genovese basil from our greenhouses makes a great treat from June to August. At season's end, we freeze the basil leaves blended with olive oil for winter use.*

2 large bunches fresh basil
1/4 to 1/2 cup extra virgin olive oil
1 cup walnuts, organically grown
4 to 6 cloves garlic
1/2 to 1 cup freshly grated parmesan cheese
1/2 pound tofu
dash of tamari or salt to taste
ground black pepper to taste

BLEND THE FIRST 4 ingredients together in a food processor, adding additional olive oil to create a fine mixture. Add the remaining ingredients and blend well. Serve at room temperature with fresh cooked pasta or steamed potatoes. Also makes a great spread on toast. For variations include spinach, cilantro, or parsley added to the "green" part.

**Debra Martin & Bill Booth**
HORTON ROAD ORGANICS

| | |
|---|---|
| **mushroom magic** | During September and October in the cool hollows in woods grow one of the most versatile and delicious of mushrooms, the Chanterelle. You may even be lucky enough to find a few in July and August, given a few good rains. There are many different kinds of chanterelles. The two most favored are the white chanterelle with its delicate almond flavor, and the yellow or pale orange chanterelle, having the distinct smell and subtle flavor of a ripe apricot. To bring out its true essence, always dry sauté in a nonstick skillet first. Once the moisture cooks off and just before they begin to brown, add butter or toss mushrooms into a sauce. |
| | For a good pocketbook reference on mushrooms, check out *All The Rain Promises and More*, by David Aurora. There are many great recipes using the Chanterelle mushroom, many of which can be found in mushroom cookbooks. Two worth mentioning are *The Wild Mushroom Recipes* by the Puget Sound Mycological Society; and *Joe's Book of Mushroom Cookery*, a classic by Jack Czarnecki. |

# Green Garlic Pesto

*Kate & Richard Wilen of Hayhurst Organic Farm and Nursery grow certified organic fruits, vegetables, dried flowers and nursery plants on 10 cultivated acres of their 80 acre farm just outside of Yoncalla. Their specialties are salad greens, zucchini, blueberries, raspberries, cherry tomatoes, dried flowers, and of course, garlic. Besides selling garlic greens, they also craft an extensive display of decorated garlic braids and flower arrangements which are available at the Lane County and Holiday Markets.*

*Both green garlic and garlic spears are seasonal favorites on our farm table. This recipe is one of our favorite toppings for pasta, as a coating for broiled chicken or fish, or for use as a spread for French bread.*

2 cups garlic greens, chopped (about 2 dozen stalks)
3/4 cup romano or pecorino parmesan cheese, grated
1/3 cup extra virgin olive oil
dash of salt
1 to 2 tablespoons fresh herbs (optional)

CHOP THE TENDEREST portion of the garlic stalks into chunks, discarding the very top of the green leaves and the root plate. Put in a food processor and puree while slowly adding olive oil. As the mixture begins to liquefy, add the cheese, salt and fresh herbs. Blend until texture is smooth. Can be refrigerated for up to a week or put in freezer for future use.

**Kate & Richard Wilen**
HAYHURST VALLEY ORGANIC FARM AND NURSERY

**a twist on garlic**

Green garlic is the young garlic shoot before the bulb is formed. The tender young stalks are a springtime delicacy with a piquant garlic flavor that is much sweeter than the spicy bite of garlic cloves. Another form of green garlic are garlic spears, the flower pod formed on hardneck varieties of garlic such as German red or Spanish roja. Prior to the opening of the flower, these pods and their stalks are tender and ooze a wonderful garlic taste. Whether used in a stir fry or soups, they provide a zesty bridge between the end of last year's spent garlic and the pungent cloves of the summer harvest.
HAYHURST VALLEY ORGANIC FARM AND NURSERY

# New Potato Waffles Divine

*Most of our potatoes are dug as "new potatoes" before the skins are cured and while the starches are still sweet and juicy. We favor a yellow flesh potato for this recipe although any will do such as Yellow Finn or Yukon Gold.*

5 medium new potatoes, grated
1 onion, thinly chopped
1 egg
1/2 cup cheddar cheese, grated
1 tablespoon apple cider vinegar
2 tablespoons flour
salt, pepper, dill to taste

COMBINE THE ABOVE ingredients and cook in a waffle iron for about 5 minutes, or until golden brown. Serve with a side of steamed greens and toppings of salsa or sour cream.

**Debra Martin & Bill Booth**
HORTON ROAD ORGANICS

# Chanterelle Frittata

*Organically grown gourds abound at The Gourd Patch. For over 9 years Freeman Rowe has been selling all sorts and sizes of dried and decorated gourds at the Lane County Farmers' Market. Also a mycological expert (fungi specialist) Rowe has many mushrooms, including chanterelles, and brings an assortment of wild berries to the market like tayberry, silvanberry and huckleberry.*

*The flavor of the chanterelle mushroom is especially enhanced in dishes which combine mushrooms with eggs and cheese.*

2 cups chanterelles, chopped
1 tablespoon butter, margarine, or olive oil
4 eggs, lightly beaten
salt and pepper to taste
1/2 cup cheddar cheese, grated

MELT BUTTER in a frying pan which can be covered with a lid. Sauté the chanterelles until tender. If there is excess juice, pour it off and save for later use in gravies or sauces. Add salt and pepper to the beaten eggs. Pour the egg mixture over the evenly spread sautéed chanterelles in the bottom of the pan. Cover. Cook slowly. When the eggs are almost set, sprinkle the cheese over the top of the eggs. Cover again. Once the cheese has melted, remove eggs from the pan with a pancake turner or spatula. Serve hot, cheese side up. Serves 2.

**Freeman Rowe**
THE GOURD PATCH

LANE COUNTY FARMERS' MARKET

# Garlic Green Soup

*Selling at the Lane County Farmers' Market since 1979, Clark Wilde is well known for his certified organic elephant garlic, Spanish Roja garlic, golden delicious apples, rhubarb, and horseradish. A one-man operation, he must work a lot. Maybe that's why his place is called Full Moon Farm. Make up a batch of this delicious early springtime soup.*

2 or 3 garlic green stalks with tops
1 large celery stalk with leaves
4 medium potatoes with skins
1 tablespoon oil
4 to 5 cups chicken stock or
  vegetable broth
1 cup milk
1/2 cup yogurt
freshly ground black pepper
paprika or chili powder
1 tablespoon fresh parsley, chives,
  or watercress, chopped

CHOP OR THINLY SLICE the garlic green stalks, celery and potatoes; sauté in a large pot for 5 minutes. Add stock or broth, bring to a boil, then simmer for 20 to 30 minutes. Puree vegetables in blender or mash together. Add milk and yogurt and heat well. Do not boil. Garnish as desired with seasonings and serve either hot or cold. Serves 4 to 6.

**Clark Wilde**
FULL MOON FARM

| garlic storage tips | Outside of winter squash, no other vegetable stores quite as well in its natural state as garlic. A prime head of garlic kept in the right conditions can sometimes keep up to a year. Three important factors determine the storage life and that depends on the type of garlic, the appearance of the garlic before storage and the conditions in which it's stored.

First you need to know if the garlic you're buying is a hardneck or softneck type. For long-term storage, choose softnecks. The storage life of a hardneck can vary from 2 months to 6 months.

Look for heads that are firm and free from any sign of mold or spoilage. The bulb should be intact and protected by the paper-like wrappers. Individual cloves do not keep well and neither does a bulb where the cloves are showing signs of separation. Stems should be cut within 1 to 2 inches of the bulb. A bulb with a part of the stem left on will always last longer than one with the stem removed.

Store garlic in a cool (40 to 55 degrees), dry and well-ventilated place. Garlic will quickly deteriorate with moist air, so it should never be stored in the refrigerator.

# Cottage Cheese Potato Salad

*If you're looking for tasty and unique jams and jellies, then come visit Somebody's Grandmother at the Lane County Farmers' Market. Letha Paden started selling her jams, breads, brownies, cookies and other baked goods over 13 years ago. Her jams and jellies are in high demand and include the common and exotic like strawberry, peach, kiwi, mint, huckleberry, raspberry, and Jalapeno.*

*A creamy potato salad that really hits the spot.*

1/2 gallon new potatoes with skins
8 ounces sour cream
16 ounces small curd cottage cheese
1 bunch green onions, chopped (tops and all)
salt and pepper to taste

IN A LARGE POT, cook small potatoes with skin on. Let them cool, then peel and slice. In a large bowl, add all ingredients, including potatoes. Mix well and chill. Serves 8 to 10.

**Letha Paden**
SOMEBODY'S GRANDMOTHER


# Green Bean Salad

*Located east of Cottage Grove is Stuners Farm with 5 of its 20 acres in production. Gardening since she was a child, Wendy Stuner now sells herb and vegetable starts, plus fresh certified organic produce like beans, corn, carrots, onions, potatoes, lettuce, berries and much more at the Lane County Farmers' Market.*

*This salad may be served warm or chilled, but I especially like it warm.*

1 pound green beans (steamed)
1 small sweet red onion, chopped
1/2 cup hazelnuts, chopped
1/4 cup sharp cheddar cheese, shredded

IN A STEAMER, snap beans into bite-sized pieces and steam. Remove beans to a medium-sized bowl and cool slightly. Then add onion, hazelnuts and cheese. Serves 4.

**Wendy Stuner**
STUNERS FARM

---

**digging new potatoes**   This is not some kind of a new potato variety. Any potato can be considered a *new potato* if it was harvested (dug-up) before becoming fully mature. New potatoes are usually smaller and always more tender. Since the potato has not yet *fully matured*, its skin hasn't yet developed, making the storage life on a new potato less than a regular potato. There's a sure indicator for knowing when new potatoes are ready simply by looking for the flowering tops. When the potato plant blossoms, new potatoes are ready for digging.

# Zucchini Rounds

*In 1991, Rick and Kris Wetherbee made their dreams into a reality when they established Camelot Farm and began growing their own organic produce along with chicken, lamb and rabbit. Somehow their vision grew as well and they now sell their certified organic produce along with vegetable starts, perennials, culinary and medicinal herbs and other plants at the Lane County market.*

*This has become Rick's favorite way to eat zucchini. Save the big ones for this.*

1 large zucchini, green or gold
olive oil
1 cup wheat germ
1 cup whole wheat flour
1/2 cup sesame seeds
1 teaspoon chili powder
1/2 to 1 teaspoon salt

CUT ZUCCHINI INTO 1/2-inch thick rounds and arrange on a nonstick baking sheet or shallow pan. Make the seasoning by mixing together wheat germ, whole wheat flour, sesame seeds, chili powder and salt. Pour into a shaker style jar. Lightly baste zucchini with olive oil and then shake on a thin coating of the seasoning mix. Bake in a hot (400 to 450 degree) oven for about 10 minutes. Remove pan from oven and turn over zucchini with a spatula. Lightly baste unseasoned side with olive oil and shake on a thin coating of seasoning mix. (Refrigerate leftover seasoning.) Return to oven and bake another 10 minutes. Serves 4 to 6.

**Kris Wetherbee**
CAMELOT FARM

# Looks Don't Count Zucchini

*This is a long-standing recipe in our family. My mother often prepared zucchini this way. My father didn't particularly like any vegetables except potatoes, but even he often took more than one helping of zucchini whenever this dish was served. This may not look good, but it's absolutely one of the best ways to enjoy zucchini!*

1 tablespoon butter, margarine,
    or cooking oil
2 slices bacon, chopped (or the
    equivalent amount of ham)
2 1/2 cups zucchini, thinly sliced
1 medium onion, sliced
2 eggs
salt and pepper to taste

MELT BUTTER IN a frying pan over medium heat. Cook bacon until half done. Add zucchini and onion, and cook until tender. If there is a lot of juice, cook until the juice is gone. Break the two eggs over the top of the cooked zucchini. Stir together until the eggs are cooked. Serve hot. Serves 2.

**Freeman Rowe**
THE GOURD PATCH

LANE COUNTY FARMERS' MARKET

# Zucchini Bake

*This recipe was first given to me by Julie Kierstead. If you use the larger zucchini, cut in half lengthwise and scrape out the pithy developing seed area with a tablespoon, using only the firm flesh of the squash.*

4 cups zucchini, coarsely grated
1/2 cup flour
1/2 cup parmesan cheese, grated
   (or any other cheese)
3 tablespoons parsley, finely chopped
3 tablespoons onion, finely chopped
1 clove garlic, finely chopped
3/4 teaspoon oregano
1/4 teaspoon black pepper
1 1/4 teaspoons salt
4 eggs, lightly beaten
12 cherry tomatoes (optional)

SQUEEZE OUT THE JUICE of the grated zucchini so that you have 4 cups of fairly dry zucchini. (This is why older zucchini are better for this recipe because the flesh of the squash is less juicy.)

Sprinkle the flour over the zucchini in a large mixing bowl. Mix in the flour. Next, mix in remaining ingredients except the beaten eggs and tomatoes. Now add the eggs and mix; pour into a greased baking dish. Place the tomatoes decoratively on the top of the mix.

Bake in a preheated 350 degree oven for 1/2 hour, or until the zucchini bake is set and the top is brown. This may take longer.

Serve hot. Will not serve very many people because it is so good!

**Freeman Rowe**
THE GOURD PATCH

# Tomato Pie

*Serve as an appetizer or as a side dish.*

1 9-inch single layer pie crust
4 large tomatoes, peeled and sliced
2 tablespoons onion, finely chopped
1/4 teaspoon basil
1/4 to 1/2 teaspoon sugar
salt and pepper to taste
1 cup Swiss cheese, grated
1/4 cup mayonnaise

BAKE THE PIE CRUST according to recipe directions. Allow crust to cool. Slice tomatoes into baked pie crust. Sprinkle with onion, basil, and sugar. Mix together in a small bowl, mayonnaise and cheese. Spread cheese mixture on top of tomatoes. Bake at 350 degrees for 20 minutes. Serves 6.

**Letha Paden**
SOMEBODY'S GRANDMOTHER

# Sweet Italian Peppers
## (for Chiles Rellenos)

*Denison Farms grows a wide variety of certified organic fruits and vegetables year-round, selling direct to 7 different farmers' markets each week during the summer, including Lane County, Corvallis, and Beaverton.*

*Denison's sweet Italian peppers make outstanding rellenos and are much easier to deal with than fresh Anaheims as the skin is thinner and doesn't need to be peeled. They are sweet and mild, and absolutely delicious. One of our customers at the market gave us this hint for using our sweet Italian peppers for chiles rellenos. Thanks Ingrid!*

CUT THE TOP of the pepper, just below the stem. With a small knife, cut out the seeds which are in a chunk right at the top. Lay the peppers on a baking sheet in the middle of the oven at around 375 degrees. Bake for about 10 minutes. Check to see how they are doing; they may need a bit longer. They should be just a bit limp, not mushy and lifeless. Take them out and allow to cool. Proceed with your favorite Chiles Rellenos recipe. Since these peppers are very sweet and mild, you may want to add hot chiles to your sauce to spice it up.

**NOTE:** When fresh, these peppers are twisted and folded. After being roasted they will straighten out. The skin can be removed if desired, but it is so thin that you can leave it. No need to cut a slit down the length of the pepper either since the opening at the top is sufficiently large to stuff through. (Recipes for Chiles Rellenos can be found on pages 53, 88, and 140.)

**Tom Denison & Elizabeth Kerle**
DENISON FARMS

| | |
|---|---|
| **elephant garlic** | So named because of its really big heads, elephant garlic is indeed a misnomer because it really isn't a type of garlic at all but is actually more like a leek. The huge, softball-sized heads can easily weigh up to a pound. Grown in much the same way as regular garlic (except that it's planted deeper), the flavor is milder and well-suited to many recipes. |

LANE COUNTY FARMERS' MARKET

# Quiche Lorainne

*For the classic quiche you should use Swiss cheese, but another cheese will suffice.*

1 unbaked pie shell
2 mediums onions, finely chopped
3 cups chanterelle mushrooms
   (white or golden), chopped
2 tablespoons butter, margarine,
   or cooking oil
1 1/2 cups Swiss, cheddar,
   or Jack cheese, grated

3 eggs, lightly beaten
1 cup cream or half & half
1/2 cup milk
1/2 teaspoon salt
1/2 teaspoon pepper
1/4 teaspoon powdered mustard
dash of cayenne

IN A SKILLET, sauté onions and mushrooms in the butter or oil. Drain off juice and reserve for later use. (The juice is excellent for use as flavoring in sauces, soups, or gravy.) In a large bowl, mix the grated cheese with the cooked onions and mushrooms. Distribute mixture evenly in the unbaked pie shell.

Mix together eggs, cream, milk and seasonings. Pour this over the ingredients in the pie shell. (No top crust is used.) Bake in a preheated 350 degree oven for 45 minutes or until golden brown on top and the contents are set. Serve hot. Serves 4.

**Freeman Rowe**
THE GOURD PATCH


# Honey-Spiced Rabbit

*Rabbit meat is similar to chicken, yet delightfully better in that it is sweeter and more closely grained in texture. The extra sauce from the baked rabbit is excellent with steamed potatoes.*

1 young rabbit, cut into
   serving-size pieces
1/4 cup honey
1/4 cup butter or margarine, melted
2 tablespoons Dijon-style mustard

1 teaspoon ginger or 1 tablespoon fresh
   ginger root, grated
1/2 teaspoon salt
1/2 teaspoon black pepper

ARRANGE RABBIT PIECES in a shallow 9x13-inch baking dish. In a small bowl, thoroughly mix together remaining ingredients and pour over rabbit; marinade, covered, for a few hours or overnight in the refrigerator. Bake, uncovered, at 350 degrees for 1 1/4 hours, basting occasionally with sauce in dish. Serves 4 to 6.

**Kris Wetherbee**
CAMELOT FARM

LANE COUNTY FARMERS' MARKET

# Italian Rabbit Sausage

*An older rabbit (stewer) is best for making sausage but younger rabbits (with added pork fat) can be substituted. When making sausage I roughly estimated on how much fat to add from the stewer, usually 1/2 to 3/4 cup fat for every 3 1/4 to 3 1/2 cups meat. This makes a very healthy and low-fat sausage.*

4 pounds boneless rabbit with fat, well chilled and cut into cubes.
1/2 cup parsley
3 teaspoons fennel seed
2 teaspoons salt
1 teaspoon garlic powder
1 teaspoon thyme
1 teaspoon black pepper
1/2 teaspoon crushed red pepper
1/2 teaspoon allspice
1/4 teaspoon nutmeg

USING THE LARGE HOLE DISC of your meat grinder, grind the well chilled rabbit and fat into a large bowl. In a smaller bowl, mix remaining ingredients and sprinkle over ground rabbit.

Mix together with hands until thoroughly blended. Shape into rolls, patties, or leave loose. Can be refrigerated up to 3 days or frozen in 1 pound packages. Makes four 1 pound packages.

**Kris Wetherbee**
CAMELOT FARM

# Pigeon Pie

*Pigeon meat is known as "squab."*
*If squab is unavailable you can substitute chicken, turkey or rabbit.*

2 pigeons, plucked
1 onion, diced
1 potato, diced
3 carrots, diced
3 tablespoons unbleached flour
3 tablespoons butter or margarine
1 cup stock
1/4 teaspoon summer savory
1/4 teaspoon salt
1/4 teaspoon black pepper
1/8 teaspoon celery seed
1/8 teaspoon sage
Pie dough for 2 crusts

PUT PIGEON WITH WATER to cover in a pot and bring to a boil. Reduce heat and simmer until meat pulls easily with a fork, about 45 minutes. Allow meat to cool, then pull meat from bone. Roll out dough for bottom crust and place in a 9-inch pie pan. Sprinkle evenly the meat, onion, potato and carrots in the pie crust. In a small saucepan, melt butter over low heat; stir in flour. Slowly stir in broth, a little at a time, to make a smooth gravy. Pour over pie, then roll out top crust and place on pie. Cut slits in top crust. Bake pie at 375 degrees for 45 minutes or until done. Serves 4.

**Rick Wetherbee**
CAMELOT FARM

LANE COUNTY FARMERS' MARKET

# Whole-Grain Asian Pear Muffins

*Asian Pears are one of our specialties and we dry plenty for later use like in these muffins.*

1 cup each wheat bran, untoasted wheat germ and rolled oats
1 cup boiling water
2 large free range chicken eggs, slightly beaten
2 cups buttermilk
1/2 cup canola oil
1 cup dried Asian pears, chopped or snipped with scissors

2 1/2 cups unbleached flour
1 cup sugar or 3/4 cup fructose
2 1/2 teaspoons baking soda
1 teaspoon apple pie spice
1 teaspoon ground cinnamon
pinch of ground cloves
1/2 teaspoon salt

IN A LARGE BOWL, combine the wheat bran, wheat germ and rolled oats. Add boiling water and stir with fork to moisten evenly; let cool 5 to 10 minutes. Stir in the eggs, buttermilk, oil and Asian pears, blending well. In another bowl, stir together remaining ingredients, then stir into wet mixture. Do not overmix.

Muffins can be baked all at once or several at a time. Keep extra batter tightly covered and store up to 2 weeks in the refrigerator, stirring before each use. To bake muffins, spray muffin pan with a non-stick spray and fill 3/4 full with batter. Bake at 350 degrees for 20 minutes. Makes 24 muffins.

**Kris Wetherbee**
CAMELOT FARM

# Broccoli Cornbread

*Delicious and creamy with nice corn flavor.*

2 packages Jiffy corn bread mix (or your favorite)
4 eggs, slightly beaten
8 ounces broccoli, chopped

1 1/2 sticks margarine
8 ounces cottage cheese
1 medium onion, chopped

STIR ALL INGREDIENTS together in a large bowl. Spray a 9x13-inch pan with a nonstick spray and pour in batter. Bake in a preheated 350 degree oven for 40 minutes, or until toothpick inserted in the middle comes out clean. Serves 8 to 10.

**Letha Paden**
SOMEBODY'S GRANDMOTHER

---

**rabbit ratings**  Ounce for ounce, rabbit has less fat, cholesterol and calories than chicken, turkey, beef, pork and lamb. Rabbit also wins the race when it comes to calcium and protein, it provides more. If you have never tried it, you're in for a treat—this smooth, fine-grained meat is sweet and incredibly tender.

# Spoon Bread

*During World War I, an appeal was made to all American women to save resources and use simple recipes. Spoon bread was a simple recipe that many used during that period.*

1 cup boiling water
1/2 cup corn meal
1/2 cup milk
1 1/2 teaspoons baking powder
1 tablespoon oil or soft butter
2 eggs, well beaten

IN A MEDIUM BOWL, pour boiling water over corn meal. Add milk, baking powder and oil, stirring to mix. Beat in eggs, then pour batter into a buttered 1 quart casserole. Bake at 400 degrees for 20 to 25 minutes. Serves 4 to 6.

**Letha Paden**
SOMEBODY'S GRANDMOTHER

# Blackberry Pie

*Blackberries are abundant at my farm and it's a good thing because blackberry is my favorite pie.*

### Crust (makes 2)

1 3/4 cups whole wheat pastry flour or unbleached flour
1/2 teaspoon salt
1/2 cup oil
3 to 5 tablespoons cold water

MIX FLOUR AND SALT in a medium bowl. Stir in oil with fork and mix well. Add just enough water to form a ball of dough. Divide in half and roll out to make two pie crusts. Line a 9-inch pie pan with one crust.

### Filling

4 cups blackberries
1/2 to 3/4 cup sugar
1/2 cup flour
1/2 teaspoon cinnamon
cinnamon and sugar reserved for topping

Mix together (you can use same bowl that crust was mixed in) all ingredients and pour into pie crust. Top with other crust and sprinkle a little cinnamon and sugar on top. Bake in a preheated 425 degree oven for 30 minutes. Serves 2 to 8 (depends on who is eating the pie!)

**Wendy Stuner**
STUNERS FARM

# Gram's Rhubarb Pie

*An organic master gardener, Linda Williams began Mariposa Enterprises and started selling her plants, herbs, flower bouquets and fresh vegetables over 11 years ago at the Lane County Farmers' Market. Both unique and common perennial and annual plants are sold along with her crafted ceramics and pottery.*

3 cups rhubarb, diced
1 1/2 cups sugar
3 tablespoons flour

1 tablespoon butter
2 eggs, well beaten (duck eggs are great)

BLEND SUGAR, flour, butter, and eggs in a large bowl until batter is smooth. Add rhubarb and mix well. Pour into your favorite pie crust and cover with a top crust. Bake in a 450 degree hot oven for 10 minutes. Reduce heat to 350 degrees and continue cooking for another half hour or so. Allow pie to cool before serving. Serves 6.

**Linda Williams**
MARIPOSA ENTERPRISES

**ready for rhubarb**

Rhubarb and tomatoes have a lot in common, yet they are just the opposite. Where tomatoes are botanically a fruit and thought of as a vegetable, rhubarb is botanically a vegetable while it's regarded, and used, as a fruit. The stalks create tempting sauces, jams, puddings and pies. A classic example is the strawberry-rhubarb pie.

Only the juicy and tart stalks should be used since the leaves and roots are poisonous and contain toxic amounts of oxalic acids. The stalks are rich in minerals, especially potassium. April and May are great months to shop for fresh rhubarb, later in the season stalks that are large can sometimes be slightly pithy or stringy. Look for stalks that are thin, but stiff and crisp. Stalks can be pink, red, or even reddish-green, but the color should be bright and clear. To keep rhubarb fresh, store it in an open plastic bag in the crisper section of the refrigerator.

To use rhubarb, always discard the leaves, then cut the edible portion diagonally across the stalk. Here's a bit of cooking advice for those serious about their rhubarb. Do not use water as the cooking liquid for rhubarb. Fruit juice, wine or even cream are great, but never water.

LANE COUNTY FARMERS' MARKET

# French Vanilla Ice Cream

*Herbs are becoming increasingly popular both for growing and for using in many recipes. Kate Penhallagon loves using herbs and also sells many different kinds of herbs plants at her Lane County Farmers' Market booth, Cottage Herbs.*

*This basic recipe is rich but not overpowering. It makes a wonderful foundation for all the herbal ice cream recipes.*

| | |
|---|---|
| 1 1/2 cups whipping cream | 3 egg yolks |
| 1 1/2 cups milk | 1 teaspoon vanilla extract |
| 2/3 cup sugar | |

IN A HEAVY 2 quart saucepan or double boiler over medium heat, stir and heat the heavy cream, milk, and sugar until the sugar dissolves. Do not boil.

In a small bowl, whisk the egg yolks lightly. While whisking, pour 1 cup of the hot cream mixture into the bowl, then pour the egg mixture back into the saucepan and place over medium-low heat. Stir constantly with a wooden spoon (don't let the mixture boil; it could curdle) for about 8 minutes, or until it begins to thicken and coats the spoon.

To test for doneness, dip a metal spoon into the mixture and run your finger across the back. The custard is done when your finger leaves a clear, clean trail. A candy thermometer should read 175 to 180 degrees.

Remove the pan from the heat and stir in the vanilla. Use the prepared base in one of the following recipes, or freeze as is according to manufacturer's instruction.

**Kate Penhallagon**
COTTAGE HERBS

# Rose Geranium Ice Cream

*The longer this is chilled in the refrigerator, the stronger the flavor will be.*

| | |
|---|---|
| 2 tablespoons rose-scented pelargonium leaves, chopped | 1 batch French Vanilla Ice Cream |
| 1 1/2 cups loosely packed rose petals, white bases removed | 1 to 3 teaspoons rose water (optional) |
| | 2 tablespoons chopped pink rose petals, white bases removed |

STIR THE CHOPPED pelargonium leaves and the 1 1/2 cups rose petals into the hot French Vanilla prepared base. Cover and chill in the refrigerator for at least 1 hour. Strain the mixture and add rose water to taste if desired. Stir in the chopped rose petals. Pour the mixture into an ice cream maker and freeze according to manufacturer's directions.

**Kate Penhallagon**
COTTAGE HERBS

# Lavender Ice Cream

*For a stronger lavender flavor, increase chilling time.*

2 rounded tablespoons fresh lavender blossoms
1 batch French Vanilla Ice Cream
1 rounded teaspoon fresh lavender blossoms, chopped
7 drops red food coloring (optional)
7 drops blue food coloring (optional)

STIR THE 2 TABLESPOONS lavender blossoms into the hot French Vanilla ice cream base. Cover and chill in the refrigerator for at least 2 hours or overnight. Strain the mixture and add the additional chopped lavender blossoms and the optional food coloring. Pour the mixture into an ice cream maker and freeze according to the manufacturer's directions.

**Kate Penhallagon**
COTTAGE HERBS

# Lemon Ice Cream

*The fresh lemon flavor of lemon verbena and lemon balm really makes this ice cream stand out.*

zest of 1 lemon
2 tablespoons freshly squeezed lemon juice
1/4 cup hard-packed lemon verbena leaves
1/4 cup hard-packed lemon balm leaves
1 batch French Vanilla Ice Cream made with only 1/2 teaspoon vanilla extract
1 tablespoon fresh lemon balm leaves, chopped

STIR THE LEMON PEEL, lemon juice and hard-packed herbs into the hot French Vanilla ice cream base. Cover and chill in the refrigerator for at least 1 hour. Strain the mixture and add the chopped lemon balm leaves for color. Pour the mixture into an ice cream maker and freeze according to the manufacturer's directions.

**Kate Penhallagon**
COTTAGE HERBS

---

**loving lavender**

Lavender has always been loved and at one time was thought to be an herb of love. There seems to be something about the fragrance that evokes familiarity and serenity. That could account for the fact that today, the majority of lavender blooms goes into perfume and other fragrance products. On the horizon is a new frontier just beginning to bloom and that is in the kitchen.

Lavender leaves excel in flavored oils and vinegars, jellies, chicken and rabbit. The chopped leaves add a pleasant addition to biscuits, cakes and ice creams; while the flowers can season sugar and fruit compotes.

# Chocolate Mint Ice Cream

*Chopped spearmint leaves swirl through every scoop of this creamy, rich chocolate ice cream. You can use peppermint instead of spearmint, but because peppermint is stronger the amounts should be reduced by half.*

1 batch French Vanilla Ice Cream
2 ounces semi sweet chocolate
2 ounces unsweetened chocolate

1 cup hard-packed fresh spearmint leaves
1/2 cup spearmint leaves, chopped

WHILE HEATING the ice cream base, melt the chocolate in a double boiler over hot but not simmering water, stirring occasionally. Remove chocolate from heat and pour about 1 cup of the prepared hot French Vanilla ice cream base into the melted chocolate and whisk until well blended. Pour the chocolate mixture back into the remaining vanilla base and whisk again. Stir in the hard-packed mint leaves. Cover and chill in the refrigerator for at least 1 hour. Strain the mixture and add the chopped mint leaves. Pour the mixture into an ice cream maker and freeze according to the manufacturer's directions.

**Kate Penhallagon**
COTTAGE HERBS

**blackberry time**

Those of us that love blackberries are lucky to live in an area where they grow wild and in abundance. Two introduced species that now commonly grow wild are the **Himalayan Blackberry** and **Evergreen Blackberry**. Usually ripening first, the Himalayan blackberry is quite juicy and sweet. The evergreen blackberry is not quite as juicy but the flavor tends to be more developed. Blackberry season may vary depending on your location, but generally begins in late July and can last through September.

Be ready to "gear up" when picking blackberries. The thorns are quite sharp! Heavy-duty long pants, a long-sleeved shirt and a glove on one hand can save a lot of wear and tear. The ultimate gear though includes heavy rubber boots (to move into the patch) and a bucket tied to your waist. After all, both hands need to be free; one to grab the vine and the other to pick berries!

Besides lots of taste, blackberries also have plenty of fiber, minerals, B vitamins and vitamin C. Look for berries that have no trace of red on them. If there is, they will be tart! Shiny blackberries may also be tart and not yet ripe. When the berry begins to lose its gloss and it pulls easily from the vine, it will be at its berry best.

Refrigerate berries immediately and wait to wash until you are ready to use them. Berries also freeze well by placing a thin layer of berries on a cookie sheet. Once individually frozen, they're ready to put in freezer bags or containers.

LANE COUNTY FARMERS' MARKET

Virginia Style Sweet Chunk Pickles

Lime Pickles

Green Tomato Mincemeat • Tomato Sauce

Tomato Catsup • Chili Sauce

Zesty Pesty • Canning Spaghetti Sauce

Freezing Corn • Fried Zucchini

Quick Pickled Beets

Pesto Pinwheels • Peppery Garlic Eggplant

Spring Green Eggs • Lukewarm Tuna Salad

Stinging Nettle Lasagna

Fresh Apple Cake

# PEOPLE'S ALL-ORGANIC FARMERS' MARKET

**LOCATION:**

Next to People's Co-op Food Store

3029 SE 21st Avenue in Portland

April through first hard frost, usually November

Wednesdays, 2:00 - 7:00 p.m.

IN 1990, KATHY BETHEL, PRODUCE MANAGER AT PEOPLE'S CO-OP FOOD STORE, WAS seeking ways to promote the increasingly dominant organic share of produce being sold at the co-op. She also wanted to offer local farmers an opportunity to sell their produce. The first Sunday Market became a reality in May, 1991.

During that first year about 15 local organic farmers gathered on the first Sunday of each month at People's Co-op to sell direct to consumers. Produce was kept fresh and cool during the market in a large walk-in cooler, courtesy of the co-op. The Sunday market encouraged consumer requests for local produce. When Pablo Kennison took over as produce manager of the co-op in the fall of 1991, People's Co-op formally became the first retail store to offer completely and only all-organic produce. The co-op itself is open every day from 9:00 am to 9:00 pm.

The First Sunday Market continued in 1992 and 1993, but as farmers' markets in general grew in popularity, People's Co-op decided to change its once-a-month market to a once-a-week affair occurring in mid-week on Wednesdays when, at the time, there were no other farmers' markets open. Since 1991, over 30 farmers have participated in the market, growing mainly by word of mouth and homemade signs placed on neighborhood streets on the day of the market.

By 1997, farmers were usually selling out, and the co-op, which for years experienced reduced produce sales on the day of the market, was enjoying steadily increased produce sales, even on the day the market is open. Organic farmers from as far away as 60 miles and from Portland itself benefit from the direct customer contacts that the All-Organic Farmers' Market provides. Products span the wide range of organic fruits, vegetables, nuts, nursery starts, baked goods and Kombucha tea. Shoppers can enjoy the scenic market surrounded by flowers, herbs, shrubs, trees, and the live organic contribution from the music community, a regular occurring feature.

# Virginia Style Sweet Chunk Pickles

*Located on the historic property of Sebastian Brutschen, Mustard Seed Farms is now the only working farm within the city of Newberg. Nancy Brown, now owner, grows many vegetables including 10 kinds of leaf lettuce and 12 varieties of cherry tomatoes in mixed colors and shapes. Brown has farmed for 30 years and in addition to selling her certified organic produce at People's All-Organic Market, she also has a community garden and a CSA. There's plenty of raspberries to bring to the market, plus monstrous giant pumpkins at the farm, weighing up to 200 or more pounds.*

*This recipe goes back four generations in my family. Though there are several steps, it is very easy to follow and the pickles always come out great.*

75 pickling cucumbers, 4 to 5-inches long, or 2 gallons of smaller pickles in large crock or container
2 cups pickling salt
water
4 1/2 tablespoons alum
9 cups vinegar
10 1/2 cups granulated sugar
1/2 pickling spice
1 1/2 tablespoons celery seed

1. Make brine of 2 cups pickling salt to 1 gallon water.

2. Boil brine and pour over cucumbers. To keep cucumbers from floating to the top of the brine, invert a dinner plate on top of container and put a pint jar of water (with lid) atop plate as a weight. If weather is hot, you might need to skim off any scum that may arise to the top each day. Let stand for 1 week.

3. Drain cucumbers and cut into chunks.

4. For the next 3 days, make a boiling hot solution of 1 1/2 gallons water and 1 1/2 tablespoons powdered alum. (Be sure to buy fresh alum every season.) Pour this solution over pickles. MAKE A NEW SOLUTION EACH DAY, throwing away the old solution.

5. On the fourth morning, drain pickles from the alum water. Heat in a large pot 9 cups vinegar, 7 1/2 cups granulated sugar, 1/2 cup pickling spice and 1 1/2 tablespoons celery seed to boiling, then pour solution over pickles.

6. On the 5th day, drain off this liquid. SAVE THE LIQUID and add 2 more cups sugar; bring to a boil again and pour over pickles.

7. On the 6th day, again drain off the liquid. SAVE THE LIQUID. Add 1 cup sugar, reheat, pour over pickles. Pack pickles into hot sterilized jars, pour hot liquid over pickles and seal. Yields 17 pints.

**Nancy Brown**
MUSTARD SEED FARMS

# Lime Pickles

*A traditional lime pickle always has a bright green color, thus the use of food coloring. Ordinarily we avoid color enhancers and additives, but in this recipe I add color.*

7 pounds pickling cucumbers, sliced (no ends)
2 pounds slack lime
2 gallons water
2 quarts vinegar
1 tablespoon celery seed
1 tablespoon whole cloves
1 tablespoon mixed pickling slices
1 tablespoon (heaping) pickling salt
4 pounds granulated sugar
1 ounce green food coloring

COVER SLICED CUCUMBERS with slack lime and water. Soak for 24 hours. Drain and rinse well. Cucumbers will be very fragile, handle with care. Cover with clear water for 3 hours. Drain and rinse again.

Make a syrup of vinegar, spices, salt, sugar and green food coloring. Simmer cucumbers in the syrup for 1 hour. Seal in pint jars with syrup. Refer to the Pickling Chart in this book or a canning book for recommended processing time. Yield: 12 pints.

**Nancy Brown**
MUSTARD SEED FARMS

**pickles with a snap**

Crisp pickles begin with fresh pickling cucumbers. They should be firm with no signs of shriveling or yellowing. Ask the grower when the cucumbers were picked. Quality pickles will come from cucumbers that were picked within a few days of use. Pickling cucumbers can be any size up to 6 inches long. The larger picklers are great for making into bread and butter or dill pickle slices, the smaller ones are good for sweet gherkin pickles. For an extra crisp pickle, try packing in one or two grape leaves into each jar. Seedless cucumbers (sometimes called burpless) also result in a pickle that's crunchy.

# Green Tomato Mincemeat

*This is a great recipe when you have a lot of those green tomatoes to deal with.*

- 8 quarts green tomatoes, chop first then measure
- 8 quarts sour apples, core, chop and then measure
- 5 pounds granulated sugar
- 1 pound raisins or currants (or combine)
- 2 cups molasses
- 2 whole oranges, chopped in blender with no extra water added, will be mushy
- 2 cups shortening or ground suet
- 2 cups vinegar
- 2 tablespoons salt
- 2 tablespoons ground cinnamon
- 1 tablespoon ground cloves
- 2 teaspoons ground nutmeg

CHOP TOMATOES and put in a very large pot. Cover with water and bring to a boil, then boil for 15 minutes. Drain well. Repeat this process twice more to bleach out the green tomato color. Chop and add apples to tomatoes. Add all the other ingredients, stir completely and bring mixture to a boil. Reduce heat and simmer until mixture is as thick as you want for pies. Stir frequently with a long handled wooden spoon.

**CAUTION:** If the mixture sticks or burns on the bottom, the whole batch will taste burnt! Seal in sterilized jars.

I usually chop and combine the ingredients on the first day and start cooking. Turn it off overnight. Start it cooking again the second morning and usually by evening, the mixture is thick enough to be sealed into jars. Refer to the Pickling Chart in this book or a canning book for recommended processing time. Yields 13 quarts.

**Nancy Brown**
MUSTARD SEED FARMS

---

**squash mix-ups**

It seems squash is the bearer of more jokes than any other vegetable. The tales of terror do not stop with the zucchini that ate Manhattan or the abandoned zucchini litter discovered by the neighbor. Gardeners also share shocking stories of mutilated and deformed squash that look something like a vegetable from the "Outer Limits." Scared stiff by this encounter, they become leery of ever planting any two different types of squash together ever again.

Just like all bad horror flicks, realty is always unlike the made-up monsters. You can plant zucchini and crooknecks together, or even pumpkins with butternuts. The resulting fruit you harvest that year will still be exactly what you planted. Different squash varieties can easily cross-pollinate, but the resulting fruit is not what's affected, it's the seed. Prolific produce can often get ahead of the best of gardeners and if that cross-pollinated fruit is left to rot on the soil where the seeds can then spill out, then next year's squash may just become the talk of the town.

PEOPLE'S ALL-ORGANIC FARMERS' MARKET

# Tomato Sauce

*When making this sauce, put small amounts of the mixture into the blender when blending—it squirts!*

13 pounds ripe tomatoes, roma-type is best
2 medium sized onions
1/4 teaspoon cayenne pepper
2 cups cider vinegar
1 1/2 tablespoons broken cinnamon stick
1 tablespoon whole cloves
3 cloves garlic, finely chopped
1 tablespoon paprika
1 cup granulated sugar
2 1/2 teaspoons salt

WASH AND SLICE TOMATOES and boil in a large pot until soft (about 15 minutes). Into another pan, slice the onions. Cover with a small amount of water and cook until tender. Puree cooked tomatoes and onions, or put through food mill or sieve. Mix tomato and onion pulp. Add the cayenne pepper. Boil this mixture rapidly until it has been reduced to about half of its original volume.

Meanwhile, place vinegar in an enamel pan; add a spice bag containing the cinnamon, cloves, and garlic. Simmer for 30 minutes, then bring to the boiling point. Place cover on pan until ready to use. When tomato mixture has cooked down to half its original volume, add vinegar mixture, of which there should be 1 1/4 cups. Add the paprika, sugar, salt, and boil rapidly until desired consistency is reached. This should require about 10 minutes. Pour sauce while boiling hot into sterilized jars and seal at once. Refer to the Pickling Chart in this book or a canning book for recommended processing time.

**Nancy Brown**
MUSTARD SEED FARMS

# Tomato Catsup

2 gallons tomatoes, roma-type best
4 tablespoons salt
3 cups sugar
1 quart vinegar
2 tablespoons mustard
1 teaspoon red pepper flakes
1 large onion, finely chopped
4 teaspoons mixed pickling spices

PEEL TOMATOES by dipping a few at a time in rapidly boiling water, then dunking immediately in cold, clean water; skin will slip off easily. Chop up the tomatoes, add the remaining ingredients and cook until it is as thick as you desire. Refer to the Pickling Chart in this book or a canning book for recommended processing time. Yield: 9 bottles.

**Nancy Brown**
MUSTARD SEED FARMS

# Chili Sauce

*Delicious on meat loaf or any beef dish. Add to mayonnaise to make a "mock" Thousand Island dressing along with a dash of lemon juice.*

24 ripe tomatoes
6 large onions, chopped*
3 green bell peppers, chopped*
1 red bell pepper, chopped*
1 1/2 cups granulated sugar
1 1/2 tablespoons salt
1 tablespoon cinnamon
1/2 teaspoon ground cloves
1/2 teaspoon ground allspice
3 cups vinegar

PEEL TOMATOES by dipping a few at a time in briskly boiling water, then dunking immediately in cold, clean water; skins will strip right off. Chop tomatoes and put into a large kettle.

Add the remaining ingredients and bring to a boil. Reduce heat and simmer for approximately 3 hours. Stir occasionally with a wooden spoon. Refer to the Pickling Chart in this book or a canning book for recommended processing time.

* The onions and peppers can be chopped in a food processor, or chunks can be chopped in a blender if you add water so mixture will swirl, then pour contents into a strainer and thoroughly drain before adding to rest of recipe.

**Nancy Brown**
MUSTARD SEED FARMS

# Zesty Pesty

*Growing at SunBow Farm in Corvallis is a diverse variety of over 70 certified organic vegetables and 20 herbs. In addition, Harry McKormick and Bine Schulte also specialize in lots of fresh garlic and garlic braids, and since Schulte comes from Germany, they maintain and grow original German seed. Look for SunBow Farm's fresh organic produce at the People's All-Organic Farmers' Market.*

*When you get a craving for pesto early in the season try this new recipe*

FOLLOW TRADITIONAL pesto recipe substituting fresh roquette (arugula) and parsley for the basil, and adding miso, sour cream and ground almonds in addition to the garlic, olive oil, and greens.

**Bine Schulte**
SUNBOW FARM

---

**the traditional pesto nut**  Once considered a delicacy in the colonial South, these nuts have moved their way into the most favored nut for pesto making. Pine nuts go by many names like pignolias, Indian nuts, pesto nuts, pinocchios and Mexican nuts. One of the smallest nuts, its sweet flavor is packed with protein. Most pine nuts sold today are either shelled, or blanched.

PEOPLE'S ALL-ORGANIC FARMERS' MARKET

# Canning Spaghetti Sauce

*A meatless sauce that's wonderful for those hectic days when you want a quick meal.*

5 gallon bucket tomatoes, roma-type
3 pounds onions
2 red bell peppers
2 green bell peppers
3 hot peppers
6 cloves garlic, or 2 heads elephant garlic
1 pint olive oil
1/2 cup salt
4 large cans tomato paste
6 bay leaves
2 tablespoons oregano
2 tablespoons basil
2 tablespoons parsley

COOK TOMATOES and put through a food mill. Grind onions, peppers, and chop garlic and add to tomatoes. Add remaining ingredients, stir thoroughly and cook slowly until it has cooked down to desired thickness. Remove bay leaves.

For processing sauce (no meat), put into sterilized canning jars. Adjust lids. Put into pressure canner and raise to 10 pounds pressure. Turn off heat once the pressure is reached. Let cool off heat, down to 0 pressure. Remove jars. Yields 14 quarts.

**Nancy Brown**
MUSTARD SEED FARMS

| butternut squash | Creamy like butter with a sweet, mild flavor, butternut squash cooks up moist and delicious. The skin takes on a salmon-colored hue and the shape is long and round with an eye-catching bulging bulb on the end. They tend to have the longest storage potential of all squashes. The longer they're stored, the sweeter they become. |
|---|---|

PEOPLE'S ALL-ORGANIC FARMERS' MARKET

# Freezing Corn

*We really like this because none of the "goodness" is blanched away, yet the corn is blanched. You lose less of the vitamin content when processed this way.*

4 quarts corn, raw and cut from the cob
1/2 cup granulated sugar
1 quart water
4 teaspoons salt

PUT SUGAR, WATER, AND SALT in a large pot and boil for 10 minutes. Remove from heat, add corn and let stand until it reaches room temperature. Pack corn into freezing containers, including the liquid, and freeze promptly.

**Nancy Brown**
MUSTARD SEED FARMS

# Fried Zucchini

*This takes very little oil in that it is not a deep-fried recipe.*

medium to large zucchini (not too big that it has developed seeds)
beaten eggs
Pride-of-the-West batter mix *
Italian seasoning
canola oil
grated cheese (optional)

THE AMOUNTS NEEDED depends upon the number of people being fed. Slice the zucchini crosswise into 1/2-inch thick rounds. Use 2 small shallow bowls for dipping zucchini. In the first bowl, put beaten eggs. In second bowl, put some Pride-of-the-West batter mix (dry form). Heat an electric skillet with a little canola oil to 325 degrees.

Now for the messy part. One at a time, dip the zucchini rounds first in the beaten egg, then in the dry batter mix. Covering will be thin and tend to drip. Place in hot skillet, bumper to bumper, until skillet is full with a single layer of zucchini. Cook until brown on bottom. Turn each piece over. Sprinkle with Italian seasoning and brown on second side. Reduce temperature to 200 degrees, add a small amount of water and put on lid. Steam until zucchini is tender but not mushy. Test with a fork. Put on serving platter and sprinkle with grated cheese. Serve immediately. CAUTION: Zucchini is very hot in the middle. Be sure children don't burn their tongues.

*Pride-of-the-West batter mix is sold in most seafood departments of the grocery store. Comes in 1 pound packages.

**Nancy Brown**
MUSTARD SEED FARMS

PEOPLE'S ALL-ORGANIC FARMERS' MARKET

# Quick Pickled Beets

*I got this recipe 30 years ago from my friend Alice Maurer. It's the quickest way I know to pickle fresh cooked beets, a small amount at a time, and with very little effort.*

1/2 cup vinegar
1/2 cup liquid from 1 pint of beets
2 tablespoons sugar
2 whole cloves
1/2 teaspoon salt
3 whole peppercorns
1/4 bay leaf
1 pint beets, drained and liquid reserved

IN A POT, bring to a boil all ingredients except the drained beets. Remove from heat, add beets and chill. Yield: 1 pint.

**Nancy Brown**
MUSTARD SEED FARMS

### the tomato debate

As president, Ronald Reagan stated that catsup served in school lunchroom cafeterias met the required serving for a vegetable. However, botanically speaking, the tomato is actually a fruit, or more specifically, a berry.

Whether the tomato is a fruit or a vegetable is a debate that began back in 1883 with the Tariff Act which allowed the duty-free importation of fruits, but not vegetables. Three years later an importer named John Nix protested when a customs agent levied a duty on his imported tomatoes, even though Nix knew they were botanically fruits.

This controversy went all the way to the Supreme Court and in 1893 Justice Horace Gray ruled the tomato a vegetable: "Botanically speaking, tomatoes are the fruit of the vine, just as are cucumbers, squashes, beans and peas. But in the common language of the people...all these vegetables...are usually served at dinner...and not, like fruits, generally as dessert." So by law from that day forward the tomato became a vegetable.

# Pesto Pinwheels

*In a small neighborhood of Portland lies Tenino Farm where Laura Napruszewski and John White grow and sell a variety of organic vegetables. They first started growing and selling to neighbors and then soon expanded their marketing in 1994 to People's All-Organic. Traditional vegetables are plentiful like greens, roots, corn, peppers, eggplant and tomatoes, and they also keep an active interest in exploring new varieties.*

*Summer brings lots of basil and pesto making. Here's a great way to use some of that pesto.*

pie crust for 2 crusts
   (your favorite recipe)
2 cups pesto (your favorite)
2 cups dried tomatoes

1/2 cup fresh garlic, crushed or finely minced
olive oil
salt, fresh or dried basil and oregano
pignolia nuts or nuts of your choice

HAVE PIE CRUST DOUGH ready and pesto ready. Place dried tomatoes in a quart saucepan, preferably a Pyrex type. Cover tomatoes with water. Bring water to boil and cook, stirring occasional on simmer until all the water is gone and tomatoes are very tender. Add 3 tablespoons olive oil and sauté garlic, herbs and salt along with tomatoes. Mixture should become soft and paste like but not gummy. Cool 1 1/2 hours.

Roll out pastry dough into a big square, 1/4-inch thick. First spread dough with pesto, then tomato mixture, then sprinkle on nuts. Roll tightly from one end to the other. Transfer roll to a surface which can be covered and placed in the refrigerator 3 to 4 hours. Slice the roll into 1-inch thick pinwheels. Place on a well oiled baking sheet and bake in a preheated 400 degree oven until pastry is golden brown.

**Laura Napruszewski**
TENINO FARM

---

**how hot is hot?**

The heat of a pepper can vary immensely all the way from the mild Anaheim to the fiery hot Habanero. Measured in units of heat, the Scoville pepper scale registers the mild Anaheim at 1,000 to 1,500 units, medium hot Jalapeno at 35,000 to 45,000 units, and flaming Habanero, thought to be the hottest pepper, at 200,000 to 300,000 units. The following peppers are listed in order of heat, with the hottest pepper being first.

1. Habanero
2. Scotch Bonnet
3. Thai Paper Dragon
4. Super Chili
5. Tabasco
6. Fire
7. Mushroom
8. Cayenne Long Red Slim
9. Cherry Bomb
10. Serrano Chili
11. Garden Salsa
12. Early Jalapeno
13. Hot Banana
14. Ancho
15. Tam Jalapeno
16. Mulato Isleno
17. Anaheim Chili
18. Passilla Bajio

PEOPLE'S ALL-ORGANIC FARMERS' MARKET

# Peppery Garlic Eggplant

*Serve this dish with polenta, pasta, rice, or alone in a bowl with some chewy, crusty bread.*

4 big red onions, chopped
8 to 10 cups cubed eggplant,
    globe type or Japanese long
    (I use both)
lots of olive oil
lots of salt

1/2 tablespoon freshly ground black pepper
1/2 cup pressed garlic (mixed in a bowl
    with 1/2 teaspoon salt)
tomato juice
2 teaspoons crushed chili peppers

IN A BIG STOCK POT, sauté the onions in plenty of olive oil, first at a high flame to get started, then turn down to low and cook very slowly for 1 hour or so until the onions become very translucent. While onions are cooking, layer eggplant chunks in a colander alternately with liberal sprinklings of salt. After at least 1/2 hour when the dark, bitter liquid from the eggplant is visibly draining, rinse with water and pat dry. You may need 2 or 3 colanders, or you can do the eggplant in separate batches, but allow yourself plenty of time.

Add eggplant, garlic and salt mixture, and peppers to onions and add more olive oil if needed. Cover up to one-half the vegetables with fresh tomato juice (I use the liquid left over from baking tomatoes). Cook until eggplant is very tender and falling apart. Add more liquid if needed but only if eggplant is sticking to the pot. Stir frequently and keep lid on when not stirring. Serves 6 to 8.

**Laura Napruszewski**
TENINO FARM

| | |
|---|---|
| **more on miso** | Miso is simply a paste made by fermenting soybeans along with other ingredients. Depending on the type of miso, the "other ingredients" may include barley or brown rice. Sometimes used in place of soy sauce for dips and spreads, its versatility also lends to desserts, seasonings, sauces, soups and stews. |
| | Store miso in a cool place. Refrigeration or boiling can destroy the living enzymes that help aid digestion. |

PEOPLE'S ALL-ORGANIC FARMERS' MARKET

# Spring Green Eggs

*Roger Konka has been growing specialty greens, salad mixes and mushrooms for over 7 years at his farm, The Green Dude. In addition, he also sells other vegetables, flowers and fresh eggs at the Portland market and People's All Organic market.*
*Great served for breakfast, lunch or dinner.*

olive oil
4 eggs, beaten
2 to 3 cloves garlic, minced
4 baby leeks, sliced

1/4 pound shitake mushrooms, chopped
1 large bunch spinach, rinsed and chopped
1 sprig rosemary, chopped

SAUTÉ GARLIC IN OLIVE OIL; add leeks and mushrooms and continue to sauté for 5 minutes. Mix in spinach and rosemary; cook until spinach wilts. Fold in beaten eggs and stir until cooked. Serves 2 to 4.

**Roger Konka**
THE GREEN DUDE

# Lukewarm Tuna Salad

*Here's an original twist to an old-time favorite.*

3 cups uncooked elbow noodles
1/2 pound royal burgundy beans,
　　cut in 1-inch pieces and steamed

1 cup German original purple onions, diced
1 6 ounce can tuna
oregano, basil, mayonnaise and vinegar to taste

AFTER COOKING the noodles, layer them in the bottom of a casserole or dish. Top noodles with steamed beans and sliced onions. Add the tuna and toss with mayonnaise, vinegar, and herbs to taste. Eat lukewarm or chilled. Serves 4.

**Bine Schulte**
SUNBOW FARM

---

**the purple green bean**

Yes, there are purple "snap beans" that can also be called green beans. Purple on the vine and when eaten raw, they change their color to a deep green when steamed or cooked. This is the perfect blanch indicator when freezing beans. Royal Burgundy is one popular variety that produces straight 6 inch beans. The deep midnight purple color is just as striking in salads as it is in crunchy texture and juicy flavor. Once cooked, they turn a deeper green than other snap beans.

Choose pods that are firm but not bulging and with seeds that are still small. Look for good, sharp color and crisp pods that feel slightly fuzzy.

PEOPLE'S ALL-ORGANIC FARMERS' MARKET

# Stinging Nettle Lasagna

*Formally a Koi fish farm in the 70's, Julia Butler has turned fish into organic produce and the farm into Osmo Gaia Produce. Most things Butler grows are specialty produce you just can't find in the stores, but she also brings peas, greens, carrots, and blackberries to the People's All-Organic Farmers' Market. The medicinal benefits of herbs has captivated Butler's interest and she loves cooking with stinging nettles.*

*This lasagna not only tastes good, but is also good for you.*

1/2 pound lasagna noodles
1 1/2 cups ricotta cheese, crumbled
1 1/2 quarts tomato sauce
1/2 pound stinging nettles
2 cups mozzarella cheese, shredded
1 tablespoon basil
1 tablespoon oregano
1/2 teaspoon salt
1/2 teaspoon pepper

PREHEAT OVEN to 375 degrees. Cook lasagna noodles in large pot until done. Rinse noodles in colander and allow to drain. Place 3 inches of water in same pot and put stinging nettles in metal colander that will fit inside the pot. Steam slightly to take out the "sting" of the nettles. Mix together tomato sauce, basil, oregano, salt, and pepper in a bowl.

In a 9x13-inch ovenproof pan, layer the following; noodles, ricotta cheese, nettle greens, tomato sauce, and mozzarella cheese. Repeat layers. Bake at 375 degrees for 35 to 45 minutes. Serves 6.

**Julia Butler**
OSMO GAIA PRODUCE

---

**nettle news**

Nettle plants are also known as "stinging nettles" and rightly so. The plant contains hollow needle-like hairs attached to sacs filled with chemical irritants that sting when a person brushes up against a plant. That's why protective clothing (especially gloves) should be worn when harvesting the plant. Despite their powerful sting, nettle is a powerful plant with a multitude of uses.

Nettle has a long history of use as a cloth and was in high demand in Germany during World War I when cotton was in short supply. Also used medicinally, nettle is now being studied for treatment of high blood pressure, asthma and hay fever.

The fresh tender shoots are said to be without sting and can be eaten raw or tossed in salads. Use leaves as a vegetable, in casseroles or steamed like spinach. Once boiled or steamed the leaves will lose their sting, but the effects don't always disappear when the plant is dried.

PEOPLE'S ALL-ORGANIC FARMERS' MARKET

# Fresh Apple Cake

*When you want a healthy treat, this one's sure to please. It's quick, easy, and ooh so delicious.*

4 cups sliced apples, preferably Gravenstein or other sweet/tart and juicy variety
2 cups whole wheat pastry flour
1 teaspoon or more cinnamon
2 teaspoons baking powder
dash of salt
1 cup oil
2 eggs
dollop of dark honey

### Topping

1/2 to 1 cup chopped almonds
cinnamon and sugar

SIFT TOGETHER the dry ingredients in a large mixing bowl. Mix together wet ingredients in a small bowl. Add wet ingredients and apple together with dry ingredients and pour into a well-oiled 9x13-inch baking dish. Sprinkle on top of batter 3 handfuls of chopped almonds and a mixture of cinnamon and sugar. Bake in a preheated 350 degree oven for 35 to 40 minutes or until toothpick inserted in the middle comes out clean. Serves 8 to 12.

**Bine Schulte**
SUNBOW FARM

PEOPLE'S ALL-ORGANIC FARMERS' MARKET

## pickling chart

Keep in mind that when you are canning, processing time can change depending on the altitude of where you live. Listed are some guidelines for favorite pickling recipes. Refer to a canning book or contact your local Master Food Preserver extension agent with any questions you may have on canning.

| product | style | jar size | Minutes of process time at altitudes of | | | |
|---|---|---|---|---|---|---|
| | | | 0-1,000 | 1,001-3,000 | 3,001-6,000 | Above 6,000 ft |
| Dill pickles | Raw | Pints | 10 | 15 | 15 | 20 |
| | | Quarts | 15 | 20 | 20 | 25 |
| Quick Dills | Raw | Pints | 10 | 15 | 15 | 20 |
| | | Quarts | 15 | 20 | 20 | 25 |
| Quick Sweet pickles | Hot | Pints or quarts | 5 | 10 | 10 | 15 |
| Quick Sweet pickles | Raw | Pints or quarts | 15 | 20 | 20 | 25 |
| Bread and Butter pickles | Hot | Pints or quarts | 10 | 15 | 15 | 20 |
| Sweet Gherkin Pickles | Raw | Pints | 5 | 10 | 10 | 15 |
| Pickled Asparagus | Raw | Pints or quarts | 10 | 15 | 15 | 20 |
| Pickled Dilled Beans | Raw | Pints | 5 | 10 | 10 | 15 |
| Pickled Beets | Hot | Pints or quarts | 30 | 35 | 40 | 45 |
| Pickled Hot Peppers | Raw | Half-pints or pints | 10 | 15 | 15 | 20 |
| Pickle Relish | Hot | Half-pints or pints | 10 | 15 | 15 | 20 |

Source: OSU Extension Service

Sea Berry Juice • Mountain Ash Juice

Cornelian Cherry Preserves • Sautéed Sunchoke Pesto

Watercress Soup

Wilted Spinach Salad with Seasonal Garnish

Royal Potato Salad • Fava Beans

Thai Minted Eggplant • Roasted Leeks • Pickled Beets

Roast Salmon with Pesto Crust and Red Onion Relish

Chili Rellenos

Roasted Halibut with Salad of
Asparagus, Spring Onions, Fava Beans, and Fresh Herbs

Seared Salmon on Mediterranean Couscous
with Cucumber Raita

Oven-Roasted Mussels with Saffron Tomato Vinaigrette

Cornmeal Poundcake with
Summer Berry Compote and Mascarpone Cream

Chocolate Espresso Sorbet with Fresh Berries

Abiqua Blueberry Crisp • Rhubarb Coffeecake

# PORTLAND FARMERS' MARKET

**LOCATION:**
Albers Mill Parking Lot on the Willamette River
1200 NW Front Avenue
May through October
Saturdays, 8:00 - 1:00

**SECOND LOCATION:**
Pioneer Courthouse Square, downtown Portland
July through September
Wednesday's 11:00 - 3:00

EXCITEMENT AWAITS AT THE PORTLAND FARMERS' SATURDAY MARKET, located right alongside the scenic Willamette River. Going into its seventh season, the market offers specialty food and produce, baked goods, lots of fruits and vegetables, and plenty of bedding and landscape plants and flowers for the anxious gardener. The market offers a 16-week run of Chef in the Market, a cooking series that began in 1992. Every Saturday through the heart of the season, the market hosts a free 30-minute cooking demonstration taught by chefs from local restaurants. Last year also saw the debut of the first Bread Festival showcasing Portland area bakeries. The market atmosphere is like that of a community brimming with family, friends and familiarity. Not just a social outing but social event. With nearly 50 farmers and specialty food vendors, you'll be sure to find just what you need.

Right in the heart of downtown Portland is the Wednesday Farmers' Market, now in its second year. Situated on the brick patio of Pioneer Courthouse Square, farmers and vendors bring their specialty items for downtown shoppers. Likewise the Wednesday market draws thousands of office workers on their lunch breaks to farm-fresh produce rather than packaged fast food. Last year the market hosted a Berry Festival where they gave away 1,000 free berry shortcakes with the help of downtown business community volunteers. And if it's berries you want, you'll find plenty of strawberries, blueberries, raspberries, blackberries and more. Take a break with the family and join in the fun at the market.

# Sea Berry Juice

*If you're looking for the unusual, look at Portland Market's Jim Gilbert of One Green World. Well known for the fuzzless varieties of kiwi he sells both as plants and as fruit, he also brings unique fruiting plants from the former Soviet Union and Eastern Europe. His uncommon finds not only bring beauty to the landscape, but also some pretty tasty treats. Jim notes in his catalog about Oregon, "As Oregon's liquid sunshine beats down, as rivers rise and snow falls in the mountains, I am reminded of the incredible diversity of plants and climates here on our Spaceship Earth."*

*Sea Berry is a fruiting bush grown on a large scale in former East Germany, China, Russia and other regions. The fruit is valued as a tasty juice and the seeds are pressed for oil, used for treating burns and other skin injuries.*

1. Harvest the fruit after it has turned bright orange, usually late August to early September. Harvest it before it softens as the soft fruit is more difficult to pick.

2. Wash fruit

3. Crush fruit in a large kettle and strain out the juice, separating seeds and pulp.

4. Heat juice to about 120 degrees and add an equal amount of sugar. (Honey may be used or less sugar for a tarter juice.)

ONCE THE SUGAR is dissolved, juice can be bottled using approved methods or mixed with water for fresh consumption. Try mixing 30% to 50% juice with flavored or unflavored mineral water. Makes a wonderful and refreshing drink!

**Jim Gilbert**
ONE GREEN WORLD

# Mountain Ash Juice

*The common Mountain ash bears attractive, but bitter tasting orange fruit. Our Eastern European and Russian varieties on the other hand bear large tasty fruit that is not bitter. Mountain Ash fruit is high in Vitamins A and C, niacin, pectin and trace elements. Fruit of cultivated varieties is eaten fresh and used in preserves, jam, pastry and wine.*

SORT OUT SOUND ripe fruit, remove stems and twigs, and wash, first in warm water and then under tap water. Put cleansed fruit in a kettle. Add water at the rate of 1 pint for every 2 pounds of fruit. While stirring regularly, raise temperature to 185 to 195 degrees. Keep at this temperature until fruit softens, cool to 115 to 120 degrees and strain out the juice. To store, heat the juice to 195 degrees, pour into hot jars and quickly seal. When using juice, add sugar to taste. Yield: 3 2/3 to 4 pounds of fruit makes 1 quart of juice.

**Jim Gilbert**
ONE GREEN WORLD

# Cornelian Cherry Preserves

*Fruit of cultivated varieties can reach 1 1/2 inches long with a unique sweet-tart flavor resembling that of a good pie cherry. Besides being delicious eaten fresh and in baked goods, it is used to make delicious preserves, juice, wine and pickled as an olive substitute.*

    1 pound ripe fruit                                    4 cups water
    3 cups sugar

WASH FRUIT, add warm water and fruit to large saucepan and heat at 175 to 180 degrees for 3 to 5 minutes. Drain off water and use to make sugar syrup (boil sugar in water until dissolved). Add fruit to hot syrup and let stand for 3 to 4 hours. Bring to a boil for 3 to 4 minutes, let stand for 5 to 8 hours and repeat 2 to 3 times. Preserves are ready when drops of syrup stand when dropped on a cool plate. These preserves are a real delicacy, used to sweeten tea, as a topping for ice cream, and simply eaten.

**Jim Gilbert**
ONE GREEN WORLD

# Sautéed Sunchoke Pesto

*They grow everything they can and they grow it organically. That's the philosophy of Frederick and Deborah Oerther of The Oerther Family Farm. Besides seasonal produce, you'll also discover garlic, herbs, compost, worms, plant starts and seeds at their farm, and at their Portland Farmers' Market booth. Instruction is offered in organic gardening, composting and soil regeneration. The Oerthers have been farming their land for over 20 years, always organic.*
*Makes a unique and wonderful pesto.*

    1/3 cup olive oil                                4 to 6 medium basil leaves, minced
    1/3 cup water                                   10 to 12 sunchokes, minced or finely chopped

OVER MEDIUM HIGH HEAT, sauté basil and sunchokes with olive oil in a hot pan for 5 minutes, adding water as needed. Cook until done, preferably until sauce becomes thick. Serve on a small bed of toast, rice, potatoes, or noodles.

**Deborah Oerther**
THE OERTHER FAMILY FARM

---

**spinach standouts**    Spinach ranks high on the nutrition scorecard but the winner doesn't go to iron. Rich in beta-carotene, one cup of raw spinach supplies nearly 70 percent of the RDA. There's still plenty of iron to this healthy vegetable along with vitamin B6, vitamin C, folic acid, potassium and calcium.

---

**PORTLAND FARMERS' MARKET**

# Watercress Soup

*If you love specialty greens, salad mixes and mushrooms, then you'll love The Green Dude. Besides growing gourmet greens and salad mixes, Roger Konka sells other vegetables in addition to flowers and fresh eggs at the Portland market and People's All Organic market.*

*A delicate blend of gourmet treats makes this soup a winner.*

| | |
|---|---|
| 4 cloves garlic, minced | 1 1/2 cups cream or milk |
| 5 baby leeks, chopped | salt and pepper to taste |
| 1 1/4 pounds shitake mushrooms, sliced | cayenne pepper (optional) |
| | olive oil |
| 1 large bunch watercress, chopped | parmesan cheese |
| 2 tablespoons flour | |

HEAT OLIVE OIL In wok or heavy skillet; sauté garlic, baby leeks, shitake mushrooms until soft. Add watercress and sauté briefly. Sprinkle flour over all and add the cream or milk, stirring continually. Simmer 10 minutes, stirring occasionally. Season to taste with salt and pepper. Sprinkle parmesan cheese on top. Serves 2.

**Roger Konka**
THE GREEN DUDE

# Wilted Spinach Salad with Seasonal Garnish

*Fresh spinach is always a welcome culinary treat and so is this salad.*

| | |
|---|---|
| 3 cups fresh spinach | 1/2 cup carrots, grated |
| 1/3 cup water | 2 to 6 cloves garlic, minced |
| 1/3 cup vinegar | 1/2 cup seasonal vegetables |
| 1/2 cup green onions, chopped | (radishes, cucumbers, mushrooms, |
| 3 drops lemon juice | turnips, thinly sliced) |

WASH AND STEM SPINACH. Place whole leaves in large salad bowl. Create a hole in the middle of the bowl and put in all ingredients except vinegar and water. Mix vinegar and water together and heat to a boil in a small saucepan. Mix seasonal vegetables and spinach leaves together in bowl. Pour heated liquid evenly all over salad. Put cover over salad bowl for 30 seconds. Ready to serve.

**Deborah Oerther**
THE OERTHER FAMILY FARM

---

**it's still zucchini**

Thank the Italians for introducing zucchini to this country. Now popular worldwide, zucchini graces the tables of France as courgette, the Spanish fondly call it calabacin, and in England it's the baby marrow. The traditional Mid East style of zucchini is Cousa, and can go by the variety names of "Zahra," "Magda" or "Kuta." Popular Italian varieties are "Seneca Milano," "Lagenaria Longissima," "Cocozelle" and "Costata Romanesco."

PORTLAND FARMERS' MARKET

# Royal Potato Salad

*This potato salad is colorful and fun to eat.*

| | |
|---|---|
| 6 to 8 cooked peeled white potatoes, chopped | 1/2 cup green onions, chopped |
| 6 to 12 cooked unpeeled purple potatoes, chopped (about 1/2 pound) | 1/2 cup dill pickles, chopped |
| | 1/2 cup lite ranch dressing |
| | 1/2 cup lite mayonnaise |
| 1/2 cup carrots, grated | 1/2 cup water or pickle juice |
| 1/2 cup celery, chopped | 1 teaspoon yellow mustard |
| | dash of Italian seasoning |

MIX TOGETHER all vegetables except 1/2 of the cooked and unpeeled purple potatoes. Next mix all liquids together and carefully fold into vegetables. Mince the other 1/2 of the purple potatoes and decorate the top of the salad with circles which spiral into the center of the bowl. Sprinkle white parts with olives, green or black, and Italian seasoning. Chill and serve.

**Deborah Oerther**
THE OERTHER FAMILY FARM

# Fava Beans

*A family farm since the 1940s, Winters Farms grows an assortment of popular and unusual berries; many vegetables including sweet corn, beans—green, wax and horticultural, summer and winter squashes, carrots, peppers and tomatoes; plus fresh herbs including several varieties of basil. Wholesale customers and brokers are an important part of their business in addition to the Beaverton and Portland Farmers' Markets.*

*This recipe was given to me by one of our customers, Roxanne Piekenbrock.*

SHELL FAVA BEANS and blanch for a couple of minutes. Remove hull from beans. Sauté beans in olive oil with garlic, minced prosciutto (Italian ham) or regular ham and rosemary. Toss with cooked hot pasta and serve with freshly grated parmesan cheese and black pepper.

**Inge Winters**
WINTERS FARMS

---

**from green to bean** — Talk about versatility. A bean actually can be used in three different forms—string, shell and dried. All beans can be used in each form but some beans are better when used in one form over another. The string bean stage is really stringless, it has been since 1894. This is the young stage (also called snap beans) when the pod is still tender and the bean is eaten whole. When the pod becomes tough and rubbery (the shell stage), the still tender fresh beans are shelled and promptly cooked. Once the bean has fully formed and matured, the vine is allowed to dry, the bean is removed from the pod and then used as "dried beans".

# Thai Minted Eggplant

*Starting off with Ph.D's in genetics and botany, Carole Laity and Sheldon Marcuvitz gave up their careers in scientific research to do what they love best—growing food. And grow food they do at Your Kitchen Garden, their 11 acre farm where they provide pesticide-free produce to Portland area restaurants and customers at the Portland Farmers' Market. They grow over 200 varieties of vegetables and 15 varieties of heirloom tomatoes, along with heirloom shelling beans and many European and Oriental specialties.*

*Oriental eggplants are sweet and delicious and can be served in a number of ways. Try them barbecued in slices about a half-inch thick with your favorite dip, or as tempura, slice or (for Bambino) whole. This recipe is a Thai dish with a strong, hot flavor. If it's too pungent, reduce the amount of garlic or fish sauce.*

6 Japanese eggplants or
   24 Bambino eggplants
vegetable oil
1/3 cup lime juice
1/3 cup Thai fish sauce

2 tablespoons sugar
4 cloves garlic, crushed
1/4 cup mint, chopped
1/8 cup Thai basil, chopped

CUT THE JAPANESE EGGPLANTS into 3/4 inch rounds, brush with oil and grill or broil until browned (3 to 4 minutes per side). Baby eggplants may be grilled whole. Stir the other ingredients together in a small bowl. Serve the eggplants hot, drizzled with the sauce. Serves 6.

**Carole Laity**
YOUR KITCHEN GARDEN

---

**magnificent mints**

There are several different varieties of mints, at last count well over 600. Still when it comes to culinary creations and soothing teas, there are just a few cultivars that are notable. Those most familiar are peppermint (Mentha x piperita) and spearmint (M. spicata).

Peppermint is the source behind that original peppermint flavor found in personal products like toothpaste, oils and mouthwash to food items like candy, gum, and herbal tea. English mint (M. x piperita var. vulgaris) and white mint (M. x piperita var. officinalis) are varieties of peppermint. Peppermint is well known for its digestive properties and well favored in cooking.

Similar in use to peppermint, spearmint and curly mint's milder flavor is more thought of as the versatile culinary mint. Pineapple mint (M. sauvolens var. variegata) is a white-leaved version of apple mint (M. suaveolens). Both mints impart a delicate fruity flavor to drinks, fruit salads and cream cheese. A unique mint that's also stunning in the garden, is orange mint (M. x piperita var. citrata), also know as bergamont mint. It makes a wonderful herbal sun tea and vinegar.

PORTLAND FARMERS' MARKET

# Roasted Leeks

*Roasted leeks are simple and absolutely delicious. It's our favorite way to eat leeks.*

8 medium or 16 baby leeks
butter

salt and pepper

CLEAN OUTER LEAVES from leeks. If using medium leeks, split in half lengthwise and clean under running water. Baby leeks may be left whole but check carefully for dirt or sand. Heat butter in an oven-proof sauté pan and add leeks. Sauté for a few minutes, turning until well glazed and slightly golden on the outside. Place in preheated 375 degree oven and roast about 20 minutes or until tender and golden, turning once. Serves 4.

**Carole Laity**
YOUR KITCHEN GARDEN

# Pickled Beets

*Beets are really coming into their own and when you make this tasty dish,
you'll want plenty more.*

8 medium or 16 baby beets
2 pints vinegar
1 teaspoon black peppercorns

1 teaspoon allspice berries
1 teaspoon grated horseradish
1 teaspoon salt

COOK THE BEETS, cool, skin and slice. (If desired baby beets may be left whole.) Pack in preserving jars. Put the vinegar, spices, horseradish and salt into a pan. Bring to a boil and then cool. When the vinegar has cooled, pour over the beets and seal at once. If the spiced vinegar mixture doesn't quite cover the beets, the jars may be topped with additional cold vinegar.

**Carole Laity**
YOUR KITCHEN GARDEN

| | |
|---|---|
| **from bottom to top** | Hold on to those beet tops because they're packed with nutrition and flavor. With only half the calories, beet tops have more vitamins A, B1, B2, and C, plus more calcium and iron than the roots. Similar in taste to Swiss chard, the tender somewhat buttery texture of the tops are great in salads, lightly steamed or braised. If you like greens with a little less flavor intensity, use the tops from the gold or white beets instead. |

**PORTLAND FARMERS' MARKET**

# Roast Salmon with Pesto Crust and Red Onion Relish

*Philippe Boulot may have grown up in France, but he's an avid sport fisherman, and like many northwesterners, he loves to come up with a new way to prepare salmon. The following recipe comes from the Portland Farmers' Market Chef in the Market series where every year, chefs from local restaurants give cooking demonstrations that include farm fresh produce.*

*This is quite easy and turns out delicious if you follow the directions carefully. It's especially important to use a non-stick frying pan and heat it very hot, or the pesto won't get a crispy top. (The pan is hot enough when, if you hold your hand about 3-inches above the surface, you can only hold it there for 3 or 4 seconds.)*

*The red onion relish isn't essential, but it adds a nice, sharp contrast to the rich salmon and herbs.*

### Red Onion Relish:

- 1/4 cup extra virgin olive oil
- 3 medium red onions, diced (about 4 cups)
- 1 teaspoon minced fresh ginger
- 1/2 cup lemon juice (1 to 2 lemons)
- 2 teaspoons red chili garlic paste (found in Asian groceries or the Asian products aisle)
- 2 tablespoons soy sauce
- 2 teaspoons capers, rinsed and drained
- 1 teaspoon green onion, thinly sliced (white part only)
- 1 teaspoon cilantro, finely chopped
- 1 teaspoon parsley, finely chopped

MAKING THE RELISH: Heat the oil in a heavy saucepan over medium-high heat. Add the diced onion and sauté, stirring, until it is soft and transparent but does not begin to brown. Add the ginger and garlic and sauté for 1 minute more. Stir in the lemon juice and cook until most of the liquid has boiled off. Stir in the chili garlic paste, soy sauce, capers, green onion, cilantro, and parsley. Remove from heat, transfer to a bowl, cover and refrigerate until ready to use. The relish can be made up to 2 days in advance.

### Pesto Crust:

- 1/2 cup fresh basil leaves, packed
- 1/2 cup fresh white bread crumbs
- 1/4 cup pine nuts
- 1/4 cup imported parmesan cheese, grated
- 2 cloves garlic
- 1/4 cup bacon or pancetta (unsmoked Italian bacon), chopped
- 1/4 cup extra virgin olive oil
- salt and freshly ground pepper to taste

MAKING THE PESTO CRUST: Place the basil leaves, bread crumbs, pine nuts, cheese, garlic and bacon in the bowl of a food processor fitted with a steel blade. With the motor running, slowly add the oil through the feed tube and process until the mixture is crumbly and well combined. Transfer to a bowl. Stir in salt and pepper to taste. Cover and refrigerate until ready to use. Can be made a day in advance.

# Roast Salmon with Pesto Crust and Red Onion Relish
## (continued)

6 pieces salmon fillet, skin on, approximately 6 ounces each
(do not use salmon "steaks")

PREPARING THE SALMON: Preheat oven to 425 degrees. Have the pesto and the salmon fillets very cold. Press a layer of pesto, about 1/8 to 1/4-inch thick, on the flesh side (not the skin side) of each fillet. If necessary, wet your fingertips with a little water to keep the pesto from sticking to your hands.

Heat a dry, non-stick skillet over high heat until very hot. Do not use any oil. Place each fillet, pesto side down, in the hot skillet and allow the outside layer of the pesto to brown. Let brown well but do not allow to burn. Remove each fillet from pan, turn over, and place, crust side up, in a single layer on a baking dish. Bake, uncovered, for 10 to 15 minutes, depending on the thickness of the fillet and how you prefer it cooked.

To serve, place a portion of red onion relish on each of six serving plates. Lay a fillet on top of relish and serve. Serves 6.

**Philippe Boulot, executive chef**
THE HEATHMAN HOTEL, PORTLAND

**drying fresh garlic**

Fresh-harvested garlic needs to be seasoned so it will store properly and that process is called curing. Garlic is cured by either hanging the garlic (stalks attached) in bundles, or stacking it loosely on drying screens located in a dry, airy and shady spot. Left in the sun to dry, garlic can literally cook, ruining the keeping quality.

The curing process can take as little as two weeks or as long as six weeks depending on the size of the bulb, air temperature and how much moisture there is. Garlic that is well cured can last a long time, with softnecks (especially early California) lasting up to a year, and hardnecks lasting 4 to 6 months.

PORTLAND FARMERS' MARKET

# Chili Rellenos

*Kris Koa and Robert Burns began Unicorn Meadows back in 1987 and now grow a vast selection of certified organic vegetables like beans, peas, potatoes, corn, tomatoes, and peppers, with an emphasis on fancy salad greens. Offering a fine selection of herbal honeys and a great line of oils, vinegars and cordials, they also have an annual plant sale and Christmas Bazaar. Many of their products are also included in their mail order catalog. Look for their specialty items throughout the season during the Portland Wednesday Market at the Pioneer Courthouse.*

*This recipe is one that you make once a year for a special occasion. It may be lots of work but it's worth every bite!*

36 whole fresh Anaheim chiles, roasted (try roasting them over the grill)

1 large brick jack cheese, cut into 1/2 to 3/4-inch squares by 3-inches long to form sticks

3 dozen farm fresh eggs, reserve 3 eggs

1/2 gallon corn oil

BEAT 3 EGG WHITES in a large bowl until stiff. In a separate bowl, beat 3 egg yolks until they are beaten to a fluffy consistency. Very carefully, add egg yolks by drizzling into egg whites, then gently fold in. To maintain as much air as possible, only do 3 eggs at a time and do each batch at the very last minute.

Take roasted, peeled chiles and gently stuff with cheese sticks.

Heat 2-inches of oil in skillet until the oil moves about (without smoking) in the pan. One at a time, dip stuffed chile into egg mixture and gently lower into hot oil. Deep fry, dip and splash oil on top of floating chile. When top of chile is light yellow, very carefully turn it over to fry evenly on the other side.

Float no more than 3 chiles at a time in a standard wok or other large skillet. Drain chiles by placing folded paper towels on top of folded newspaper. Put chiles on paper towels and when drained, place in a casserole. Don't let the chiles linger too long on the paper towels as they will stick and pull off your coating.

### Prepare sauce:

1 sweet onion, sliced

2 cloves garlic, minced

36 ounces tomato sauce (preferably homemade)

dash of freshly ground cinnamon

Blacken onion in a saucepan, then add garlic. Mix in tomato sauce and cinnamon, then simmer 15 minutes. When done, add sauce to casserole dish and bake at 350 degrees for 30 minutes or until bubbling. Invite hungry guests and serve hot with homemade tortillas.

**Kris Koa**
UNICORN MEADOWS

---

**keep beets from bleeding**

When it comes to bleeding beets, red is the runny culprit. You can help keep the red from bleeding into your other food with these tips: add a bit of lemon juice or vinegar to your cooking water the next time you throw in the beets, this helps to stabilize the red pigment and hold in that color. And when preparing beets, leave an inch of the leaf stalk attached to discourage bleeding. If all else fails, use beets of a different color like gold or white.

# Roasted Halibut
## with Salad of Asparagus, Spring Onions, Fava Beans, and Fresh Herbs

*The following recipe comes from the Portland Farmers' Market Chef in the Market series where every year, chefs from local restaurants give cooking demonstrations that include farm fresh produce.*

*This spring or summer salad makes a delicious first course, or a light main dish. Don't be afraid to add or substitute other market produce, such as boiled tiny new potatoes, or fresh basil.*

### For the halibut:

- 1 1/4 pounds fresh halibut or other firm-fleshed fish (salmon, swordfish), trimmed
- olive oil
- sea salt

### For the salad:

- 16 to 24 asparagus spears
- 24 to 30 tender green beans
- 1 cup fava beans or cooked dried beans, such as cranberry beans or white cannelloni
- 2 cups salad greens, washed and dried
- 1 red bell pepper
- 4 small ripe tomatoes
- 1/4 cup extra virgin olive oil
- grated zest and juice of 1 lemon
- 1 tablespoon balsamic vinegar
- 2 tablespoons parsley, chopped
- 2 green onions, cut on the bias into 1/2-inch pieces
- 1 tablespoon chopped fresh thyme, oregano, or rosemary
- salt and freshly ground black pepper to taste

TRIM THE ASPARAGUS SPEARS and green beans. Blanch by plunging into a pot of boiling water for 2 to 3 minutes, then draining and rinsing well with cold water to stop cooking and set bright green color. If you're using fava beans, blanch briefly using the same method, then squeeze each bean out of its covering.

Halve the bell pepper, trim off the stem and any ribs and seeds, then broil, skin side up, very near the broiler element, until thoroughly blackened. Set aside to cool in a paper bag. When cool, peel blackened skin off completely. Cut pepper into long strips and set aside.

Cut tomatoes into small wedges or dice. Set aside.

Just before serving, place all vegetables, greens and fresh herbs in a large bowl. Toss gently with 1/4 cup olive oil, lemon juice and zest, balsamic vinegar, and salt and pepper. Portion out onto 4 good-sized serving plates. Divide asparagus, green beans and tomatoes evenly, and arrange carefully on plates.

Heat a non-stick frying pan and add some olive oil. Sauté the halibut until browned on one side; turn over, season and finish cooking. Fish can also be grilled or cooked in the oven.

When fish is cooked, cut into serving-size pieces and arrange on salad. Serve immediately. Serves 4.

**Mark Gould, executive chef**
RED STAR TAVERN AND ROAST HOUSE, PORTLAND

# Seared Salmon on Mediterranean Couscous with Cucumber Raita

*The following recipe comes from the Portland Farmers' Market Chef in the Market series where every year, chefs from local restaurants give cooking demonstrations that include farm fresh produce. Couscous, a North African specialty, is made of durum wheat semolina, and quickly steams into a fluffy side dish. Look for it boxed in the supermarket or in bulk at natural food stores. In this recipe, the couscous is brightly colored with saffron. Raita is of Indian origin, and provides a cool, creamy side dish for the salmon.*

*Two simple preparations add new flavors to a Pacific Northwest favorite, salmon. This recipe calls for rich goat's milk yogurt, but you can also use regular, low-fat or non-fat cow's milk yogurt.*

### Couscous

- 1 cup couscous
- 1 cup chicken broth, homemade or canned
- pinch saffron
- pinch curry powder (choose hot or mild, to your taste)
- pinch cinnamon
- 2 tablespoons raisins
- 1 tablespoon pine nuts, briefly toasted on the stove in a skillet
- 2 tablespoons carrot, diced in 1/4-inch or smaller pieces
- 2 tablespoons zucchini, diced in 1/4-inch or smaller pieces
- 2 tablespoons chopped olives

PLACE COUSCOUS in a large heatproof bowl. In a saucepan, heat broth with spices to boiling. Immediately pour over couscous and cover bowl tightly with plastic wrap. After 5 minutes, open plastic wrap and fluff the couscous lightly with a fork. Stir in raisins, pine nuts, diced vegetables and olives.

### Raita

- 1 English cucumber
- kosher salt
- 1 medium Walla Walla onion, diced
- 1/2 cup fresh mint leaves, chopped
- 1/2 cup fresh cilantro leaves, chopped
- 2 cups plain goat's milk or cow's milk yogurt

PEEL CUCUMBER, slice lengthwise and seed. Slice into thin rounds, and spread in a colander set in the sink or over a large bowl. Sprinkle with kosher salt and let stand about 15 minutes, until the cucumber gives up its liquid. Rinse off salt and pat dry. Combine all raita ingredients in a mixing bowl, taste, and add salt and freshly ground pepper to taste.

---

**green potatoes**   When potatoes are exposed to light during growth or in storage, tubers will turn green. This green color indicates that a poisonous substance known as solanine is present. Small amounts of green on a potato can simply be cut away, making the rest of the potato safe for eating. A really green potato should not be eaten but it can be used as seed for planting.

# Seared Salmon on Mediterranean Couscous with Cucumber Raita
## (continued)

### Salmon

SALMON IS BEST simply grilled for this recipe. If a grill is not available, follow the directions below.

> 4 salmon fillets, 6 to 8 ounces each, skin removed
> Peanut oil or other neutral oil for sautéing
> flour
> salt and pepper

Start a sauté pan heating on the stove with 1 tablespoon of oil. Put a handful of flour in a bowl and toss salmon in flour. Shake off excess flour and set fillets aside. When pan is very hot, place salmon fillets, presentation side down, in pan. Do not crowd fillets; cook them separately if necessary so they all brown properly. Sauté until bottom is crisp and fish is starting to look opaque around the edges, about 2 to 3 minutes for a 1-inch fillet. Turn over and cook to medium-rare.

To serve, place a bed of couscous on a plate and place salmon on couscous. Edge plate with raita. Serves 4.

**NOTE:** Couscous can be served at room temperature or hot. To reheat couscous, place in microwave for 30 seconds, or heat on the stove briefly with a little extra broth or water. Do not overcook, or it will lose its fluffy texture and become gummy.

**Vitaly Paley, chef/owner**
PALEY'S PLACE, PORTLAND

| nothing "fishy" going on | Fish that is fresh should not have a fishy or strong odor to it, but rather an aroma that's mild. Everything about the fish should be bright and clear, from the prominent eyes to the pink or red gills. Say no to fish with sunken eyes that are cloudy or hazy. The firm flesh should have a "bounce" to it when touched. |
|---|---|

PORTLAND FARMERS' MARKET

# Oven-Roasted Mussels with Saffron-Tomato Vinaigrette

*The following recipe comes from the Portland Farmers' Market Chef in the Market series where every year, chefs from local restaurants give cooking demonstrations that include farm fresh produce.*

*This marvelous dish is a year-round favorite at Wildwood. At the restaurant, they roast the mussels in a wood-burning brick oven, which isn't something most of us have at home. This also tastes great made on the stove or on an outdoor grill.*

| | |
|---|---|
| 4 pounds mussels or clams | salt and freshly ground pepper to taste |
| 1/2 cup good-quality white wine vinegar | 2 to 4 fresh tomatoes, chopped |
| | 2 shallots, thinly sliced |
| pinch saffron | 2 to 3 cloves garlic, thinly sliced or minced |
| 1/2 cup extra virgin olive oil | 1 lemon |
| 1 cup vegetable oil | 1/2 cup parsley, chopped |

PLACE VINEGAR and saffron threads in a small saucepan and warm gently over low heat until saffron "blooms" and vinegar turns bright yellow. Whisk in oils and salt and pepper to taste.

Scrub mussels well and place in a large heavy pot with a tight-fitting lid. Mussels should be in 1 or 2 layers on bottom of pot, not heaped up. Add vinaigrette, tomatoes, shallots and garlic. Cover pot and place over high heat. Cook, checking frequently and removing mussels from pot as soon as they open so they don't overcook. When all mussels are open, remove from heat. Taste broth and squeeze in fresh lemon juice as desired. Stir in chopped parsley, salt and freshly ground pepper to taste. Divide the mussels into 4 serving dishes and pour hot broth over. Serve immediately with crusty sourdough bread or toast. Serves 4 generously.

**Cory Schreiber, chef/owner**
WILDWOOD, PORTLAND

---

**an account of eggplant**

The most common color of eggplant today is purple, but it wasn't always that way. The white eggplant prevailed early on and the small fruits resembled eggs and for that reason came the name "egg" plant. Once peeled, eggplants can quickly brown just like apples, bananas, and potatoes do. The enzyme that causes the browning is restrained by salt, which is why a recipe will sometimes instruct for the eggplant to be salted. (This may also be done to reduce bitterness).

Older eggplant can be pithy, soft or seedy. It's those developing seeds that can leave a bitter taste in your mouth. Fruit can be used while quite small and these are sometimes the best. Look for eggplant with a glossy, smooth skin and good, sharp color. If the skin is dull or the fruit is soft, it's probably overmature.

# Cornmeal Poundcake with Summer Berry Compote and Mascarpone Cream

*The following recipe comes from the Portland Farmers' Market Chef in the Market series where every year, chefs from local restaurants give cooking demonstrations that include farm fresh produce.*

*Fresh summer berries accent this delectable poundcake.*

### Cornmeal Poundcake:

3 1/2 cups confectioner's sugar
3/4 pound unsalted butter, creamed
4 whole large eggs
2 large egg yolks

1 teaspoon vanilla
2 cups flour
1 cup polenta or coarse cornmeal

### Summer Berry Compote:

4 pints mixed berries

3/4 cup sugar

### Mascarpone Cream:

1/2 cup mascarpone
1 cup heavy cream

3 tablespoons sugar

FOR THE POUNDCAKE: Butter and flour a large loaf pan. Beat together the butter, sugar and vanilla until light and creamy. Add the eggs and egg yolks, one at a time, until blended. Add the polenta and flour and beat lightly just until smooth. Pour mixture into pan and bake in a 325 degree oven until a toothpick comes out clean, about 1 1/4 to 1 1/2 hours. Unmold onto a wire rack to cool.

*For the compote:* While the cake is baking, place 3/4 of the berries and the sugar in a large saucepan and cook over medium heat, stirring occasionally, until the sugar dissolves and forms a syrup with the berry juices, about 10 to 15 minutes. Leave to cool.

*For the cream:* Beat the cream, sugar and mascarpone until soft peaks form.

To serve, cut the cake into 1-inch slices. Top each slice with a large spoonful of the compote and some of the syrup. Scatter some of the uncooked berries around the cake, then top with a large dollop of the cream. Serves about 12.

**Chef Ken Gordon**
DEMO AT THE PORTLAND FARMERS' MARKET
SATURDAY, JULY 5TH, 1997

# Chocolate Espresso Sorbet with Fresh Berries

*Several relatively inexpensive and effective ice cream machines turn out an excellent product. If you don't have an ice cream machine, you can freeze the mixture in ice cube trays, then whiz the frozen cubes in a food processor just before serving. The sorbet will be fluffy and icy rather than smooth—so you can call it a granita, instead—but it will still taste great. A granita will not hold in the freezer; it must be served immediately.*

*The following recipe comes from the Portland Farmers' Market Chef in the Market series where every year, chefs from local restaurants give cooking demonstrations that include farm fresh produce.*

*The better the chocolate, the better the sorbet. Most supermarket cocoas are not flavorful enough to make a good sorbet; some excellent cocoas are available from specialty food mail order companies.*

2 cups sugar
1 cup cocoa
1 teaspoon cinnamon
pinch of salt

4 cups water
1/2 cup espresso or strong coffee
1 tablespoon coffee liqueur or hazelnut liqueur (optional)

### For the Garnish:

1 cup mixed fresh berries or cherries
mint sprigs

chopped toasted hazelnuts

IN A LARGE SAUCEPAN, stir together all ingredients and bring to a boil, stirring constantly. Cool in the refrigerator until thoroughly cold. Freeze in an ice cream machine according to manufacturer's instructions. To serve, scoop into a bowl and garnish with fruit, mint and toasted hazelnuts.

**Mark Gould, executive chef**
RED STAR TAVERN AND ROAST HOUSE, PORTLAND

---

**how sweet it is**

Currently research is being done to measure just how sweet an onion is. The process involves the use of a laser beam, and when aimed at an onion, the end result will measure for sugars. The percent of sugars alone doesn't necessarily indicate a sweet onion. A pungent onion can have the same amount of sugars as a sweet onion, but the pungency will overpower the sweetness, making the sugars less detectable. A sweet onion with a sugar content of 8% is a very sweet onion.

What makes some onions sweet while others are pungent and tear-provoking? There's just one answer and that is sulfur. The more sulfur compound an onion has, the more pungent (and less sweet) it will be. A low sulfur potential is already predetermined by the genes found in sweet onions.

# Abiqua Blueberry Crisp

*First planted over 50 years ago, Forsters' Blueberry Hill began with a vision and grew into a family affair when the Forsters took over in 1960. Twenty years later, Susan Maginnis joined the ranks as "the boss," and soon other products like strawberries, raspberries, eggs, and fresh produce were added. For the past 5 years, their fresh berries and produce appear at the Portland Farmers' Market.*

*This recipe can also be made with apples, peaches, or blackberries. It's quick, easy, and low in sugar but high in taste. Always a favorite at any pot-luck.*

4 pounds fresh or frozen blueberries
1 cup unbleached flour
1 cup rolled oats
2/3 cup brown sugar
2 teaspoons cinnamon
1 teaspoon nutmeg
4 tablespoons soft butter or margarine

POUR BERRIES INTO the bottom of a 10x13-inch baking dish. In a medium bowl, mix together flour, oats, brown sugar, cinnamon, and nutmeg. Cut in butter until mixture resembles crumbs, then sprinkle evenly over berries. Bake 1 hour at 350 degrees. Serves 6.

**Susan Maginnis**
FORSTERS' BLUEBERRY HILL

**native sunchokes**  Not an artichoke at all, sunchokes (also know as Jerusalem artichoke) are related to sunflowers. The sweetest tubers are dug after a frost and look similar to a miniature, lumpy sweet potato. Look for sunchokes at the beginning of market season into July. Tubers should be firm with no evidence of shriveling. They lose moisture quickly and become limp, so store them in plastic bags in the refrigerator. Slice them into salads, puree for soup, mash, fry or bake. When thinly sliced in stir fry, they taste a bit like water chestnuts.

**PORTLAND FARMERS' MARKET**

# Rhubarb Coffeecake

*Rose Hubler's home-baked goods have taste baked right into them because they're made with real ingredients and not artificial flavors. Working out of her home licensed kitchen, Hubler bakes an assortment of goods like sweetbreads, pies, and scones for several coffee shops in addition to the Portland Farmers' Market.*

*You'll give rhubarb a second look after trying out this simple, yet hearty and delicious sweetbread.*

| | |
|---|---|
| 2 3/4 cups unbleached flour | 2/3 cup oil |
| 1 1/2 teaspoons baking powder | 1 cup brown sugar |
| 1/2 teaspoon baking soda | 2 eggs |
| 1 teaspoon salt | 1/2 cup sugar |
| 1 1/2 cups rhubarb, diced | 1 cup milk |
| 1/2 cup walnuts, chopped | 1 teaspoon vanilla |

### Topping

| | |
|---|---|
| 2 tablespoons sugar | 2 teaspoons butter |

PREHEAT OVEN to 350 degrees. In a small bowl, blend the topping ingredients together and set aside. In a medium bowl, blend together flour, baking powder, soda, and salt. Stir in the rhubarb and nuts.

In a separate bowl, beat the oil, sugar, and eggs together until light, then blend in milk. Mix the wet ingredients with the dry, stirring just enough to blend. Don't overmix. Stir in the vanilla.

Pour the batter into a 9x5-inch nonstick loaf pan and drizzle the butter sugar topping over the loaf. Bake 1 hour or until a toothpick inserted in the center comes out clean. Makes 1 loaf.

**Rose Hubler**
MORSELS

---

**cooking with sage**

With the invigorating essence of lemon lightly touched with pine and camphor, the strong flavor of sage equally compliments strongly flavored foods. Used in stuffing, soups, breads, omelets, vinegar and most all vegetables, sage is a natural for sausages and other meats, aiding in the digestion of fats.

Dried sage is a little less lemony than fresh, bringing a slightly different flavor in cooking. The best varieties for cooking are the common garden sage and big-leafed sages such as Berggarten or Holt's Mammoth.

Good tea sages are Spanish, purple and variegated. With splashes of yellow, the mild-flavored gold variegated sage can be used like garden sage, and for a fruity treat try pineapple sage. The flavor is light with a pineapple aroma and is excellent for sun tea or other refreshing drinks; meats like chicken, rabbit and pork; or with fruit in jams, jellies, desserts or fruit salads.

**a collection of basil**

Basil's wonderfully rich and spicy sweet flavor offers a culinary array of versatility. There are many varieties of basil, each having a slightly different flavor, but they all can be used fresh or in cooking, dried or frozen. One basil lover even says cinnamon basil makes the best pesto. The following chart gives a description of some of the more well-known varieties and their common uses.

### CINNAMON (MEXICAN SPICE)
Slight cinnamon taste and distinct fragrance with a hint of citrus
Culinary, in fruit compote, herbal tea, potpourri

### FINISSIMO VERDE (GREEN GLOBE)
Delicate, sweet and spicy with tiny leaves
Excellent culinary with tender stems, good for pesto

### GENOVESE
Italian type, intense spicy fragrance with 3-inch leaves
Popular culinary and pesto with strong flavor that holds up well to cooking

### HOLY BASIL
Clove-scented leaves
Used in salads or cold dishes, never in cooking

### ITALIAN LARGE
Italian type, somewhat sweeter than Genovese, large leaves
Preferred by some chefs, also for sandwiches

### LEMON
Delicate lemon flavor with floral tones
Herbal vinegar, chicken, fish, baked goods, tea, fruit, ice cream

### LETTUCE LEAF
Large, mildly flavored leaves
Good culinary, stuffed, salads

### MAMMOTH
Heavenly aroma, sweet basil flavor with very large leaves
Salad, cooking, pesto. Praised by Italian chefs

### OPAL
Basil flavor with touch of citrus zest
Excellent culinary, vinegar, salads

### PURPLE RUFFLES
Sweet, mild cinnamon-like flavor
Good flavor, salads, vinegar

### RED RUBIN
Biggest leafed purple basil with good traditional flavor
Unique pesto, cooking, salad, vinegar

### SIAM QUEEN (THAI, LICORICE)
Great robust flavor and aroma, strong and spicy with licorice and clove overtones
Excellent in Thai cuisine, fish, soup, stir fry, flavored rice wine vinegar

### SWEET
Popular variety with typical sweet flavor
Great culinary, pesto

PORTLAND FARMERS' MARKET

Honey Butter • Blueberry-Apple Butter

Hot Spiced Blueberry Sauce • Blueberry Syrup

Honey Jelly • Kiwi Breakfast Syrup

Huckleberry Jam • Honey Granola

Berry Cordial • Refreshing Herbal Sun Tea

Corn Chowder • Diet Tomato Cabbage Soup

Pear/Jicama Salad • Vinaigrette Dressing

Dressing for Salad Mix • Lemon-Mint Couscous Salad

Zucchini Stuff • Cracked Wheat Bread • Vegetable Pizza

Frozen Horseradish Garnish • Meat-Potato Quiche

Blueberry Freezer Bread • Blueberry Applesauce Bread

Cinnamon Pear Muffins • Strawberry Pie

Berry Pie • Pearberry Pie

Elegante Pear Tart • Bonnie's Cobbler

French Pear Tarte • Marionberry Crumble • Berry Leather

Oregon Pear Tree Cake • Heavenly Strawberry Cream

Chocolate-Dipped Strawberries

# MORE FARMERS' MARKETS

### GRESHAM FARMERS' MARKET

LOCATION:
Between 2nd & 5th on
Roberts Avenue, Downtown Gresham
May through October
Saturdays, 8:30 - 2:00

STARTING ITS 12TH YEAR, THE GRESHAM MARKET IS A favorite weekly event for shoppers and vendors alike. With over 100 vendors joining in during the season, there's plenty of fresh-picked produce along with healthy plants, quality crafts and lively entertainment.

### HARRISBURG FARMERS' MARKET

LOCATION:
Harrisburg's Riverfront,
255 Smith Street at First
Downtown Historic District
Year-round
Wednesdays, 10:00 - 2:00

A VARIETY OF FRESH GARDEN PRODUCE, BAKED goods, agricultural products and plants, plus craft items are featured at the Harrisburg Wednesday Farmers' Market. There are even some Saturdays that are set aside for their Rye Grass celebration and Trusty Rusty Pick-Up Truck Contest. Last year began the market's first year indoors, and this year the market will be open throughout the year with added boutiques and community events. Here the market is more than just a place to shop, it's an event that brings community and people together.

### HILLSBORO FARMERS' MARKET

LOCATION:
2nd and E. Main on Courthouse Square
May through October
Saturdays, 8:00 - 1:00

SINCE 1982 THE HILLSBORO FARMERS' MARKET HAS been providing quality produce, herbs, plants and crafts to hundreds of people every Saturday during the season. The market atmosphere is almost as much a social outing as it is a place of business with plenty of shade and areas to relax. Over 100 vendors participate, with an average of 45 on any given Saturday. There are also master preservers, master gardeners, musical entertainment and plenty of free information.

### HOOD RIVER FARMERS' IN THE PARK

LOCATION:
Jackson Park, 13th and May Streets
Mid-June through mid-October
Saturdays, 9:00 -2:00

JACKSON PARK IS A FAVORITE CENTRAL CITY PARK and an ideal location for the Hood River Farmers' In The Park market. Sponsored by the Hood River Growers & Shippers Association, the market first started in 1991 and has become a favorite attraction for both the community and tourists alike. Local farmers and crafters from the Columbia Gorge fill the park with a picturesque display of mouth-watering produce, luxuriant plants and hand-crafted items. Be sure to visit August 14 -16 during the "Gravenstein Apple Days" celebration, an annual event that involves the entire valley.

## LA GRANDE FARMERS' MARKET

LOCATION:
Sunflower Book Store Lawn
1114 Washington Avenue, La Grande
Mid-June through mid-September
Saturdays, 9:00 - 12:00

LOCATED IN THE GRANDE RONDE VALLEY IN EASTERN Oregon is a small gathering of farmers and crafters. The valley is blessed with rich soil which is every gardeners dream for growing produce. On Saturday mornings they gather together to sell locally grown produce, fresh flowers and handmade crafts at the farmers' market in La Grande. People say the only disappointing thing about the market is that fall arrives and the market ends.

## LINCOLN COUNTY SATURDAY FARMERS' MARKET

LOCATION:
Lincoln County Fairgrounds, Newport
May through October
Saturdays, 9:00 -12:00

THE DESIRE FOR LOCAL FRESH FARM PRODUCE LED TO the creation of the Lincoln County market in 1978. Assisted from the beginning by the OSU Extension Service, the idea of a farmers' market progressed from a dream in the minds of a few enthusiastic farmers to today's thriving weekly event. At the peak of the season, hundreds of buyers descend upon the displayed produce, baked goods and other quality products brought every Saturday.

## TUALATIN LAKESIDE MARKET

LOCATION:
Tualatin Commons on the Lake,
Nyberg Road and Seneca
June through October
Saturdays, 9:00 - 1:00

EVERY SATURDAY DURING THE MARKET SEASON nearly 20 vendors surround a crystal blue lake with their produce, plant and craft booths. Shoppers looking for fresh, in-season produce will find it at the Tualatin Lakeside market along with other garden craft items like the ever-popular cement stepping stones. Season's Nursery is well known for its topiaries and seasonal wreaths, and for outstanding peonies go visit Brothers Peony. And Lee Berry Farms brings a variety of colorful berries along with their delicious jams and jellies.

## WEEKEND GARDEN MARKET

LOCATION:
Tri-Met Park & Ride,
158th & Cornell Rd.
at Highway 26, North Beaverton
May through October
Saturdays, 9:00 - 3:00

NOW A POPULAR AND THRIVING MARKET, THE WEEKEND Garden Market offers all types of produce, plants, flowers, crafts and other food items. Several fun, educational festivals throughout the year have become favorite family destinations. Last year's festivals included Oregon Entrepreneur Fest, Nature Fest '97, Herb Fest '97 and The Great Pumpkin Fest. Other impromptu events and community activities take place at the market during the year, such as kids' bike races and a "sample the farm in the city" day.

# Honey Butter

*A family farm for over 45 years, Gloria Lamon and her husband Shirley have been keeping bees since 1960. Here at Lamon Bee Acres they also do custom extracting and have had many field trips from local school children. Their spun honey, honey butter and honey popcorn are featured at the Gresham Farmers' Market.*

*Blend in chopped nuts or crushed strawberries for a flavorful twist.*

| | |
|---|---|
| 1 pound butter | 1/2 to 3/4 cup honey |

LET BUTTER SOFTEN to room temperature. Beat butter with a mixer at medium speed until fluffy. Slowly add honey to butter beating on high. Refrigerate in containers.

**Gloria Lamon**
LAMON BEE ACRES

# Blueberry-Apple Butter

*Selling at the Gresham Farmers' Market for many years, Alota Phelps brings quite a bounty of blueberries along with many different hand-crafted items.*

*Delicious served on toast, pancakes, bagels or biscuits.*

| | |
|---|---|
| 6 to 8 pounds apples, sliced | 8 cups blueberries |
| 4 cups sugar | 1 tablespoon allspice |

PLACE APPLES IN A PAN and add water to cover. Cook until soft. Press through a sieve or food mill. Measure eight cups of apple pulp and mix with berries, sugar and allspice. Cook until thick and smooth. Pour into sterile containers and process for 10 minutes in a boiling water bath.

**Alota Phelps**
GRESHAM FARMERS' MARKET

---

**elegant shallots**

The classic flavor of shallots is a delicate blend of mild onion and garlic. Shallots are a type of multiplying onion, yet in appearance and growth they more closely resemble garlic. A shallot is comprised of several smaller cloves or bulbs.

Because they are distinctly more tender, shallots also cook quicker than onions. Their culinary value is unsurpassed and is highly esteemed for sauces and also prized in wine cookery. With its slightly pink skin and flesh, French shallots are traditionally used in cooking while brown shallots (sometimes called multiplier onions) are valued for their greens, often used for flavoring soups.

The season for fresh shallots begins in July. Look for shallots that are firm with smooth outer skin like onions. Avoid shallots that show signs of sprouting. When kept in a cool, dry and well-ventilated area, shallots can easily keep for several months.

# Hot Spiced Blueberry Sauce

*This sauce is delicious on ice cream.*

1 cup blueberries
1/4 cup sugar
1/2 teaspoon cinnamon
1/4 teaspoon nutmeg

COMBINE BLUEBERRIES, sugar, cinnamon and nutmeg in a saucepan. Bring to boiling point and boil for 5 minutes, stirring occasionally. Serve hot.

**Alota Phelps**
GRESHAM FARMERS' MARKET

# Blueberry Syrup

*Use this syrup as a topping for ice cream, poured over pound cake,
or served over pancakes or waffles.*

1 1/4 cups prepared blueberry juice
1 tablespoon lemon juice
1 3/4 cups sugar OR
    1 1/2 cups sugar and 1/4 cup light corn syrup

COMBINE THE JUICES and sugar in a saucepan. Bring to a rolling boil and continue boiling for one minute. Remove from heat and skim off any foam. Pour into clean, hot 1/2 pint or pint canning jars, leaving 1/2 inch head space, and seal. Process in boiling water bath canner for 10 minutes. Yields 3 cups.

**Alota Phelps**
GRESHAM FARMERS' MARKET

# Honey Jelly

*Simple to make, simply wonderful.*

3 cups honey
1/2 bottle liquid pectin
1 cup water

COMBINE HONEY WITH water in a saucepan and bring to a boil. Continue boiling for 1 minute. Add pectin and bring to a rolling boil. Boil for another 30 seconds. Remove from heat and pour into sterilized jars and seal.

**Gloria Lamon**
LAMON BEE ACRES

# Kiwi Breakfast Syrup

*A small community lying between the eastern Coburg Hills and the western Coast Range is also the home to Susie Coen and her farm, Susie's Garden. In an area that was once known as the Rye Grass Capital of the World, she raises kiwi, horseradish and cut flowers along with chicken, duck and quail eggs for the Harrisburg Farmers' Market.*

*Kiwi fruit makes an effective meat tenderizer, or use it as a garnish on cakes or creme pies. Fresh kiwi should never be used in gelatin as it will not "set up". This breakfast syrup brings a new outlook to French toast and pancakes.*

3/4 cup honey
1/4 teaspoon grated orange rind
1 tablespoon melted butter or margarine

1/4 cup apple or peach juice
3/4 cup diced kiwi

COMBINE ALL THE ingredients in a saucepan and stir over medium heat until mixture is fairly smooth. Makes about 1 1/2 cups syrup.

**Susie Coen**
SUSIE'S GARDEN

| **honey hints** | Store honey at room temperature. Keep tightly covered and in a dry place. |
| --- | --- |
| | If honey becomes granulated, place the container in hot water until the honey has cleared up. |
| | When measuring honey, first coat the measuring utensil with a small amount of oil to prevent the honey from sticking. |
| | Never add water to honey in the container, this may cause it to spoil. Honey will never go bad if handled and stored properly. |
| | When baking with honey, lower temperature 25 degrees to prevent over browning. |
| | Ice cream with honey and nuts for a topping is very good. |
| | **LAMON BEE ACRES** |

MORE FARMERS' MARKETS

# Huckleberry Jam

*Over in Summerville, George Gooder and his wife are busy picking gallons of fresh huckleberries to keep up with the demand for their huckleberry jam. He grows many different fruits for his jam and jelly making including apples, pie cherries, peaches, apricots, rhubarb and five kinds of berries. In addition to selling his jams and jellies, Gooder also sells a variety of vegetables at the farmers' market in La Grande.*

*After you make this recipe the only thing left to do is clean up the mess, make some biscuits and enjoy your huckleberry jam.*

- 3 pints huckleberries
- 1 package pectin
- 2 teaspoons lemon juice
- 1 teaspoon margarine
- 4 cups sugar

CRUSH THE BERRIES well and measure out 4 cups of pulp into a pot or kettle. Mix in pectin and lemon juice. Stir well as you bring mixture to a boil, then add margarine. (This is done to prevent a scum from forming.) Add the sugar and stir constantly.

Bring the mixture to a second rolling boil, then continue cooking for 3 minutes longer. (If you live at sea level, boil 1 minute; add 1 more minute for each 1000 feet of elevation.) Remove mixture from heat and fill hot half-pint jars to within 1/2-inch from the top. Place a hot lid and a ring on the jar and using a towel, tighten the lid very tight. Place the jars on a counter upside down. This will heat the lid seals on to the top of the jars. After about 10 minutes, the jars can be uprighted. A good seal is important for safe keeping of the jams. This will make six 8 ounce jars.

**George Gooder**
LA GRANDE FARMERS' MARKET

# Honey Granola

*Makes a great healthy snack loaded with energy. Enjoy!*

- 6 cups rolled oats
- 1 cup shredded coconut
- 1 cup wheat germ
- 1/2 cup shelled sunflower seeds
- 3/4 cup chopped nuts
- 1 teaspoon cinnamon or nutmeg
- 1/2 cup cooking oil
- 1/2 cup honey
- 1/3 cup water
- 1 1/2 teaspoons salt (optional)
- 1 1/2 teaspoons vanilla extract
- 1 cup raisins

COMBINE OATS, coconut, wheat germ, sunflower seeds, nuts and spices in a large bowl. In a smaller bowl, mix together oil, honey, water, salt and vanilla. Pour over dry mixture, stirring well to coat. Spread mixture on 2 greased baking sheets. Bake at 350 degrees for 30 to 40 minutes; stir frequently. Remove from oven and allow to cool. Add raisins and store in an airtight container. Yields 10 cups.

**Gloria Lamon**
LAMON BEE ACRES

# Berry Cordial

*A family farm since 1869, Heidi and Craig Lee grow fresh produce along with raspberries, marionberries, boysenberries, strawberries, tulips, daffodils and Christmas trees. Here a family that farms together, stays together and so does the family at Lee Berry Farms. Heidi and Craig's 4 daughters are continuing that tradition by helping to pick and sell produce at the Tualatin Farmers' Market.*

*Serve as an after-dinner drink or over ice cream or dessert.*

| | |
|---|---|
| 1 quart raspberries, marionberries or boysenberries | 1 fifth vodka<br>2 cups sugar |

MIX BERRIES, vodka and sugar together in a gallon jar. Cover and let stand three weeks, shaking occasionally. Strain into a glass decanter.

**Lee Berry Farms**
TUALATIN FARMERS' MARKET

# Refreshing Herbal Sun Tea

*Five years ago, Richard and Joan Perry began The Weekend Garden Market. The whole family participates in running the market and making it a popular destination for children as well as adults. The Perry's also own a natural soap company and sell their spring plants at the Market.*

*This recipe is a huge hit at our HERB FESTIVALS.*

PACK A ONE GALLON glass sun tea container with a generous handful of fresh lemon balm, spearmint or peppermint herbs, or any combination of the above herbs, both leaves and stems. Fill container with water, replace lid and place in full sun for 5 to 6 hours. Remove from sun, strain into pitcher or decanter and add one 12 ounce can of frozen pineapple juice and one 12 ounce can of frozen lemon juice and stir. Pour over ice and garnish with an herb sprig.

**Joan Perry**
THE WEEKEND GARDEN MARKET

---

**first grain cultivated by man**

An important crop worldwide, wheat can be ground into flour, cracked, or left whole. There are essentially two types of wheat and they differ by their gluten content. Hard wheat is high in gluten and excellent for bread making. Soft wheat, being low in gluten and higher in starch, is often referred to as "pastry wheat". Another type of soft wheat, Durum wheat, is sometimes called "semolina" and is commonly used in pasta products.

When an ingredient listing says the product contains "wheat flour" or is "wheat bread", it only means the flour came from wheat, not oats or rye for instance. However that flour is not the whole wheat. For a product containing the whole wheat (wheat germ, bran and all), the product should say "whole wheat" or "100% whole wheat".

# Corn Chowder

*A third generation family of farmers, Vicki & Charlie Hertel grow a variety of produce on 250 acres at Vicki's. All the farm and nursery work is done by family and their produce is fresh and picked daily. Perennial, vegetable and bedding plants along with fresh lettuce, peas, beets, carrots, beans, tomatoes, pumpkins and squash are brought to the Hillsboro Farmers' Market. At Vicki's, they specialize in very early field grown tomatoes, the freshest corn, painted pumpkins and hand-painted garden signs.*

*The freshest ingredients make a flavorful chowder that is also fast and healthy. Make a large batch, it's even better the next day.*

4 cups sweet corn (fresh from the cob is best!)
4 medium potatoes
2 cups milk
3 tablespoons butter
salt and pepper to taste

COVER POTATOES WITH water in a pot and bring to a boil. Cover and simmer until tender. Drain potatoes (reserve liquid for sauces, breads or stock). Return to pot and mash into bite-sized chunks. Add milk, butter, corn, salt and pepper. Simmer until corn is tender. Serves 6.

**Vicki Hertel**
VICKI'S

# Diet Tomato Cabbage Soup

*Long-time regulars at the Gresham market, Lonnie and Ollie Hager bring a breathtaking display of fuchsias, tree fuchsias and unique bonsai fuchsias, along with specialty indoor cactus plants.*

*A hearty soup that's rich and flavorful.*

1 1/2 cups tomato juice
2 cups water
1/4 cup celery, chopped
3 cups cabbage, shredded
1/2 cup onion flakes
1 tablespoon parsley
1 tablespoon sweet pepper
2 cubes beef bouillon
1 teaspoon artificial sweetener
1 can mushrooms with liquid
16 ounce can French green beans with liquid
dash garlic powder
salt and pepper to taste

COMBINE IN A LARGE POT all ingredients, reserving mushrooms and beans. Bring to a boil and simmer over low heat until cabbage is tender. Add mushroom and beans; continue cooking until heated through. Ladle into soup bowls. Serves 4.

**Lonnie Hager**
GRESHAM FARMERS' MARKET

# Pear/Jicama Salad

*Delicious served anytime. For the dressing, use the vinaigrette recipe that follows.*

3 green onions, chopped
1 cup jicama root, shredded
1/2 medium red bell pepper, chopped
2 Bosc pears, cored and diced
1 stalk celery, chopped
radicchio lettuce, torn into bite-sized pieces
romaine lettuce, torn into bite-sized pieces
pine nuts

IN A LARGE SERVING BOWL, toss together romaine and radicchio lettuce, celery, pears, pepper, jicama and green onion. Sprinkle desired amount of pine nuts on top. Serve chilled.

**Thom Nelson, Executive Director**
**Hood River Growers & Shippers Assn.**
HOOD RIVER FARMERS' MARKET

# Vinaigrette Dressing

*Excellent as a dressing over any salad. Try it over potato or coleslaw.*

| | |
|---|---|
| 1/2 cup olive oil | 1/8 teaspoon freshly ground pepper |
| 1/4 cup garden herb vinegar | 1/4 teaspoon prepared mustard |
| 1/8 cup red wine | 1/2 teaspoon basil, chopped |
| 1/2 teaspoon salt | pinch sugar |

COMBINE ALL INGREDIENTS together in a bottle.

**Thom Nelson, Executive Director**
**Hood River Growers & Shippers Assn.**
HOOD RIVER FARMERS' MARKET

# Dressing for Salad Mix

*Old MacDonald may have had cows, pigs and horses, but over at Ojalla Creek Farm where Marvin and Carol Willey have lived for 10 years are animals of a different sort. Cashmere goats, angora rabbits, alpacas and chickens provide plenty of eggs and fiber for spinning. The Willey's also have an ample garden and grow vegetables along with featured marionberries and assorted greens for the Lincoln County Farmers' Market.*

*Great served on cottage cheese, salad greens or fruit salads. Good eating!*

| | |
|---|---|
| 1 cup salad oil | 1 tablespoon chopped chives or dried onion or fresh onion |
| 1/2 cup sugar | |
| 1/3 cup cider vinegar | 1 teaspoon salt |
| 1 tablespoon poppy seed or sesame seed or chopped basil | 1 teaspoon mustard |

BLEND ALL OF THE ABOVE in a mixer on high speed. It looks creamy when done but clears up when it sets in the refrigerator. Also it gets thick so stir before using.

**Carol Willey**
OJALLA CREEK FARM

---

**a word on horseradish**

Horseradish has a thin skin and therefore doesn't keep well once it's dug up. However, it can be left in the ground all winter, digging as needed. Apply a thick mulch to make the digging easier in areas that are prone to freezing. If the root is dug up and not used right away, keep it stored in the crisper drawer of the refrigerator.

The flavor comes through best when the horseradish is ground or shredded. You can use a food processor or even do it by hand, just be sure to work at arms length! Chopping can be done in a blender, but the quality and flavor are just not as good.

SUSIE COEN

# Lemon-Mint Couscous Salad

*This is a delicious solution for controlling lemon balm and mint that seem to race through the garden with wild abandon.*

10 ounce package couscous
2 cups chicken broth
4 tablespoons fresh spearmint, chopped fine
4 tablespoons fresh lemon balm, chopped fine
4 large lemon balm leaves
4 large cloves garlic, chopped fine
16 ounce can peas, drained
2 cups fresh tomatoes, diced
1/2 cup green chiles, chopped fine
6 ounce can tomato paste
1/2 cup vinaigrette
1 tablespoon curry powder
1 tablespoon cumin
1 lemon

BRING CHICKEN BROTH to a boil in a saucepan, add couscous and immediately remove from heat. Stir well, cover and set aside for 5 minutes; broth will be absorbed. Fluff with a fork.

Place couscous in a large bowl and toss in mint, lemon balm, garlic, peas, tomatoes and chiles. In a separate bowl, mix well tomato paste, vinaigrette, curry powder and cumin. Toss into couscous mixture.

Place couscous in a serving bowl. Garnish with 4 lemon balm leaves arranged in a cross pattern on top. Place 4 thin lemon slices on top of lemon balm leaves. Squeeze remaining lemon over top of salad. Chill, serve and enjoy.

**Richard Perry**
THE WEEKEND GARDEN MARKET

---

**peeling peppers perfectly**

Hot peppers are a favorite, except maybe when it comes to peeling. Those tough skins should be removed if you're going to use the pepper fresh. By blistering the skin, it becomes easier to remove and heat will help with that. You can even use the heat from your backyard barbecue grill.

When roasting peppers, avoid using charcoal lighter fluid and if available, use wood charcoal instead of briquettes. Once the glowing coals are covered with a white ash, it's time to put on safety glasses (chiles have been known to explode). Using tongs, lay peppers on the grill preferably close to the coals. Keep turning the peppers until they're blackened on all sides, then throw them for 5 minutes into a paper bag creating a "sweat lodge". Here the steaming action will help loosen the skin.

Once steamed, the skin will easily slide off under cold running water. Protect your hands with rubber gloves first to avoid that painful chile burn. If you carefully cut around the stem, the seeds and membranes should pull out willingly. Now you can use them in your favorite recipe, or toss into freezer bags where they will keep in the freezer for six months or longer.

MORE FARMERS' MARKETS

# Zucchini Stuff

*This recipe was given to me by my mother-in-law when the kids were young.
They started calling it "Zucchini Stuff".*

5 young (7 to 8-inch) zucchini,
  green or yellow
2 eggs, beaten

2 tablespoons butter
1/4 pound saltine cracker crumbs
salt and pepper to taste

DICE ZUCCHINI into a large bowl. Add eggs and cracker crumbs. Stir until well mixed. Melt butter in a large nonstick skillet. Sauté zucchini mixture in skillet over medium heat until browned. Cover and simmer until done, about 30 minutes. Season to taste. Serves 6 to 8.

**Vicki Hertel**
VICKI'S

# Cracked Wheat Bread

*Yvonne Bender Baked Goods is well known at the Harrisburg Farmers' Market and holiday bazaars. In her home-based business, Yvonne Bender creates tempting baked goods and enticing jams and jellies. Her goods are awaited with anticipation from her specialty breads to her Bread n' Butter Pickles and Zucchini Relish.*
*This cracked wheat bread is a best-seller with a crunch in every bite.*

2 cups cracked wheat
1 cup water
2 packages yeast
1 cup warm water

1 1/2 teaspoons salt
2 tablespoons sugar
2 tablespoons vegetable oil
4 to 5 cups flour

SOAK CRACKED WHEAT in 1 cup water several hours or overnight. Dissolve yeast in 1 cup warm water. Add yeast water along with the salt, sugar and oil to soaked cracked wheat mixture and mix well. Add flour to make a dough that is not sticky. Knead until smooth and elastic, about 10 minutes, adding more flour if needed. Place in oiled bowl, cover, and let rise in warm place until doubled. Punch down and turn; let rise again. Shape into two 20 ounce loaves (there should be some leftover dough, reserve for Vegetable Pizza). Place loaves in two greased 8x5-inch bread pans. Let rise until well crowned. Bake at 375 degrees for 25 minutes or until well browned. Brush tops with melted butter. Yields 2 loaves.

**Yvonne Bender**
YVONNE BENDER BAKED GOODS

# Vegetable Pizza

*This is a warm-weather favorite with my family. Served with chips and iced tea in our backyard, it's an almost perfect lunch.*

*Take leftover dough (about 8 ounces) from Cracked Wheat Bread recipe and roll out into a circle. Place in a 12-inch pizza pan, stretching and pressing dough flat to fit. Prick all over with a fork and let rise in a warm place until almost doubled. Bake at 375 degrees for 17 to 20 minutes; cool. Use now or freeze for later. To serve, cover with the following filling.*

8 ounce package cream cheese, softened
1/3 cup mayonnaise
1/4 to 1/2 teaspoon dill weed
1/2 teaspoon minced onion
shredded lettuce
assorted chopped vegetables such as tomatoes, cucumber, carrots, broccoli, cauliflower, olives, mushrooms, whatever you like
grated cheese

MIX TOGETHER the first four ingredients and spread on the baked bread shell. Cover with shredded lettuce and your choices of the assorted vegetable toppings. Sprinkle with grated cheese. Cut into wedges to serve. Serves 4 to 6.

**Yvonne Bender**
YVONNE BENDER BAKED GOODS

### freezing berries

Even in the dead of winter you can enjoy the delightful taste of summer with fresh-frozen berries. The freezer is a natural for preserving the juicy flavor of berries. Blueberries can be put directly in freezer bags or containers. Other berries need to be "flash frozen" first so the berries won't stick together and leave you with a solid block of berries.

Rinse berries and allow to drain thoroughly. Then place berries in a single layer on a cookie sheet, allowing enough room so berries aren't crowded. Place the cookie sheet in the freezer for 24 hours, after which time the berries will be individually frozen. Berries can now be placed in freezer bags or containers and returned to the freezer. Berries will remain separated so you can take out just the amount you need for pancakes, muffins, pies, fruit salads or even fresh eating.

# Frozen Horseradish Garnish

*This garnish is always ready to serve and will help liven up beef stew, pork, roasts or steaks.*

4 6-inch pieces horseradish root
vinegar
1 cup ricotta cheese
1 cup heavy cream
2 teaspoons sugar (or less to taste)
1/4 teaspoon sea salt
touch of freshly ground white peppercorn

PEEL AND COARSELY grate horseradish, then put in a bowl along with several splashes of vinegar to cover; set aside. Meanwhile, in a medium bowl beat the ricotta cheese with a wooden spoon until soft. In another bowl whip the cream until stiff peaks form; add to ricotta cheese. Add the sugar, salt and white pepper. Combine this mixture with the horseradish mixture and freeze, covered, for about 3 hours. Remove from freezer, mix again, and return to freezer until ready to serve. Scoop out garnish with a melon baller or spoon and serve. Makes 2 1/2 to 3 cups.

**Susie Coen**
SUSIE'S GARDEN

# Meat-Potato Quiche

*Another favorite, Meat-Potato Quiche is quick to assemble and
when served with a salad and bread or rolls, makes a delicious meal.*

3 tablespoons vegetable oil
3 cups raw potato, coarsely shredded
1 cup Swiss or cheddar cheese, grated
3/4 cup cooked and diced chicken, ham, or sausage
1/4 cup chopped onion
1 cup evaporated or rich milk
2 eggs
1/2 teaspoon salt
1/8 teaspoon pepper
1 tablespoon parsley flakes

IN A 9-INCH PIE PAN, mix together the oil and potato. Press evenly into a pie crust shape. Bake at 425 degrees for 15 minutes or until just beginning to brown. Layer on the cheese, meat and onion. Beat together milk, eggs, salt and pepper in a small bowl. Pour over other ingredients in pie shell and sprinkle with parsley flakes. Return to oven and bake at 425 degrees about 30 minutes or until lightly browned. Allow to cool 10 minutes before cutting into wedges. Serves 4 to 5.

**Yvonne Bender**
YVONNE BENDER BAKED GOODS

---

**horseradish history**  Not yet recognized for its culinary value, horseradish was used for centuries as a medicinal herb. The Germans and Danes are credited for bringing horseradish from the medicine cabinet to the kitchen, at which time its use was perfected in a fish sauce. Later its journey went westward and in the 1600's became accepted by Britain where it now continues to be a favorite condiment for roast beef.

# Blueberry Freezer Bread

*This is a great bread to have handy for those hectic days.
The storage life in a 0 degree freezer is about 6 months.*

3 cups unsifted all-purpose flour
2 teaspoons baking powder
1 teaspoon baking soda
1/2 teaspoon salt
2/3 cup vegetable shortening
1 1/3 cups granulated sugar
4 eggs
1/2 cup milk
1 1/2 teaspoons lemon juice
1 cup crushed pineapple, well-drained
2 cups fresh blueberries, rinsed and drained
1 cup nuts, chopped
1/2 cup flaked coconut

SIFT TOGETHER FLOUR, baking powder, baking soda and salt in a bowl. Set aside. In another bowl, cream shortening until light and fluffy. Gradually beat in sugar, then stir in eggs, milk, lemon juice and pineapple. Beat in dry ingredients and fold in blueberries, nuts and coconut. Pour dough into 6 greased and floured 6 x 3 1/4 x 2 1/4-inch pans. Bake in a preheated oven at 350 degrees for 40 to 45 minutes. Unmold and cool on a rack. When thoroughly cool, wrap breads in freezer wrap or place in freezer bags, removing as much air as possible. Seal tightly and label with date. Yields 6 loaves.

**Alota Phelps**
GRESHAM FARMERS' MARKET

# Blueberry Applesauce Bread

*Applesauce helps make this bread incredibly moist.*

3 cups flour
1 cup sugar
1 tablespoon baking powder
1 teaspoon salt
1/2 teaspoon baking soda
1/2 teaspoon mace
2 eggs, beaten
1 cup applesauce
1/4 cup melted shortening
2 cups blueberries

SIFT TOGETHER FIRST six ingredients in a large bowl. In a medium bowl, mix eggs, applesauce and shortening. Add the wet ingredients to the dry ingredients and gently fold in floured blueberries. Bake in a greased 13 x 4 x 3-inch loaf pan at 350 degrees for 50 to 60 minutes.

**Alota Phelps**
GRESHAM FARMERS' MARKET

# Cinnamon Pear Muffins

*This recipe placed 3rd at the 1994 Oregon State Fair. The annual cooking contest is sponsored by the Hood River Growers & Shippers Association.
Use your favorite pear variety for this recipe.*

2 cups all-purpose flour
1/2 teaspoon salt
2 teaspoons baking powder
1/2 cup graham flour
1/2 cup sugar
1 teaspoon cinnamon
2 eggs, beaten
1 1/2 cups milk
1 tablespoon oil
1 cup pears, chopped

IN A LARGE BOWL, sift together all the dry ingredients, then set aside. In another bowl, mix together all the wet ingredients. Stir gently into dry ingredients until batter is slightly lumpy. Do not overmix. Fill non-stick muffin pan 3/4 full and bake at 400 degrees for 20 minutes. Makes 2 dozen.

**Judith Bartel**
SALEM, OREGON

# Strawberry Pie

*Serve this topped with fresh whipped cream.*

1 baked pie shell
1 quart strawberries, sliced
1 cup water
1/2 cup sugar
2 tablespoons cornstarch
4 tablespoons strawberry Jello

BRING TO A BOIL the water, sugar and cornstarch in a saucepan. Continue boiling for 1 minute. Remove from heat and cool for 1 minute. Stir in strawberry Jello and allow to cool. Gently fold in strawberries, pour into baked pie shell and refrigerate until set. Serves 8.

**Lee Berry Farms**
TUALATIN FARMERS' MARKET

---

**color coordinated beets**

Beets come in a colorful display of different shapes and tastes. The classic red beet can range in hues from a crimson to a deep burgundy red. Some farmers say the white beet is just about as sweet as you can get. There's also a golden beet that has a hint of a sweet potato flavor, one that is quite purple in color, and there's even a striking Italian type with interior rings that alternate in shades of bright pink and white.

Shapes can also vary from perfectly round to cylindrical. Some feel the cylindrical beets have even a milder flavor and are more tender than the round red beets. But no matter what the color or shape is, usually the smaller beets, about baseball size or smaller, will be the most tender.

# Berry Pie

*Use marionberries, boysenberries, or loganberries for this pie.
A mixture of all three is especially tasty.*

pastry for a 2 crust pie
4 cups berries
1 cup sugar
1/4 cup flour

2 teaspoons tapioca
1 tablespoon lemon juice
1/2 teaspoon cinnamon
butter

LINE A 9-INCH PIE PAN with pastry. Combine berries, sugar, flour, tapioca, lemon juice and cinnamon. Let mixture stand in bowl for 15 minutes. Turn into pie shell and dot with butter. Cover with top crust, slit to allow steam to escape. Bake in a preheated 450 degree oven for 10 minutes. Reduce heat to 350 degrees and bake for another 35 to 40 minutes. Serves 6 to 8.

**Lee Berry Farms**
TUALATIN FARMERS' MARKET

# Pearberry Pie

*A delicious blend of blackberries and pears, this recipe won 1st place at the 1996 Oregon State Fair.
The annual cooking contest is sponsored by the Hood River Growers & Shippers Association.*

3 cups pears, diced
3 cups blackberries

1 cup sugar
4 tablespoons corn starch

### Pastry for 2 double crust pies

4 cups flour
2 teaspoons salt
1 tablespoon lemon juice
1 1/2 cups shortening

1 egg
1/3 cup water
1 teaspoon sugar
milk

IN A LARGE BOWL, mix pears, blackberries, sugar and corn starch. Set aside.

In another large bowl, blend flour and salt. Cut in shortening with a pastry blender until it resembles coarse meal. In a separate bowl, combine egg, lemon juice and water, mixing well. Stir liquid into flour mixture a little at a time, using only as much as you need to make a ball when the dough is gently pressed together.

Roll out half of dough to fit two 8-inch pie plates for bottom crust. Fill each pie crust with half of filling. Roll out two top crusts with remaining dough, 1-inch larger than pie plate. Put on top of filling, then cut design in top crust to let out steam. Fold edge under and seal.

Brush with milk and sprinkle with 1 teaspoon of sugar; top of pie will be browner if you brush it with milk and glisten if you sprinkle it with sugar. Bake at 400 degrees for about 30 minutes or until golden brown. Makes 2 pies.

**Arlene Thorp**
MONMOUTH, OREGON

# Elegante Pear Tart

*This recipe placed 2nd at the 1996 Oregon State Fair. The annual cooking contest is sponsored by the Hood River Growers & Shippers Association.*

| | |
|---|---|
| 1/4 cup butter, softened | 3 tablespoons sugar |
| 2 tablespoons sugar | 1/4 cup butter, softened |
| 1/2 teaspoon grated lemon rind | 1/2 teaspoon grated lemon rind |
| 1/2 teaspoon vanilla extract | 1/2 teaspoon almond extract |
| 1 egg yolk | 3 ounces cream cheese, softened |
| 3/4 cup flour | 1 egg |
| 1/4 cup ground almonds | 5 canned pear halves |
| 1/4 cup melted currant jelly | 18 strawberries, halved |
| 1/2 cup flour | |

CREAM 1/4 CUP BUTTER and 2 tablespoons sugar in bowl until light and fluffy. Add 1/2 teaspoon lemon rind, vanilla and egg yolk. Beat until smooth. Stir in 3/4 cup flour and almonds. Roll on floured surface and fit in tart pan. Bake at 375 degrees for 10 minutes. Brush with 2 tablespoons jelly.

Combine flour, 3 tablespoons sugar, 1/4 cup butter, lemon rind, almond flavoring, cream cheese, and 1 egg in mixer bowl. Beat 1 minute at medium speed. Pour over pastry. Arrange pear halves cut sides down over filling. Score pears with a knife. Bake at 375 degrees for 15 to 17 minutes or until center is set. Arrange strawberries between pears. Spoon remaining melted jelly over fruit. Cut into wedges. Serves 8.

**Mary M. Heinrichs**
SALEM, OREGON

---

**an insight into berries**

BLACKBERRIES grace much of the Northwest and can be trailing, upright or even thornless (believe it or not!). Availability depends on location but can begin in July and continue through September. Different varieties will produce a difference in taste. Use for pies, jams, jellies and fresh eating.

BLUEBERRIES are a long-lived bush that gives a very striking effect in the landscape. Great for fresh eating, pies and jams. Available July through September, sometimes October.

BOYSENBERRIES are a type of blackberry. The fruit is large, reddish-black with a delightful hint of raspberry flavor. Great fresh, frozen, in pies or preserves.

CRANBERRIES are cousins to the lingonberry and blueberry. A familiar sight at Thanksgiving, these shiny red berries ripen in September or October.

GOOSEBERRIES are famous in pies, jams, jellies, pudding or as a sauce. Translucent striped fruit can be green, pink or red. Berries are large, round and high in Vitamin C.

HUCKLEBERRIES are a shrub native to the Northwest. Related to blueberries, the fruit is slightly smaller and makes delicious pies, jams, jellies or syrups.

JOSTABERRIES have a flavor that grows on you when eaten fresh and also make terrific jam. The taste is reminiscent of grape and kiwi, and the fruit ripens during June and July. The purple-black berry is a cross between a black currant and a gooseberry.

# Bonnie's Cobbler

*This is a favorite and so easy to fix.*

2 cups flour
1 cup sugar
4 teaspoons baking powder
1/2 teaspoon salt

1 cup milk
1 teaspoon vanilla
2 tablespoons butter, softened
marionberries

MIX TOGETHER all ingredients except marionberries and spread in a large dish or pan. Scatter 1 to 2 cups of marionberries on top of the mixture.

### Bring to boil:

1 1/2 cups water
1 cup sugar

Pour over the top of berries. I sometimes omit some of this mixture if it looks like the cobbler will be too juicy and especially if using frozen marionberries. Bake at 375 degrees for 30 to 45 minutes or until done. Serves 4 to 8.

**Carol Willey**
OJALLA CREEK FARM

---

**an insight into berries**

LIGONBERRY is an evergreen ground cover with tart red berries that are used for preserves, syrups and wine.

LOGANBERRIES have a unique and highly-prized flavor. Thought to be a cross between a blackberry and a red raspberry, the large, elongated maroon fruit is eaten fresh, canned, used in pies and for wine.

MARIONBERRY, a type of blackberry, has an excellent but sweet wild berry flavor and is delicious fresh, or for use in canning, freezing, pies, jam and wine. Ripens slightly before other blackberries.

RASPBERRIES begin ripening in June, with the everbearing type producing into fall. Mostly red, there are also gold and black varieties. The texture is somewhat dry with a perfumed aroma.

SALMON BERRIES are plentiful in the Pacific Northwest forests and the first berries to ripen. Related to raspberries, the flavor of the golden berry is less pronounced.

STRAWBERRIES are in high demand and it's easy to understand why. Thank goodness this bright red berry is ready in early June, and by planting different varieties, berry production can continue through September.

TAYBERRY is a cross between a loganberry and a black raspberry. The large reddish-black berries are very long on size and flavor.

# French Pear Tarte

*This delightful tart won 1st place at the 1994 Oregon State Fair. The annual cooking contest is sponsored by the Hood River Growers & Shippers Association.*

| | |
|---|---|
| 3 medium pears | 1 1/2 cups sugar |
| 3/4 cup water | 1 vanilla bean |

PLACE PEARS PEELED, halved, and cored in syrup made by boiling sugar, water and vanilla bean, stirring until clear. Reduce heat. Simmer until pears are just tender, about 5 minutes. Remove pears. Drain well.

### Buttery Pastry

| | |
|---|---|
| 1 cup all-purpose flour | 1 egg yolk |
| 2 tablespoons powdered sugar | 1/2 teaspoon vanilla extract |
| 6 tablespoons butter | 1 tablespoon water |

Sift together the flour and sugar in bowl. Cut in butter until mixture forms coarse crumbs. In another bowl, beat together egg yolk, vanilla and water. Gradually add to flour mixture, stirring until pastry clings together. Form pastry into a ball and roll out on a floured surface to a circle about 13 inches in diameter. Line an 11-inch springform tart pan with pastry. Trim edges even with rim of pan. Bake at 400 degrees until pastry begins to brown, about 8 to 10 minutes.

### Filling

| | |
|---|---|
| 1 cup butter | 3/4 cup sugar |
| 1 egg | 1 tablespoon Kirsch or rum |
| 1/2 cup walnuts, finely ground | 1 tablespoon flour |

Cream butter with sugar in bowl until light and fluffy. Beat in egg and Kirsch or rum, nuts and flour. Spread the mixture evenly in pastry shell. Cut pears crosswise into 1/4-inch thick slices, but keep them assembled in halves. Arrange halves, spreading out atop butter mixture in shell to form a flower. Bake at 400 degrees for 25 minutes or until filling is set and well browned.

### Raspberry Glaze

| | |
|---|---|
| 2 cups raspberries | 1/4 teaspoon salt |
| 1/4 cup water | 2 tablespoons cornstarch |
| 1 teaspoon lemon juice | 1/2 cup sugar |

Crush raspberries in a saucepan and add water, simmer for 5 minutes. Strain through a sieve, measuring out 1 cup juice (add a little water if less than 1 cup). Pour raspberry juice back in saucepan and add lemon juice and salt. Mix in cornstarch with sugar. Cook, stirring constantly until thick and clear. Cool slightly. Pour over tart. Serves 10 to 12.

**Dee Hansen**
KEIZER, OREGON

# Marionberry Crumble

*This is farmer Lee's favorite. Ice cream or whipped cream are good toppings for the crumble.*

2 quarts marionberries, fresh or frozen and thawed
2 cups sugar
5 tablespoons cornstarch
1 teaspoon vanilla
1 cup butter
1 1/2 cups brown sugar
1/2 teaspoon salt
2 cups uncooked oatmeal
1 1/2 cups flour
1 teaspoon baking powder

COMBINE THE FIRST four ingredients together in a saucepan and cook until thick. Set aside. Mix together remaining ingredients (except butter) in a bowl, then cut in butter until mixture is crumbly. Pat half crumb mixture into a 9 x 13-inch pan. Pour berry filling onto crust and top berries with remaining crumb mixture. Bake at 375 degrees for 45 minutes or until golden. Serves 8 to 12.

**Lee Berry Farms**
TUALATIN FARMERS' MARKET

# Berry Leather

*The leather will keep for about 1 month at room temperature,
4 months in the refrigerator and 1 year in the freezer.*

berries                                    sugar

CRUSH BERRIES AND add 2 1/2 tablespoons sugar or honey for each cup of berries. Blend until smooth. Cover a large jelly roll pan with plastic wrap and pour berries to a depth of 3/16-inch. Dry in preheated oven at the lowest setting, leaving the door slightly ajar. Drying time will be about 12 hours.

When the berry mixture is firm to the touch, try peeling the fruit from the plastic. If no puree adheres to the plastic, the leather is sufficiently dry. To store, roll up the sheets of leather with the plastic wrap. Cover and seal.

**Lee Berry Farms**
TUALATIN FARMERS' MARKET

---

**perfect pears**   If someone wants to sell you a "tree-ripened" pear, you'd better pay them with Monopoly money. Unlike Asian pears and other fruits, European pears should be harvested before they are ripe, otherwise the fruit will be mushy. For best quality, pears should be picked when they are mature but still hard and then ripened off the tree. This can take from a few days to a few weeks, depending on the variety. Pears bruise easily so handle with care.

# Oregon Pear Tree Cake

*Nicely spiced with a wonderful pear flavor, this cake took 1st place at the 1995 Oregon State Fair. The annual cooking contest is sponsored by the Hood River Growers & Shippers Association.*

| | |
|---|---|
| 1 cup fresh Bartlett pears (about 4) | 1 teaspoon vanilla extract |
| 1 tablespoon orange juice | 1 cup buttermilk, room temperature |
| 1 teaspoon lemon juice | 1 teaspoon baking soda |
| 1 tablespoon sugar | 3 cups plus 6 tablespoons cake flour |
| 1/2 teaspoon rum extract | 1/2 teaspoon salt |
| 1 cup butter, softened | 1 teaspoon allspice |
| 2 cups sugar | 1 teaspoon cinnamon |
| 5 eggs, separated | 1 teaspoon nutmeg |
| 1 teaspoon almond extract | 1 cup pecan, chopped |

Cook pears in orange juice, lemon juice and sugar in a saucepan until tender. Add rum extract. Mash slightly as for applesauce and set aside to cool.

Cream butter in large mixing bowl; gradually add sugar, beating until light and fluffy. Add egg yolks, almond extract and vanilla extract; beat well. Dissolve baking soda in buttermilk; stir well. In a separate bowl, sift together flour, dry spices and salt; reserve 1/2 cup. Combine flour/spice mixture with creamed mixture alternating with buttermilk, beginning and ending with flour mixture. Mix well after each addition. Dredge pecans in reserved 1/2 cup flour. Fold pecans and cooled pear sauce into batter. Beat egg whites until stiff peaks form; gently fold into batter. Pour into 3 waxed paper lined and greased 9-inch cake pans. Bake at 350 degrees for about 35 minutes or until a wooden pick inserted in the center comes out clean. Cool in pans for 10 minutes; remove and let cake cool completely on racks. Fill and ice with following.

### Fresh Pear Filling

| | |
|---|---|
| 1 cup fresh Bartlett pears, pared and cubed (2) | 1 teaspoon cinnamon |
| | 1 teaspoon salt |
| 1 tablespoon sugar | 2 teaspoons cornstarch, dissolved in |
| 1 tablespoon orange juice | 1 tablespoon water |
| 1 teaspoon lemon juice | 1 tablespoon butter |
| 1 teaspoon nutmeg | 1 teaspoon rum extract |

In a medium size pan over medium heat, cook pears along with sugar, orange juice, lemon juice and spices until pears are tender, stirring occasionally. Add cornstarch, stir and cook until thickened. Add butter and rum extract. Chill; spread between cake layers.

---

**buying cabbage** — Look for firm, solid heads that are heavy for their size. Savoy type cabbage is crinkly with thin leaves that cook quickly and are favored for fresh salads. Red cabbage has thick leaves and is excellent braised with wine, fruit, or sweet and sour dishes. Green cabbage is the most common and is superb cooked, steamed, in soups and stews, sauerkraut or coleslaw.

# Oregon Pear Tree Cake
## (continued)

### Almond Cream Icing

1 cup milk
5 tablespoons flour
1 cup butter

1 cup sugar
1 teaspoon almond extract
chopped pecans

BLEND FLOUR WITH MILK in saucepan; gently cook to a very thick paste, stirring constantly. Do not allow to boil. Let stand at room temperature until cool. Cover with plastic wrap after cooking to eliminate crusting on top. Cream butter, sugar and almond extract together in large bowl until light and fluffy. Add the milk/flour paste, beating about 10 minutes until sugar is completely dissolved and mixture is consistency of whipped cream. Ice sides and top of cake. Decorate sides with chopped pecans.

**Florence Neavoll**
SALEM, OREGON

# Heavenly Strawberry Cream

*Spoon into sherbet glasses for a creamy and fruity treat.*

1 1/2 cups strawberries, sliced
1 cup sugar
1 egg white
1/4 teaspoon salt
1/4 teaspoon almond extract
1 pint dairy sour cream

BEAT TOGETHER IN A BOWL the berries, sugar, egg white, salt and almond extract with an electric mixer until mixture is light and fluffy and forms soft peaks. This may take about 5 minutes. Fold in sour cream and served chilled.

**Lee Berry Farms**
TUALATIN FARMERS' MARKET


# Chocolate-Dipped Strawberries

*Chocolate and strawberries—who can resist!*

2 pints strawberries, rinsed and hulled
1 cup semi-sweet chocolate pieces
2 tablespoons shortening

DRAIN BERRIES on paper towels until dry. Over hot, not boiling, water, stir chocolate and shortening until melted; keep warm. Insert pick in stem end of berry. Dip tapered end of berry into chocolate, then lift out quickly. Briefly hold dipped berry over chocolate to let excess run off while twirling slightly. Place dipped berry on waxed paper. Remove pick. Let stand at room temperature until chocolate is set. Berries can be refrigerated for several hours.

**Lee Berry Farms**
TUALATIN FARMERS' MARKET

MORE FARMERS' MARKETS

# Farmers' Markets in Oregon

### Central Oregon

**BEND FARMERS' MARKET**
PO Box 1262
Jacksonville, OR 97530
541-899-1415
Debra Osborne

*Location:* Brooks Street Riverfront Plaza
at Mirror Pond in Downtown Bend
July 1 - September 23
Wednesdays, 5:00 - 8:00 PM

### Eastern Oregon

**LA GRANDE FARMERS' MARKET**
1207 "M" Avenue
La Grande, OR 97850
541-963-8049
Jenny Nicholson

*Location:* Sunflower Book Store Lawn
1114 Washington Avenue, La Grande
Mid-June through mid-September
Saturdays, 9:00 - 12:00

### Mid-Columbia River Gorge

**HOOD RIVER FARMERS' IN THE PARK**
Hood River Growers & Shippers Assn.
PO Box 168
Odell, OR 97044
541-354-2565
Thom Nelson

*Location:* Jackson Park, 13th and May Streets
Mid-June through mid-October
Saturdays, 9:00 -2:00

### Oregon Coast

**ASTORIA FARMERS' MARKET**
Rt. 1 - Box 709
Astoria, OR 97103
503-325-0027 (W) 503-325-1272 (H)
Deborah Seymour

*Location:* 20th & Marine Drive on Riverfront, Astoria
May 30 through October 24
Saturdays, 9:00 -2:00

**LINCOLN COUNTY SATURDAY FARMERS' MARKET**
21821 Siletz Hwy.
Siletz, OR 97380
541-444-2059
Richard, Barbara Hilp
OSU Extension
29 SE 2nd
Newport, OR 97365
541-265-4107
Bill Rodgers

*Location:* Lincoln County Fairgrounds, Newport
May 2 through October 31
Saturdays, 9:00 -12:00

### Portland Metro

**BEAVERTON FARMERS' MARKET**
PO Box 4
Beaverton, OR 97075
503-643-5345
Ginger Rapport

*Location:* 5th & Hall Blvd., behind the Fire Station,
between Hall & Tucker and 3rd Avenue & 5th
May 9 through October 31
Saturdays, 8:00 -1:30

*Second Location:* Same as above
July 1 through September 30
Wednesdays, 3:00 - 7:00 PM

**CANBY GROWERS' MARKET**
PO Box 35
Canby, OR 97013
503-266-4600
Heidi Henry

*Location:* First Avenue Carpark, Corner of
Holly and First, Canby
Second week in May through October

**GRESHAM FARMERS' MARKET**
PO Box 422
Gresham, OR 97030
503-727-9828
Ollie Hager

*Location:* Between 2nd & 5th on Roberts
Avenue, Downtown Gresham
May 9 through October 31
Saturdays, 8:30 - 2:00

### Portland Metro

**HILLSBORO FARMERS' MARKET**
860 NE Queens Lane
Hillsboro, OR 97124
503-640-5553
Patrick Rossetti

*Location:* 2nd and E. Main on Courthouse Square
May 2 through October 24
Saturdays, 8:00 - 1:00

**HOLLYWOOD FARMERS' MARKET**
PO Box 13233
Portland, OR 97213-0233
503-233-3313  FAX 503-284-0862
Randall Baker

*Location:* Washington Mutual Parking Lot
4333 NE Sandy Blvd., Portland
May 30 through October 10
Saturdays, 8:00 - 1:00

**PEOPLE'S ALL ORGANIC FARMERS' MARKET**
3029 SE 21st Avenue
Portland, OR 97202
503-232-9051  FAX 503-236-5388
Pablo Miles

*Location:* 3029 SE 21st Avenue in Portland
April 1 through first hard frost, usually November
Wednesdays, 2:00 - 7:00 PM

**PORTLAND FARMERS' MARKET**
PO Box 15064
Portland, OR 97293
503-705-2460
Anne Cederberg

*Location:* Albers Mill Parking Lot on the
Willamette River
1200 NW Front Avenue
May 9 through October 24
Saturdays, 8:00 - 1:00

*Second Location:* Pioneer Courthouse Square,
Downtown Portland
June 17 through September 26
Wednesday's 11:00 - 3:00

**SANDY FARMERS' MARKET**
PO Box 1166
Estacada, OR 97023
503-630-4058
Linda Fulop

*Location:* Downtown Sandy on Hoffman
Avenue, Between Eastbound and
Westbound Lanes of Hwy 26 across from City Hall
June 7 through October 25
Sundays, 10:00 - 3:00

**TIGARD FARMERS' MARKET**
PO Box 230106
Tigard, OR 97223
503-639-1656
S. Carolyn Long or Stan Baumhofer 503-245-5220

*Location:* Burnham Street between Hall Blvd.
and Main Street
June 6 through October 24
Saturdays, 8:00 - 1:30

**TUALATIN LAKESIDE MARKET**
22360 SW Mandan Dr.
Tualatin, OR 97062
503-692-6492
Polly Stukey

*Location:* Tualatin Commons on the Lake,
Nyberg Road and Seneca, Tualatin
June 13 through October 3
Saturdays, 9:00 - 1:00

**WEEKEND GARDEN MARKET**
678 S. 18th Avenue
Cornelius, OR 97113
503-359-1705
Joan Perry

*Location:* Tri-Met Park & Ride, 158th &
Cornell Rd. at Highway 26,
North Beaverton
May 2 through October 31
Saturdays, 9:00 - 3:00

## Southern Oregon

**DOUGLAS COUNTY SATURDAY MARKET**
PO Box 224
Roseburg, OR 97470
541-863-4854
Judy Byrd

*Location:* Roseburg Valley Mall by "The Bon Marche"
Stewart Parkway & Garden Valley Blvd., Roseburg
April through last Saturday of October
Saturdays, 9:00 - 1:00

**GRANTS PASS GROWERS' MARKET**
PO Box 1027
Grants Pass, OR 97526
541-476-5375
Marti Fate

*Location:* Corner of F and 4th
Mid-March through mid-November
Saturdays, 9:00 - 1:00

*Second Location:* Same as above
June through September
Tuesdays, 9:00 - 1:00

**ROGUE VALLEY FARMERS' MARKET**
PO Box 1262
Jacksonville, OR 97530
541-899-1415
Debra Osborne

*Location:* Downtown Medford, Main Street between Bartlett and Front
July 23 through November 19
Thursdays, 5:00 - 8:00 PM

**ROGUE VALLEY GROWERS' & CRAFTERS MARKET**
5600 Adams Road
Talent, OR 97540
541-535-3257
John Stewart

*Location:* Ashland: Water Street under the Lithia St./Siskiyou Blvd. overpass,
1/2 block North of the Plaza
April 7 through November 3
Tuesdays, 8:30 -1:30

*Second Location:* Medford: Medford Center parking lot outside Emporium, corner of Stevens and Biddle Road
April 2 through November 5
Thursdays, 8:30 - 1:30

**ROGUE VALLEY GROWERS' & CRAFTERS MARKET** (continued)

*Third Location:* Jacksonville: 4th Street and California
May 2 through October 24
Saturdays, 9:00 - 2:00

**UPPER ROGUE FARMERS' MARKET**
PO Box 1262
Jacksonville, OR 97530
541-899-1415
Debra Osborne

*Location:* Highway 62 and Indian Creek Road, Shady Cove
May 8 through September 4
Fridays, 4:00 -7:30 PM

## Willamette Valley

**CORVALLIS SATURDAY FARMERS' MARKET**
PO Box 2602
Corvallis, OR 97339
541-752-1510
Lawrence or Rebecca Landis

*Location:* Riverfront Park "Blue Lot", First Street between Jackson and Monroe Avenue, Downtown
Mid-April through late November
Saturdays, 9:00 - 1:00

**FARMERS' MARKET AT WEST VALLEY FARMERS**
2741 N. 99 W
McMinnville, OR 97128
503-472-6154
Sue Reschly

*Location:* West Valley Farmers parking lot, 274 N 99W
August through September
Saturdays, 8:00 - Noon or till all is sold

**HARRISBURG FARMERS' MARKET**
PO Box 502
Harrisburg, OR 97446-0502
541-995-6923
Susie Coen

*Location:* Harrisburg's Riverfront,
255 Smith Street at First
Downtown Historic District
Year-round
Wednesdays, 10:00 - 2:00

**INDEPENDENCE FARMERS' MARKET**
PO Box 515
Independence, OR 97351
503-838-2859
Pat Whitener

*Location:* Riverview Park on the Waterfront, just North of the Boat Ramp
May 2 through October 10
Saturdays, 9:00 - 1:00

**INDOOR FARMERS' MARKET**
24076 Ervin Rd.
Philomath, OR 97370
541-929-4167
Don & Chris Peterson

*Location:* Community Center, Old Independent Schoolhouse
June 11 through September 24
Thursdays, 2:30 - 5:30

**LANE COUNTY FARMERS' MARKET**
76 W. Broadway
Eugene, OR 97401
541-686-8885
Noa O'Hare

*Location:* E. 8th and Oak Streets in Downtown Eugene
April 4 through November 21
Saturdays, 9:00 -5:00

*Second Location:* Same as above
July 7 through October 13
Tuesdays, 10:00 - 4:00

**MID-WILLAMETTE GROWERS' ASSOCATION**
26675 Starr Road
Monroe, OR 97456
541-847-5641
Jack Lawrence

*Location:* Corvallis: Benton County Fairgrounds
110 SW 53rd Street
May 6 through November 18
Wednesdays, 8:00 - 1:00

*Second Location:* Albany: Corner of Broadalbin and Water Streets
May 2 through November 21
Saturdays, 8:00 - Noon

**SALEM PUBLIC MARKET**
8245 72nd Avenue NE
Salem, OR 97305
503-393-3758
Donna Heilman

*Location:* 1240 Rural Street SE
All Year
Saturdays, 8:30 - Noon

**SALEM SATURDAY MARKET**
116 Marion Street, NE
Salem, OR 97305
503-371-3631
DeLynn Anderson

*Location:* Gilbert House Children's Museum Parking Lot, Under the Marion Street Bridge, 116 Marion St., NE
July 11 through October 24
Saturdays, 9:00 - 2:00

**NATIONAL FARMERS' MARKET DIRECTORY**

USDA/AMS/TMD/WMDB
Room 2642-South
PO Box 96458
Washington, D.C. 20090-6456
202-720-8317

Organized by state, this directory lists known farmers' markets operating in the United States. It is available at no charge.

# Resource Listing

**BROOKLANE SPECIALTY APPLES**
1535 SW Brooklane
Corvallis, OR 97333
541-754-8039
Monine & Bob Stebbins

Hosts 2 to 3 cider making parties each season for mail list customers.

**EDEN'S GATE FARM**
15090 Hwy 238
Applegate, OR 97530
541-846-7565 or 541-846-9019
Cathy & Bill Dunlap

Mail order catalog with nearly 20 garlic varieties. Produce stand and gift/craft store open Wednesday through Sunday, 10:00 - 5:00.

**GOODWIN CREEK GARDENS**
P.O. Box 83
Williams, OR 97544
541-846-7357
Jim & Dottie Becker

Specializing in plants and seeds for rare lavenders, herbs and everlastings; scented geraniums and medicinals; hummingbird and butterfly plants; their 50 page catalog is $1.00

**HORTON ROAD ORGANICS**
93851 Horton Rd.
Blachly, OR 97412
541-925-3019
Bill Booth & Debra Martin

Offers a CSA (Community Supported Agriculture) program.

**LAMON BEE ACRES**
31833 SE Kelso Rd.
Boring, OR 97009
503-668-6772
Gloria & Shirley Lamon

Custom Honey Extracting.

**MOUNTAIN SPRING FARMS**
12584 Hwy 99 South
Myrtle Creek, OR 97457
541-863-6799
Buck & Judy Lovett

Offers a CSA (Community Supported Agriculture) program.

**MUSTARD SEED FARMS**
4020 Portland Rd.
Newberg, OR 97132
503-538-4284
Nancy Brown

Offers a CSA (Community Supported Agriculture) program.

**ONE GREEN WORLD**
Box 1080
Molalla, OR 97038
503-651-3005   FAX 503-651-3882
Jim Gilbert

Mail order catalog with unique fruits from the former Soviet Union & Eastern Europe.

**RARE TREES NURSERY**
1253 N. Old Pacific Hwy.
Myrtle Creek, OR 97457
541-863-4409 or 863-6780

Walk through tour of the Rare Trees Nursery Arboretum, including rare trees from many parts of the world.

**THE OERTHER FAMILY FARM**
16168 Sunnyside Rd.
Clackamas, OR 97015
503-658-5132
Frederick & Deborah Oerther

Seasonal produce farm stand, open daily (except Saturdays) 11:00 - Dusk. Finished compost/topsoil available. Call ahead.

**THE THYME GARDEN HERB SEED CO.**
20546 Alsea Hwy.
Alsea, OR 97324
541-487-8671
Email -thymegarden@proaxis.com.
Web page -www.proaxis.com/~thymegarden
Rolfe & Janet Hagan

Mail order catalog with 600 varieties of herb seeds, plants, teas, seasoning blends, roots and dried herbs; catalog $2.00. Display herb garden open mid-April to mid-August from 10:00 - 5:00 everyday till June 1; Friday -Monday from June 2 through August 15.

**UNICORN MEADOWS**
16391 S. Carus Rd.
Beavercreek, OR 97004-9616
503-632-6516
Robert Burns & Kris Koa

Offers a CSA (Community Supported Agriculture) program, annual plant sale, Christmas Bazaars, and mail order catalog including seasonal produce, fresh and dried herbs, herbal honeys, oils and vinegars. Catalog $1.50.

# Bibliography

### *Books*

Better Homes & Gardens. *Heritage Cook Book.* Meredith Corporation, 1975.

Bremness, Lesley. *The Complete Book of Herbs.* Viking Penguin, 1988.

Castleman, Michael. *The Healing Herbs.* Rodale Press, 1991.

Liebster, Gunther. *MACMILLAN BOOK OF Berry Gardening.* Macmillan Publishing Company, 1986.

Melzer, Werner. *Beekeeping.* Barron's Educational Series, Inc. 1989.

Morse, Roger A. *The ABC & XYZ of Bee Culture, 40th Edition.* The A.I. Root Co., 1990.

National Gardening Association. *Gardening: The Complete Guide to Growing America's Favorite Fruits & Vegetables.* Addison-Wesley Publishing Company, 1986.

Nugent, Nancy. *The Prevention Total Health System: Food and Nutrition.* Rodale Press, Inc., 1983.

Readers Digest. *Eat Better, Live Better.* The Reader's Digest Association, Inc., 1982.

Rupp, Rebecca. *Blue Corn and Square Tomatoes.* Garden Way Publishing, 1987

Spitzer, Theodore Morrow, and Hilary Baum. *Public Markets and Community Revitalization.* ULI—Urban Land Institute and Project for Public Spaces, Inc., 1995.

Taylor, Ronald J. *Northwest Weeds.* Mountain Press Publishing Company, 1990.

### *Catalogs*

Goodwin Creek Gardens. PO Box 83, Williams, Oregon 97544. 541-846-7357.

Nichols Garden Nursery. 1190 North Pacific Highway, Albany, Oregon 97321-4580. 541-928-9280.

Northwoods Nursery. 27635 Oglesby Road, Canby, Oregon 97013. 503-266-5432.

Pinetree Garden Seeds. Box 300, New Gloucester, Maine 04260. 207-926-3400.

Territorial Seed Company. PO Box 157, Cottage Grove, Oregon 97424. 541-942-9547.

Totally Tomatoes. PO Box 1626, Augusta, Georgia 30903. 803-663-0016.

### *Other*

National Honey Board, Longmont, Colorado.

Oregon Department of Agriculture, Salem, Oregon.

U.S. Apple Association, McLean, Virginia.

# Index

## A
*a collection of basil ... 149*
*a twist on garlic ... 99*
Abiqua Blueberry Crisp ... 147
*an account of eggplant ... 144*
*an insight into berries ... 168 - 169*
Apple Butter ... 27
Apple-Rose Hip Tea ... 58
apples
    *and their uses ... 39*
    Apple Butter ... 27
    Apple-Rose Hip Tea ... 58
    Blueberry Applesauce
        Bread ... 165
    Blueberry-Apple Butter ... 153
    Fresh Apple Cake ... 55, 128
    Green Tomato Mincemeat ... 118
    Honey of an Apple Cake ... 36
    Monine's Incredible Apple
        Pie ... 35
    One Bowl Apple Cake ... 36
    Swiss Apple Tart ... 23
Apricot Balsamic Dressing ... 70
arugula
    Arugula Mayonnaise ... 14
    Greens and Beans with Pasta ... 19
    Warm Spinach Salad with
        Arugula ... 85
    *what is ... 19*
    Zesty Pesty ... 120
asparagus
    *advice ... 73*
    Pickled Asparagus ... 73
    Roasted Halibut with Salad of
        Asparagus, Spring Onions,
        Fava Beans, and Fresh Herbs
        ... 141
Aztec Pudding ... 89

## B
bacon
    Broccoli Bacon Salad ... 29
    Baked Chiles Rellenos ... 53

Baked Stuffed Squash ... 88
Ballymaloe Brown Bread ... 34
basil
    *a collection of ... 149*
    Horton's Fluffy Pesto ... 98
    Lemon Basil Grilled Chicken ... 54
    Pesto ... 42
    Pesto Forever ... 75
    Pesto Pinwheels ... 124
    Pesto Stuffed Chicken Breasts ... 75
    Sauteed Sunchoke Pesto ... 133
    *storage tips ... 50*
    Tiella ... 51
beans
    *from green to bean ... 135*
    Greens and Beans with Pasta ... 19
*bee by-products ... 72*
beef
    Beef Stew ... 45
    Pastrami ... 76
beets
    *color coordinated beets ... 166*
    *from bottom to top ... 137*
    *keep beets from bleeding ... 140*
    Pickled Beets ... 137
    Quick Pickled Beets ... 123
berries
    *an insight into ... 168 - 169*
    Berry Cordial ... 157
    Berry Leather ... 171
    Berry Pie ... 167
    Berry Wonderful Clafouti ... 78
    Blackberry Pie ... 109
    *blackberry time ... 113*
    Chocolate Espresso Sorbet with
        Fresh Berries ... 146
    Cornmeal Poundcake with
        Summer Berry Compote and
        Mascarpone Cream ... 145
    Cran-Raspberry Sauce ... 70
    *freezing berries ... 163*
    Fruit Bobbler ... 79

berries (continued)
    Huckleberry Jam ... 156
    Pearberry Pie ... 167
    Sea Berry Juice ... 132
    *shopping for blueberries ... 84*
beverages
    Apple-Rose Hip Tea ... 58
    Berry Cordial ... 157
    Mountain Ash Juice ... 132
    Refreshing Herbal Sun Tea ... 157
    Rose Petal-Lemon Verbena
        Tea ... 94
    Sea Berry Juice ... 132
*bird feeding ornaments ... 79*
*blackberry time ... 113*
Blue Corn Bread ... 92
Blue Corn-Blueberry Pancakes ... 93
blueberries
    Abiqua Blueberry Crisp ... 147
    Blue Corn-Blueberry
        Pancakes ... 93
    Blueberry Applesauce
        Bread ... 165
    Blueberry Freezer Bread ... 165
    Blueberry Salsa ... 26
    Blueberry Syrup ... 154
    Blueberry-Apple Butter ... 153
    Hot Spiced Blueberry Sauce ... 154
    *shopping for blueberries ... 84*
breads
    Ballymaloe Brown Bread ... 34
    Blue Corn Bread ... 92
    Blue Corn-Blueberry
        Pancakes ... 93
    Blueberry Applesauce
        Bread ... 165
    Blueberry Freezer Bread ... 165
    Broccoli Cornbread ... 108
    Brown Honey Scones ... 94
    Chewy Egg Dumplings ... 64
    Cinnamon Pear Muffins ... 166
    Cracked Wheat Bread ... 162

*Sidebar information is italicized*

breads (continued)
- Dilly Rolls ... 92
- Irish Soda Bread ... 34
- Irish Soda Bread, a story ... 33
- New Potato Waffles Divine ... 100
- Serena's Zucchini Bread ... 65
- *sourdough starter ... 64*
- Spoon Bread ... 109
- Stuffing for Poultry ... 63
- Whole-Grain Asian Pear Muffins ... 108
- Zucchini Bread ... 93

broccoli
- Broccoli Bacon Salad ... 29
- Broccoli Cornbread ... 108

Brown Honey Scones ... 94
*bulgur beginnings ... 91*
Butternut Ginger Soup with Kale ... 16
*butternut squash ... 121*
*buying cabbage ... 172*

## C

cabbage
- *buying cabbage ... 172*
- Cabbage Vegetable Soup ... 46
- Diet Tomato Cabbage Soup ... 158
- Steamed Green Cabbage and Potatoes ... 18
- Sweet and Sour Red Cabbage ... 17

cakes
- Cornmeal Poundcake with Summer Berry Compote and Mascarpone Cream ... 145
- Fresh Apple Cake ... 55, 128
- Honey of an Apple Cake ... 36
- One Bowl Apple Cake ... 36
- Oregon Pear Tree Cake ... 172
- Rhubarb Coffeecake ... 148

candy
- Citrus Candied Walnuts ... 66

Canning Spaghetti Sauce ... 121
casseroles
- Summer Harvest Casserole ... 20
- Tabouli-Stuffed Grape Leaves Casserole ... 32
- Zucchini Casserole ... 87

celery
- *the celery craze ... 55*

Chanterelle Frittata ... 100

cherries
- Cornelian Cherry Preserves ... 133

Chewy Egg Dumplings ... 64
Chicken Noodle Soup ... 44
Chile Rellenos Bake ... 88
Chili Rellenos ... 140
Chili Sauce ... 120

chocolate
- Chocolate Espresso Sorbet with Fresh Berries ... 146
- Chocolate Mint Ice Cream ... 113
- Chocolate-Dipped Strawberries ... 174

cilantro
- Cilantro Pesto ... 84
- Tabouli with Cilantro ... 86
- *where to find coriander and cilantro ... 83*

Cinnamon Pear Muffins ... 166
Citrus Candied Walnuts ... 66
Collard Greens with Pasta and Feta ... 30
*color coordinated beets ... 166*

condiments
- Apple Butter ... 27
- Arugula Mayonnaise ... 14
- Blueberry Salsa ... 26
- Blueberry Syrup ... 154
- Blueberry-Apple Butter ... 153
- Chili Sauce ... 120
- Cornelian Cherry Preserves ... 133
- Dilled Onion Slices ... 60
- Fresh Anytime Salsa ... 83
- Fresh Garden Salsa ... 84
- Frozen Horseradish Garnish ... 164
- Honey Butter ... 153
- Honey Jelly ... 154
- Huckleberry Jam ... 156
- Key Largo Rub ... 91
- Kiwi Breakfast Syrup ... 155
- Lemon Thyme Rub ... 91
- Mushroom-Leek Gravy ... 14
- Nancy's Salsa ... 43
- Pickled Asparagus ... 73
- Pickled Garlic ... 72
- Piper's Zucchini Relish ... 71
- Refrigerator Pickles ... 60
- Salsa ... 43
- Salsa De Tomatillo ... 44
- Salsa Verde ... 90
- Tomato Catsup ... 119
- Zucchini Relish ... 59

cookies
- Honey Walnut Biscotti ... 77
- Laurie's Lemon Verbena Cookies ... 65

*cooking with sage ... 148*

coriander
- *where to find coriander and cilantro ... 83*

corn
- Blue Corn Bread ... 92
- Blue Corn-Blueberry Pancakes ... 93
- Corn Chowder ... 158
- *corn-a-plenty ... 95*
- Freezing Corn ... 122
- *Hookers sweet Indian corn ... 85*

Cornelian Cherry Preserves ... 133
Cornmeal Poundcake with Summer Berry Compote and Mascarpone Cream ... 145
Cottage Cheese Potato Salad ... 102

couscous
- Lemon-Mint Couscous Salad ... 161
- Seared Salmon on Mediterranean Couscous with Cucumber Raita ... 142

Cracked Wheat Bread ... 162
Cran-Raspberry Sauce ... 70

cranberries
- *chronicles of ... 71*
- Cran-Raspberry Sauce ... 70

cucumbers
- Lime Pickles ... 117
- *pickles with a snap ... 117*
- Refrigerator Pickles ... 60
- Seared Salmon on Mediterranean Couscous with Cucumber Raita ... 142
- Virginia Style Sweet Chunk Pickles ... 116

## D

daikon
- Steamed Daikon ... 49
- *the giant radish ... 49*

dairy
- Chocolate Mint Ice Cream ... 113
- Cornmeal Poundcake with Summer Berry Compote and Mascarpone Cream ... 145
- Cottage Cheese Potato Salad ... 102

*Sidebar information is italicized*

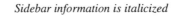

dairy (continued)
    French Vanilla Ice Cream ... 111
    Goat Milk Oatmeal Soap ... 82
    Heavenly Strawberry Cream ... 174
    Lavender Ice Cream ... 112
    Lemon Ice Cream ... 112
    Quiche Lorainne ... 106
    Zucchini Quiche ... 28
Delicata Boats ... 32
desserts
    Abiqua Blueberry Crisp ... 147
    Berry Leather ... 171
    Berry Pie ... 167
    Berry Wonderful Clafouti ... 78
    Bonnie's Cobbler ... 169
    Chocolate Mint Ice Cream ... 113
    Chocolate-Dipped Strawberries ... 174
    Citrus Candied Walnuts ... 66
    Cornmeal Poundcake with Summer Berry Compote and Mascarpone Cream ... 145
    French Pear Tarte ... 170
    French Vanilla Ice Cream ... 111
    Fresh Apple Cake ... 55, 128
    Fruit Bobbler ... 79
    Grape Pie ... 35
    Heavenly Strawberry Cream ... 174
    Honey of an Apple Cake ... 36
    Honey Walnut Biscotti ... 77
    Laura's Mom's Strawberry Pie ... 22
    Laurie's Lemon Verbena Cookies ... 65
    Lavender Ice Cream ... 112
    Lekvar ... 38
    Lekvar Bars ... 38
    Lemon Ice Cream ... 112
    Marionberry Crumble ... 171
    Monine's Incredible Apple Pie ... 35
    One Bowl Apple Cake ... 36
    Oregon Pear Tree Cake ... 172
    Pearberry Pie ... 167
    Prune Snow ... 39
    Rhubarb Coffeecake ... 148
    Rose Geranium Ice Cream ... 111
    Super Easy Strawberry Pie ... 95
    Swiss Apple Tart ... 23
    Vanilla Caramel Sauce ... 37
Diet Tomato Cabbage Soup ... 158
*digging new potatoes ... 102*
Dilled Onion Slices ... 60
Dilly Rolls ... 92

dressings
    Apricot Balsamic Dressing ... 70
    Dressing for Salad Mix ... 160
    Oven-Roasted Mussels with Saffron-Tomato Vinaigrette ... 144
    Vinaigrette Dressing ... 160
*drying fresh garlic ... 139*

## E

*egg freshness testing ... 61*
eggplant
    *an account of eggplant ... 144*
    Peppery Garlic Eggplant ... 125
    Summer Harvest Casserole ... 20
    Thai Minted Eggplant ... 136
eggs
    Chanterelle Frittata ... 100
    Chewy Egg Dumplings ... 64
    Migas ... 33
    Quiche Lorainne ... 106
    Spring Green Eggs ... 126
    Zucchini Quiche ... 28
*elegant shallots ... 153*
Elegante Pear Tart ... 168
*elephant garlic ... 105*
Elin's Creamed Albacore Tuna on Toast ... 21
espresso
    Chocolate Espresso Sorbet with Fresh Berries ... 146

## F

Fava Beans ... 135
    Roasted Halibut with Salad of Asparagus, Spring Onions, Fava Beans, and Fresh Herbs ... 141
*first grain cultivated by man ... 157*
fish
    Elin's Creamed Albacore Tuna on Toast ... 21
    Helmi's Smoked Salmon Chowder ... 15
    Judy's Smoked Fish Dip ... 15
    Lukewarm Tuna Salad ... 126
    *nothing "fishy" going on ... 143*
    Roast Salmon with Pesto Crust and Red Onion Relish ... 138
    Roasted Halibut with Salad of Asparagus, Spring Onions, Fava Beans, and Fresh Herbs ... 141

*Sidebar information is italicized*

fish (continued)
    Seared Salmon on Mediterranean Couscous with Cucumber Raita ... 142
    Swedish Open-Face Salmon Sandwiches ... 21
*freezing berries ... 163*
*freezing corn ... 122*
French Pear Tarte ... 170
French Vanilla Ice Cream ... 111
Fresh Anytime Salsa ... 83
Fresh Apple Cake ... 55, 128
Fresh Enchilada Sauce ... 53
Fresh From the Farm ... 61
Fresh Garden Salsa ... 84
Fried Zucchini ... 122
*from bottom to top ... 137*
*from green to bean ... 135*
Frozen Horseradish Garnish ... 164
Fruit Bobbler ... 79

## G

garlic
    *a twist on garlic ... 99*
    Cilantro Pesto ... 84
    *cooking with ... 18*
    *drying fresh garlic ... 139*
    *elephant garlic ... 105*
    Garlic Green Soup ... 101
    Garlic Honey Cough Syrup ... 58
    *garlic lover's guide ... 66*
    *garlic storage tips ... 101*
    Green Garlic Pesto ... 99
    Horton's Fluffy Pesto ... 98
    Peppery Garlic Eggplant ... 125
    Pesto ... 42
    Pesto Forever ... 75
    Pesto Pinwheels ... 124
    Pesto Stuffed Chicken Breasts ... 75
    Pickled Garlic ... 72
    Potato, Green Bean and Garlic Soup ... 28
    Quick 40 Clove Chicken ... 63
    *roasted garlic ... 62*
    Roasted Garlic Mashed Potatoes ... 62
    *the garlic difference ... 63*
    Tiella ... 51
    Zesty Pesty ... 120
Gazpacho A La Seville ... 46
Goat Milk Oatmeal Soap ... 82
Gram's Rhubarb Pie ... 110

**OREGON FARMERS' MARKETS**

grapes
- *connoisseur's guide to seedless ... 30*
- Grape Pie ... 35

green beans
- *from green to bean ... 135*
- Green Bean Salad ... 102
- Green Bean Tossed Salad ... 48
- Potato, Green Bean and Garlic Soup ... 28
- Shell Bean Succotash ... 18
- *the purple green bean ... 126*

Green Garlic Pesto ... 99
*green potatoes ... 142*
Green Tomato Mincemeat ... 118

greens
- Collard Greens with Pasta and Feta ... 30
- Garlic Green Soup ... 101
- Green Bean Tossed Salad ... 48
- Green Garlic Pesto ... 99
- Greens and Beans with Pasta ... 19
- Healthy Green Sauté ... 74
- Warm Spinach Salad with Arugula ... 85
- Zesty Pesty ... 120

Greens and Beans with Pasta ... 19
*growing organically ... 37*

## H

Healthy Green Sauté ... 74
Heavenly Strawberry Cream ... 174
Helmi's Smoked Salmon Chowder ... 15

honey
- Brown Honey Scones ... 94
- *honey flavors ... 77 - 78*
- Honey Butter ... 153
- Honey Granola ... 156
- *honey hints ... 155*
- Honey Jelly ... 154
- Honey of an Apple Cake ... 36
- Honey Sandwich Loaf ... 76
- Honey Walnut Biscotti ... 77
- Honey-Spiced Rabbit ... 106

*Hookers sweet Indian corn ... 85*

horseradish
- Frozen Horseradish Garnish ... 164
- *horseradish history ... 164*

Horton's Fluffy Pesto ... 98
Hot Spiced Blueberry Sauce ... 154
*how hot is too hot? ... 124*

*how sweet it is ... 146*
Huckleberry Jam ... 156

## I

ice cream
- Chocolate Espresso Sorbet with Fresh Berries ... 146
- Chocolate Mint Ice Cream ... 113
- French Vanilla Ice Cream ... 111
- Lavender Ice Cream ... 112
- Lemon Ice Cream ... 112
- Rose Geranium Ice Cream ... 111

Irish Soda Bread ... 34
- *a story ... 33*

*it's still zucchini ... 134*
Italian Rabbit Sausage ... 107
Italian Style Pac Choi ... 50

## J

jicama
- Pear/Jicama Salad ... 159

Judy's Smoked Fish Dip ... 15

## K

kale
- Butternut Ginger Soup with Kale ... 16
- *leafy kale (description of) ... 21*

*keep beets from bleeding ... 140*
Key Largo Rub ... 91
Kiwi Breakfast Syrup ... 155

## L

Lasagne with Fresh Veggies and Tomato Sauce ... 52
Laura's Mom's Strawberry Pie ... 22
Laurie's Lemon Verbena Cookies ... 65

lavender
- Lavender Ice Cream ... 112
- *loving lavender ... 112*

leeks
- *looking for ... 20*
- Mushroom-Leek Gravy ... 14
- Potato-Leek Soup ... 16
- Roasted Leeks ... 137
- Spring Green Eggs ... 126
- Watercress Soup ... 134

Lekvar ... 38
- Prune Snow ... 39

Lekvar Bars ... 38

lemon
- Lemon Basil Grilled Chicken ... 54
- Lemon Ice Cream ... 112
- Lemon Thyme Rub ... 91
- Lemon-Mint Couscous Salad ... 161

lemon verbena
- Laurie's Lemon Verbena Cookies ... 65
- Rose Petal-Lemon Verbena Tea ... 94

lime
- Lime Pickles ... 117

Looks Don't Count Zucchini ... 103
*loving lavender ... 112*
Lukewarm Tuna Salad ... 126

## M

*magnificent mints ... 136*

marionberries
- Bonnie's Cobbler ... 169
- Marionberry Crumble ... 171

Meat-Potato Quiche ... 164

Mexican style food
- Aztec Pudding ... 89
- Baked Chiles Rellenos ... 53
- Blueberry Salsa ... 26
- Chile Rellenos Bake ... 88
- Chili Rellenos ... 140
- Fresh Anytime Salsa ... 83
- Fresh Enchilada Sauce ... 53
- Fresh Garden Salsa ... 84
- Nancy's Salsa ... 43
- Salsa ... 43
- Salsa De Tomatillo ... 44
- Salsa Verde ... 90
- Sweet Italian Peppers ... 105
- Watermelon Burritos ... 20

Migas ... 33

mint
- Chocolate Mint Ice Cream ... 113
- Key Largo Rub ... 91
- Lemon-Mint Couscous Salad ... 161
- *magnificent mints ... 136*
- Thai Minted Eggplant ... 136

miso
- *more on miso ... 125*

Monine's Incredible Apple Pie ... 35
Mountain Ash Juice ... 132

mushrooms
- Chanterelle Frittata ... 100
- *mushroom magic ... 98*
- Mushroom-Leek Gravy ... 14

*Sidebar information is italicized*

mushrooms (continued)
    *Shitake ... 46*
    Spring Green Eggs ... 126
    Stuffed Mushrooms ... 61
    Watercress Soup ... 134

**N**

Nancy's Salsa ... 43
*native sunchokes ... 147*
nettles
    *nettle news ... 127*
    Stinging Nettle Lasagna ... 127
New Potatoes Waffles Divine ... 100
No Cholesterol Squash Pie ... 54
*nothing "fishy" going on ... 143*
*nut storage ... 93*
nuts
    Citrus Candied Walnuts ... 66

**O**

oatmeal
    Goat Milk Oatmeal Soap ... 82
*old-fashioned soap making ... 82*
One Bowl Apple Cake ... 36
onions
    Dilled Onion Slices ... 60
    *elegant shallots ... 153*
    *how sweet it is ... 146*
    Roast Salmon with Pesto Crust and Red Onion Relish ... 138
    Roasted Halibut with Salad of Asparagus, Spring Onions, Fava Beans, and Fresh Herbs ... 141
    Sweet Onion Pie ... 74
    *what is a scallion? ... 86*
Oregon Pear Tree Cake ... 172
Oriental Style Pac Choi ... 50
Oven-Roasted Mussels with Saffron-Tomato Vinaigrette ... 144

**P**

pac choi
    Italian Style Pac Choi ... 50
    Oriental Style Pac Choi ... 50
*parsley particulars ... 52*
pasta
    Chicken Noodle Soup ... 44
    Collard Greens with Pasta and Feta ... 30
    Fava Beans ... 135
    Greens and Beans with Pasta ... 19

pasta (continued)
    Roasted Vegetable Pasta ... 51
    Thai Pasta Salad ... 48
Pastrami ... 76
pears
    Cinnamon Pear Muffins ... 166
    Elegant Pear Tart ... 168
    French Pear Tarte ... 170
    Oregon Pear Tree Cake ... 172
    Pear/Jicama Salad ... 159
    Pearberry Pie ... 167
    *perfect pears ... 171*
    Whole-Grain Asian Pear Muffins ... 108
peppers
    Baked Chiles Rellenos ... 53
    Chile Rellenos Bake ... 88
    Chili Rellenos ... 140
    *how hot is too hot? ... 124*
    *peeling peppers perfectly ... 161*
    *pick a peck of sweet ... 23*
    Sweet Italian Peppers ... 105
    *too hot to handle ... 29*
Peppery Garlic Eggplant ... 125
*perfect pears ... 171*
pesto
    Cilantro Pesto ... 84
    Green Garlic Pesto ... 99
    Horton's Fluffy Pesto ... 98
    Pesto ... 42
    Pesto Forever ... 75
    Pesto Pinwheels ... 124
    Pesto Stuffed Chicken Breasts ... 75
    Roast Salmon with Pesto Crust and Red Onion Relish ... 138
    Sauteed Sunchoke Pesto ... 133
    Zesty Pesty ... 120
Pickled Asparagus ... 73
Pickled Beets ... 137
Pickled Garlic ... 72
pickles
    Lime Pickles ... 117
    *pickles with a snap ... 117*
    Refrigerator Pickles ... 60
    Virginia Style Sweet Chunk Pickles ... 116
*pickling chart ... 129*
pies
    Berry Pie ... 167
    Berry Wonderful Clafouti ... 78
    Blackberry Pie ... 109
    Elegant Pear Tart ... 168

pies (continued)
    French Pear Tarte ... 170
    Fruit Bobbler ... 79
    Gram's Rhubarb Pie ... 110
    Grape Pie ... 35
    Laura's Mom's Strawberry Pie ... 22
    Meat-Potato Quiche ... 164
    Monine's Incredible Apple Pie ... 35
    No Cholesterol Squash Pie ... 54
    Pearberry Pie ... 167
    Pigeon Pie ... 107
    Quiche Lorainne ... 106
    Strawberry Pie ... 166
    Super Easy Strawberry Pie ... 95
    Sweet Onion Pie ... 74
    Swiss Apple Tart ... 23
    Tomato Pie ... 104
    Zucchini Quiche ... 28
pine nuts
    Cilantro Pesto ... 84
    Pesto ... 42
    Pesto Forever ... 75
    Pesto Pinwheels ... 124
    Pesto Stuffed Chicken Breasts ... 75
    *the traditional pesto nut ... 120*
Piper's Zucchini Relish ... 71
pizza
    Vegetable Pizza ... 163
plums
    *prune plums are so wonderful!! ... 31*
potatoes
    Cottage Cheese Potato Salad ... 102
    *digging new potatoes ... 102*
    *green potatoes ... 142*
    *lore of ... 22*
    Meat-Potato Quiche ... 164
    New Potato Waffles Divine ... 100
    Potato, Green Bean and Garlic Soup ... 28
    Potato-Leek Soup ... 16
    Roasted Garlic Mashed Potatoes ... 62
    Royal Potato Salad ... 135
    Steamed Green Cabbage and Potatoes ... 18
    Tiella ... 51
poultry
    Aztec Pudding ... 89
    Chicken Noodle Soup ... 44

*Sidebar information is italicized*

poultry (continued)
    Lemon Basil Grilled Chicken ... 54
    Meat-Potato Quiche ... 164
    Pesto Stuffed Chicken Breasts ... 75
    Pigeon Pie ... 107
    Quick 40 Clove Chicken ... 63
    Stuffing for Poultry ... 63
    Tarragon Chicken ... 90
Prune Butter ... 38
prune plums
    *are so wonderful!! ... 31*
    Lekvar ... 38
    Lekvar Bars ... 38
    Prune Snow ... 39

# Q

quiches
    Quiche Lorainne ... 106
    Zucchini Quiche ... 28
Quick 40 Clove Chicken ... 63
Quick Pickled Beets ... 123

# R

rabbit
    Honey-Spiced Rabbit ... 106
    Italian Rabbit Sausage ... 107
    *rabbit ratings ... 108*
*ready for rhubarb ... 110*
Refreshing Herbal Sun Tea ... 157
Refrigerator Pickles ... 60
relish
    Piper's Zucchini Relish ... 71
    Roast Salmon with Pesto Crust and Red Onion Relish ... 138
    Zucchini Relish ... 59
rhubarb
    Gram's Rhubarb Pie ... 110
    *ready for rhubarb ... 110*
    Rhubarb Coffeecake ... 148
Roast Salmon with Pesto Crust and Red Onion Relish ... 138
Roasted Garlic Mashed Potatoes ... 62
Roasted Halibut with Salad of Asparagus, Spring Onions, Fava Beans, and Fresh Herbs ... 141
Roasted Leeks ... 137
Roasted Vegetable Pasta ... 51
roses
    Rose Geranium Ice Cream ... 111
    Rose Petal-Lemon Verbena Tea ... 94
    *the sweetest rose ... 59*
Royal Potato Salad ... 135

# S

saffron
    Oven-Roasted Mussels with Saffron-Tomato Vinaigrette ... 144
sage
    *cooking with sage ... 148*
salads
    Broccoli Bacon Salad ... 29
    Cottage Cheese Potato Salad ... 102
    Green Bean Salad ... 102
    Green Bean Tossed Salad ... 48
    Lemon-Mint Couscous Salad ... 161
    Lukewarm Tuna Salad ... 126
    Pear/Jicama Salad ... 159
    Roasted Halibut with Salad of Asparagus, Spring Onions, Fava Beans, and Fresh Herbs ... 141
    Royal Potato Salad ... 135
    Tabouli with Cilantro ... 86
    Thai Pasta Salad ... 48
    Warm Spinach Salad with Arugula ... 85
    Wilted Spinach Salad with Seasonal Garnish ... 134
salmon
    Roast Salmon with Pesto Crust and Red Onion Relish ... 138
    Seared Salmon on Mediterranean Couscous with Cucumber Raita ... 142
    Swedish Open-Face Salmon Sandwiches ... 21
salsa
    Blueberry Salsa ... 26
    Fresh Anytime Salsa ... 83
    Fresh Garden Salsa ... 84
    Nancy's Salsa ... 43
    Salsa ... 43
    Salsa De Tomatillo ... 44
    Salsa Verde ... 90
sandwiches
    Elin's Creamed Albacore Tuna on Toast ... 21
    Honey Sandwich Loaf ... 76
    Pastrami ... 76
    Swedish Open-Face Salmon Sandwiches ... 21

sauces
    Canning Spaghetti Sauce ... 121
    Chili Sauce ... 120
    Cilantro Pesto ... 84
    Cran-Raspberry Sauce ... 70
    Fresh Enchilada Sauce ... 53
    Garlic Honey Cough Syrup ... 58
    Green Garlic Pesto ... 99
    Horton's Fluffy Pesto ... 98
    Hot Spiced Blueberry Sauce ... 154
    Judy's Smoked Fish Dip ... 15
    Mushroom-Leek Gravy ... 14
    Pesto ... 42
    Pesto Forever ... 75
    Salsa Verde ... 90
    Sauteed Sunchoke Pesto ... 133
    Seared Salmon on Mediterranean Couscous with Cucumber Raita ... 142
    Tomato Catsup ... 119
    Tomato Sauce ... 119
    Vanilla Caramel Sauce ... 37
    Zesty Pesty ... 120
sausage
    Italian Rabbit Sausage ... 107
    Meat-Potato Quiche ... 164
Sauteed Sunchoke Pesto ... 133
scallions
    *what is a scallion? ... 86*
Sea Berry Juice ... 132
Seared Salmon on Mediterranean Couscous with Cucumber Raita ... 142
Serena's Zucchini Bread ... 65
shallots
    *elegant shallots ... 153*
Shell Bean Succotash ... 18
shellfish
    Oven-Roasted Mussels with Saffron-Tomato Vinaigrette ... 144
*Shitake mushrooms ... 46*
*shopping for blueberries ... 84*
smoked salmon
    Helmi's Smoked Salmon Chowder ... 15
smoking
    *history of the process ... 17*
soap
    Goat Milk Oatmeal Soap ... 82
    *old-fashioned soap making ... 82*

*Sidebar information is italicized*

sorbet
- Chocolate Espresso Sorbet with Fresh Berries ... 146

soups
- Beef Stew ... 45
- Butternut Ginger Soup with Kale ... 16
- Cabbage Vegetable Soup ... 46
- Chicken Noodle Soup ... 44
- Corn Chowder ... 158
- Diet Tomato Cabbage Soup ... 158
- Garlic Green Soup ... 101
- Gazpacho A La Seville ... 46
- Helmi's Smoked Salmon Chowder ... 15
- Potato, Green Bean and Garlic Soup ... 28
- Potato-Leek Soup ... 16
- Squash Bisque ... 47
- Watercress Soup ... 134

*sourdough starter ... 64*

spinach
- *spinach specifics ... 87*
- *spinach standouts ... 133*
- Spring Green Eggs ... 126
- Warm Spinach Salad with Arugula ... 85
- Wilted Spinach Salad with Seasonal Garnish ... 134

Spoon Bread ... 109
Spring Green Eggs ... 126

squash
- Baked Stuffed Squash ... 88
- Butternut Ginger Soup with Kale ... 16
- *butternut squash ... 121*
- Delicata Boats ... 32
- No Cholesterol Squash Pie ... 54
- *picking and storing winter squash ... 42*
- *selecting summer squash ... 26*
- Squash Bisque ... 47
- *squash mix-ups ... 118*
- Tiella ... 51

Steamed Daikon ... 49
Steamed Green Cabbage and Potatoes ... 18
Stinging Nettle Lasagna ... 127

strawberries
- Chocolate-Dipped Strawberries ... 174
- Heavenly Strawberry Cream ... 174
- Laura's Mom's Strawberry Pie ... 22

strawberries (continued)
- Strawberry Pie ... 166
- Super Easy Strawberry Pie ... 95
- Stuffed Mushrooms ... 61
- Stuffing for Poultry ... 63
- Summer Harvest Casserole ... 20

sunchokes
- *native sunchokes ... 147*
- Sauteed Sunchoke Pesto ... 133
- Super Easy Strawberry Pie ... 95
- Swedish Open-Face Salmon Sandwiches ... 21
- Sweet and Sour Red Cabbage ... 17
- Sweet Italian Peppers ... 105
- Sweet Onion Pie ... 74
- Swiss Apple Tart ... 23

## T

tabouli
- Tabouli with Cilantro ... 86
- Tabouli-Stuffed Grape Leaves Casserole ... 32

*tahini terminology ... 27*
*tamari vs. soy sauce ... 45*
Tarragon Chicken ... 90

tarts
- Elegant Pear Tart ... 168
- French Pear Tarte ... 170
- Swiss Apple Tart ... 23

tea
- Apple-Rose Hip Tea ... 58
- Refreshing Herbal Sun Tea ... 157
- Rose Petal-Lemon Verbena Tea ... 94

Thai Minted Eggplant ... 136
Thai Pasta Salad ... 48
*the purple green bean ... 126*
*the stand-alone Tomatillo ... 89*
*the tomato debate ... 123*
*the traditional pesto nut ... 120*

thyme
- Key Largo Rub ... 91
- Lemon Thyme Rub ... 91

Tiella ... 51

tofu
- Horton's Fluffy Pesto ... 98
- No Cholesterol Squash Pie ... 54

tomatilloes
- Salsa De Tomatillo ... 44
- Salsa Verde ... 90
- *the stand-alone tomatillo ... 89*
- *tomatillo types ... 89*

tomatoes
- Canning Spaghetti Sauce ... 121
- Chili Sauce ... 120
- Diet Tomato Cabbage Soup ... 158
- Fresh Anytime Salsa ... 83
- Fresh Garden Salsa ... 84
- Gazpacho A La Seville ... 46
- Green Tomato Mincemeat ... 118
- Lasagna with Fresh Veggies and Tomato Sauce ... 52
- Nancy's Salsa ... 43
- Oven-Roasted Mussels with Saffron-Tomato Vinaigrette ... 144
- Salsa ... 43
- Stinging Nettle Lasagna ... 127
- *the tomato debate ... 123*
- Tiella ... 51
- Tomato Catsup ... 119
- Tomato Pie ... 104
- Tomato Sauce ... 119

tuna
- Elin's Creamed Albacore Tuna on Toast ... 21
- Lukewarm Tuna Salad ... 126

## V

vanilla
- Chocolate Mint Ice Cream ... 113
- French Vanilla Ice Cream ... 111
- Lavender Ice Cream ... 112
- Lemon Ice Cream ... 112
- Rose Geranium Ice Cream ... 111
- Vanilla Caramel Sauce ... 37

Vegetable Pizza ... 163
Vinaigrette Dressing ... 160
Virginia Style Sweet Chunk Pickles ... 116

## W

walnuts
- Honey Walnut Biscotti ... 77
- Horton's Fluffy Pesto ... 98
- Warm Spinach Salad with Arugula ... 85

Watercress Soup ... 134

watermelon
- *how to spot a ripe watermelon ... 15*
- Watermelon Burritos ... 20

*what is a CSA? ... 47*
*what is a scallion? ... 86*

*Sidebar information is italicized*

**OREGON FARMERS' MARKETS**

*where to find coriander and cilantro ... 83*
Whole-Grain Asian Pear Muffins ... 108
Wilted Spinach Salad with Seasonal Garnish ... 134

## Z

Zesty Pesty ... 120
zucchini
    Fried Zucchini ... 122
    *it's still zucchini ... 134*
    Looks Don't Count Zucchini ... 103
    Piper's Zucchini Relish ... 71
    Serena's Zucchini Bread ... 65
    Zucchini Bake ... 104
    Zucchini Bread ... 93
    Zucchini Casserole ... 87
    Zucchini Quiche ... 28
    Zucchini Relish ... 59
    Zucchini Rounds ... 103
    Zucchini Stuff ... 162

*Sidebar information is italicized*